MY NAME IS AMERICA

The Journal of Scott Pendleton Collins

A World War II Soldier

BY WALTER DEAN MYERS

Scholastic Inc. New York

England
1944

May 25, 1944

This journal was given to me by my uncle Richard, my mother's brother. He was the only one who gave me a gift at the going-away party my folks had for me. After the party Mom said that she didn't have anything to give me and I told her that I didn't need anything. I wanted to tell her about wanting my picture on the wall, but I didn't. Maybe when all of this is over I will tell her.

On the wall in the living room, over the settee, are two pictures. One of them is of my great-grandfather, Phillip R. Collins, who fought in the Civil War and was wounded at Second Manassas. In the picture he looks strong and proud and has eyes more or less like my father's, but he looks thinner than Dad. There is a Confederate flag in the lower center of the picture.

The next picture is of Dad, who was in the army during the First World War. He was stationed in Alabama and then went to France, where he served as an ambulance driver.

I would like to have my picture on that wall. It would

make me proud to show that I have served my country, just like my dad and great-grandfather did.

Bobby Joe Hunter came to our party and everybody toasted the two of us. Afterward I drove him home and we vowed that we would stick with each other no matter what. Me and Bobby Joe didn't get along too well in school. He's the kind of guy that always has to be the star of something. He played quarterback on the football team and I mostly sat on the bench. I heard from Jerry Villency that when Bobby Joe couldn't start on the baseball team, he quit. He's been pretty decent over here, so far, and we haven't had any trouble. When we reached England, we went on pass together and we traveled to a place called Stonehenge. It was really cold and rainy there. We were both glad to leave.

May 27

Today we had a long lecture about the Nazis and what they have been doing in Europe. After the lecture, which was really kind of boring, we saw a cartoon with Hitler and Tōjō, and that was pretty funny. Lt. Rowe said that the Germans were really good soldiers and were going to be tough to defeat. Bobby Joe said that the reason the Germans looked so good was because they hadn't fought Americans. I believe that Bobby Joe is right.

I wrote to Danny and Ellen, telling them what England looks like. A captain brought the letter back to me and said that I couldn't tell them where I was. He gave me the letter and I saw that he had crossed out everything except *Dear Danny and Ellen*, at the top; the part about us marching under the Admiralty Arch; and *Your loving brother, Scott*, at the end.

There are so many soldiers here in England it isn't funny. When we go over there, we'll probably have them outnumbered two to one.

We saw Eisenhower today. He was with two other generals. I was about fifty feet away and he looked like an all right kind of guy. As soon as he left we had to pack up and move again. This time we didn't just go to another camping area. The company commander said this was going to be the final staging site.

"I'm going to shoot about fifty Germans," Bobby Joe said. "But I want to bop one of them right in the nose."

That's Bobby Joe for you. Sometimes I think he would rather hit somebody than eat. But I also know that he is a serious guy. When I told him about this journal, he went back to his stuff and showed me what his folks had given him. It is a New Testament that his dad carried through the First World War. It has his dad's name, Gordon R. Hunter, written in the front.

"I'm giving it to my son when he goes in the army," Bobby Joe said.

May 28

It's spring but the weather is still chilly and damp. We're eating field rations and there aren't enough showers to go around. There was a rumor that we were going to go back to the main camp, but the captain says we're stuck here until the invasion starts. Everybody is ready. Bill Micu (we call him Mikey) says that the Germans are probably scared stiff. He says they're just sitting there looking over the water and thinking that they're not going to get back to *der Vaterland*, which means "the fatherland."

Jerry won $200 in a poker game and a whole mess of foreign money that we've all been given. I asked Sgt. Wilson why we were given the foreign money, and he said it was in case we ran out of bullets and had to buy some from the Germans. Ha ha.

Wojo and Mikey started calling me Smoothie because I don't shave. I don't care.

May 31

This morning we loaded up with all our gear and everybody thought this was going to be it. I was mad at Wojo because he said that there is nobody in Roanoke that can play ball with even the second-stringers from Winchester. That has got to be the most stupid thing I have ever heard in my whole life. Anyway, we got on the ship and sat around all day. I cleaned my M-1 and wiped some grease from the slide that I thought I had cleaned away before.

Sgt. Wilson was running his mouth as usual. He said that if we bayoneted a German in the chest and couldn't pull out the bayonet, we could get it out by firing a shot and pulling out the bayonet on the recoil. Bobby Joe said that if we could shoot the Kraut why were we fooling around with the bayonet in the first place? That made Sgt. Wilson mad. When they talk about the Germans they use names like Kraut and Jerry. Kraut comes from sauerkraut and I don't know where Jerry comes from.

I don't really mind what Wojo said about Winchester beating Roanoke but he didn't have to make so much of it.

Evening

We didn't go again but we went over the side of the ship, down the rope ladders, and into the assault boats for practice. The sea was choppy and Corp. Hubbard, Mr. Big Time from Charlestown, got sick before he got down into the assault boat. They call the boats LCVPs — Landing

Craft Vehicle Personnel. Dumb name, but that's the army for you. One of the navy guys said it was a Higgins boat.

Corp. Hubbard showed us a company flag that he is going to carry into France and put on the highest hill he can find. That made us all feel good. We're the best in the 116th Regiment and that's a fact! I don't think anybody in their right mind will say that I am wrong.

Got a letter from home. Dolph Camilli hit three home runs over the weekend. Angie Gardiner is looking for a part-time job and asked Dad for a recommendation. Mom said that Angie was talking about me a lot.

June 3

The rumor is that the Germans have killed Hitler and the war is almost over. I don't blame them. He sounds like a creep. Sometimes I have a dream about going into a building where there are a lot of Germans and seeing Hitler sitting at this long table. In the dream he goes for his gun but I level the M-1 and blow him away.

Mikey was talking about English girls being all hot to trot for American guys. He said he had to fight them off when he was in Picadilly. That's in London.

"They were trying to tear my clothes off," he said. "And one of them looked just like Hedy Lamarr."

If I had a girl that looked like Hedy Lamarr I would

marry her faster than you could blink an eye. Another girl I would marry RIGHT AWAY is Ann Miller.

There are two English girls working with the mess crew. Neither one of them looks like Hedy Lamarr, and neither of them is even as pretty as Angie, but I like the way they talk. Very proper.

Another rumor. The invasion has already started in Italy and the 101st Airborne has gone all the way through Italy and has attacked southern Germany. Any way they put it, we don't think there will be any big fighting until about a week after we hit France. Some guys from the 29th Infantry Division said that they saw orders for boats to start taking us back to the States by the end of October. I would like to see Paris before I go back. It'll probably be my only chance.

June 4

We loaded up again. We got off the boat again. Two guys from the DUKWs, which are armored vehicles that can go in the water, said that the 101st and 82nd Airborne had already landed and that they had taken 2,809 prisoners. They said some of the prisoners had had their eyelids cut off so they could not sleep, and all they could do was fight. The Germans must be desperate!

We all got letters from Gen. Eisenhower about us

going on the invasion. The letter was serious, about how the Germans would fight savagely and everything, but it made me feel good.

June 5

The dentist pulled a tooth from Sandy Froum. Right in the front, too.

We didn't go again. We got into the boats for practice anyway and went around in circles for a little while. I wish we could go back to Dartmouth. If Mikey was right about English girls being easy, I would like to find out about it. Wojo said that French girls were nasty. Sounds good to me.

Lt. Hanken asked me if I wanted to be the backup on the machine gun. I said yes but told him that I didn't know squat about the machine gun, except that it weighed a ton more than an M-1.

Later, on the ship

It's the middle of the night and we're on our way. I'm on *The Jefferson*, which is a good sign since that is the high school I went to. The chaplain had services. Some guys are playing cards. They should play with that funny money we got. That way if they lose it won't be so bad.

About an hour after we started out, the officers were going around saying that this was it, the real thing. Guys were cheering. I did, too, because I'm tired of waiting.

The English Channel is not that big but it's big enough. Some ships got there before we did and we could hear them open fire. If anybody didn't think this was the real thing, hearing those ships open up would make them think differently. We went up on deck and saw more ships than I have ever seen in one place at one time. Overhead there were these little blimp things. They call them barrage balloons. They are connected to the ships with steel cables, so that if planes come in low they'll get hooked up in the cables.

I feel myself getting nervous, like I'm about to play a big game or something, except I know this isn't going to be a game.

During the services the chaplain said that some of us wouldn't be coming back, and he offered up a prayer for our souls.

"If anything happens to me, will you take my Bible back home?" Bobby Joe asked me.

"Yeah, sure," I said. "And if anything happens to me, you can take this journal to my folks."

"Just make sure you write down the names of all the girls you know," Bobby Joe said.

Bobby Joe could not get to first base with any girl I know for two reasons. The first reason is that he talks about himself too much. The second reason is that he is not nearly as handsome as me.

Things are getting quiet on the ship as we get ready. I told Bobby Joe that if we got to Paris we could go around and look for girls and he said okay. Then he prayed. I prayed, too.

We were told for the first time what we are supposed to do. We are supposed to get on a beach called Omaha, take care of any Germans we find there, then follow the armored guys through this ravine to a place called Vierville-sur-Mer. Then we are supposed to hold that place until they get enough equipment onshore for us to move on. All the noncoms got to look at pictures so they would know just where the ravine is.

"There are five ways off the beach," Capt. Zappacosta said. "If we can't get off one way we'll find another. Either way we need to reorganize as soon as possible. We're going to fight in squads, platoons, and companies, just as we trained. Everybody got that?"

We all said yes. Capt. Z is a good man.

The section of beach we're going to is Omaha Dog Red. That's not the real name, but that's what we're calling it.

You can always smell the sea. On a good day it has the odor of faraway places. On this ship I can smell the sea but I can also smell the guys around me. Some of them are sweating. Some are breathing so hard you can hear it. We know we're going to be fighting and some guys are going to get wounded or even killed. That is what war is all about. I am a little scared myself.

I was going to write a letter to Mom but I didn't know what to write. I think I'll write to Angie, too.

June 7

If anybody finds this notebook, please send it to my father, Mr. James Collins, care of the Norfolk and Western Railway, Roanoke, Virginia.

I do not think I am going to make it through this fighting. It is too rough. When we came in I thought the whole world was falling apart. The sea was choppy and tossing everybody around, and some of the guys were throwing up. The noise was like the worst thunderstorm you had ever heard, but instead of being up in the sky it was all around you. It was more than all around, it was inside of us, shaking us. Me, Bobby Joe, Alonzo, Mikey, and Eddie Plummer were together in the assault boat. The boats formed a circle until they were all ready to hit the beach. My mouth went dry. Bobby Joe patted my arm and I took his hand and shook it. His hand was soaking wet.

I could see Omaha Beach through the smoke and haze as our assault boat rocked in the choppy waters. The noise was unbelievable — shells hissing overhead, great booms along the shore as the navy pounded the Nazi positions. Some of the guys were getting seasick and puking their guts out. A boat up ahead had been hit. Everywhere there were guys in the water. Some were splashing their way toward shore as the bullets kicked up the water around them. Others were already dead, their bodies floating against the steel obstacles. As we stopped on a sandbar, our boat's ramp dropped. I could hear fire from the automatics slamming into its steel sides.

"Okay, this is it! Everybody out! Let's go! Let's go!"

Somebody ahead of me screamed, and I saw his body go straight back and his arms fly into the air. There was a spray of blood and I knew he was hit bad.

An officer was yelling for them to keep the boat straight, and I saw the guys in front crouching down and moving forward into the water.

"Out of the boat! Out of the boat!" somebody yelled as more guys were getting hit.

I didn't know how he meant for me to get out because I was standing so far in the back. I climbed over the side of the boat and I was scared, I can tell you that. I thought we were closer in to shore, but we weren't, and I sank down under the water. I was scared and ashamed of being so scared and wanted to get back around with the other guys. The water was about four feet deep and I got to my feet and pushed hard to get to the front of the boat. When I got there, I saw that the guys had been shot up terrible. A shock went through me.

"Get to the beach!"

I heard a voice to my right and saw an officer trying to get men from another boat to the shore. The boat they were in was on fire.

Everything was in a panic. I turned and kept going to the beach. It looked a thousand miles away. The water was halfway up my thighs and getting in my boots and the sand was slipping out from under my feet. I could see guys falling, and I didn't know if they were shot or just falling. I saw other guys get hit — I knew they were shot by the way they jerked when the bullets hit them. One guy was cut nearly in half. His mouth gaped open as he twisted. I saw his eyes staring straight up as he fell backward into the water.

I was moving as fast as I could. They had these iron things sticking out of the water and some guys were down behind one, kind of crouched together, and I wanted to get there with them, but just as I started over one of them got hit. Half his face just blew away.

Half-stumbling, half-running over people and in a half-blind frenzy, I finally felt my legs out of the water. I was on the beach. I fell and when I did, bullets hit the sand right in front of me. Somebody grabbed my shirt and pulled me to my feet and we started running toward the wall, but whoever it was who helped me didn't make it. He went backward and I stopped for a minute to look at him. No, it wasn't a minute, it wasn't even a second, because when he went back some more bullets hit him and he slid sideways and I turned and ran up on the beach. I saw some guys huddled against a wall and I ran toward them.

I got to the wall where some other guys were and we just turned and looked back on where we had been. There were guys laying all over the beach. Most were still, but some were just wounded and trying to crawl away. There were guys in the water struggling to get out. There were guys just floating.

I can't write any more right now.

June 8

This is the second day since we landed. Nothing could ever be like the first day. Officers kept trying to get us organized and a lot of them were killed. I didn't see anybody from my company and I didn't know if they were alive or dead.

Guys were dying all over the beach. The seawall, which was about four feet from where I was, gave us some protection from the machine guns firing down on us, but not from the flanks. The only reason we weren't all dead is because more and more men kept coming in and the Germans were trying to kill them before they got out of the water.

I could see a gun sticking out from up on the small hill overlooking the beach, but there was nothing to shoot at, not with an M-1. An officer was walking up and down yelling at us to get up and going.

"You're either going to get off this beach or you're going to die here!" he was screaming.

Some guys had lost their weapons and they had to run back to the beach and pick up one from one of the dead guys. They dragged a few wounded under the seawall where the rest of us were crouched. But then a few guys started moving out, and I moved with them. We were out in the open again. There were brushfires off to my left as I headed toward the small hill in front of me.

The navy guns opened up again and I could hear the shells going over my head. The ground was shaking all around me.

"29 let's go! 29 let's go!" The guy yelling was running almost straight up. When he got hit and went down, guys just went past him.

The noise was so terrible. I wanted to shut it out but knew I couldn't. Some guys started climbing up to the next level of the seawall and I followed. We got to a gully that was filled with barbed wire. It was snarled and twisted, so there wasn't any use in trying to cut it. A sergeant pushed a bangalore torpedo through the wire. It went a little way and then got stuck. A lieutenant tried to push it farther into the gully, but he was hit. You could see where the bullets had ripped into his jacket. His body was shaking, but he got up and climbed onto the wire and kept on pushing the torpedo and got it clear. Then he died. The sergeant pulled his body away and then attached another torpedo to the first. We fired at anything that didn't look natural as we waited for the torpedoes to go off.

A burst of machine-gun fire went through the barbed wire, sending up a spray of sparks and dirt, and we all crouched down quick. I had my face in the sand when the torpedoes went off.

Somehow we were off the beach and pushing up the hill. When we got up the hill, we could see the guns from the German pillbox firing down onto the beach. I was on my belly and firing at what looked like a house over to one side. There was so much smoke, it was hard to tell what you were shooting at, but the kick of the rifle made me feel good, made me feel like I was fighting back. Back in training at Camp A.P. Hill, I was big on telling everybody how I could squeeze off a shot so smooth. Here I was shooting as fast as I could. No matter what I told myself, I couldn't calm down.

The rangers broke through first, and by about two o'clock I was on the hill overlooking the beach. The same general that was trying to get us up from the seawall was trying to figure out where the gulley was that we were supposed to go through. One of the pillboxes was still being held by the Germans, and a captain was calling for a flamethrower. I was crouched down and looked back over the beach and channel. It was awesome. There were wrecks all over the place, boats and tanks just off the beach looking like monsters reaching out of the sea. Things had quieted down to a point, enough so that they were trying to gather up the dead. On one side there were bodies floating in the shallow water. From where I was, I could see them bobbing in the current. There were so many dead guys down there. So many.

The last thing I wanted to do was cry, but I couldn't help it. The tears came and came.

"You okay, soldier?" an officer asked me.

"Yeah, I'm okay," I told him.

"You're a hero, son," he said. "You made it this far."

Out in the channel were thousands of ships. In the air over them were the barrage balloons. I looked at all of it, the ships, the balloons, the men crawling up the side of the seawall. I heard the *boom-boom* of the big guns, the constant rattle of machine guns, and the *chok! chok!* of a German gun in the distance. I threw up.

June 9

The hardest thing to do is to walk past the dead. Sometimes I want to look away from them, and sometimes I have to look. Looking at some soldier lying on the ground, his arms stretched out like he is just shielding his eyes from the sun, fills me with sorrow and fear. I know that if I am killed I will lie there like that until somebody comes along with a blanket to cover me, until somebody can take a dog tag and write down my name and serial number, until somebody carries me down to the beach to be taken home.

When I see somebody I know, or think I know, it is like a stomachache; the pain makes me want to turn and twist. So many from the 116th. So many. They said that A Company was nearly wiped out. Most of the guys in A Company were from Bedford and Roanoke. God, how sad it will be when the news gets home.

I saw my first German face-to-face today. He was a noncom and he was wounded pretty bad on his right shoulder, near his neck. A medic put sulfa on it and a bandage. Three of our guys watched and he kept watching us.

I think he thought we were going to kill him. I couldn't take my eyes off him. He was a Nazi. I wanted to see if he looked different from Americans. He didn't.

The thought came to me that he might have been shooting at me. He might have aimed at me and just missed.

"Did you shoot at me?" I asked.

He said something in German and shrugged. When he moved his shoulder he winced.

We got rounded up and an officer asked us what outfits we were in. When I told him I was with the 116th he pointed out a place up the road where he thought some other 116th guys were forming up.

"Look out for snipers," he said.

I found the other 116th guys, and the sergeant told me we were going to reform as D Company. He said to grab a bite to eat and get some rest, because we were moving out as soon as the company commander got back from a briefing.

A mess truck had been moved off the beach, and we had mashed potatoes, corn, and sliced chicken. As I ate I saw more German soldiers being brought in as prisoners. They were carrying their own wounded. Some smoked cigarettes.

Tired is mostly what I felt.

Next thing I knew they were organizing us into companies and this bigheaded sergeant was yelling at us.

"On your feet! I'm Sgt. Bunch. We're moving to a second objective. It's a seaside resort. You'll love it," he said.

We formed up and spread out and started our march into France.

June 10

All night I was numb. I don't think I dreamed. I don't know if I even went to sleep. Just dozed off once in a while. When I looked around I saw the other guys around me and they looked in bad shape. A medic went around looking for wounded guys. There were soldiers who had been hit and didn't know it. I don't understand that. Some of the wounds are terrible. A ranger had the lower half of his face smashed up. His jaw was twisted and where the flesh had been blown away, there was a dark clot of dried blood. He still wore his helmet, his eyes dark and shining from under the steel rim.

A major was going around trying to get the companies straight.

"We've got the Germans backing up so fast they're falling over each other!" he said.

All around me, I see men — either dead or wounded —

lying on stretchers or on the ground. If this is what it takes to make them back up, we've got a big problem.

"We're going to veer south from Vierville-sur-Mer," the major said. "Right here."

He tapped the map with a short, stubby finger.

A couple of guys looked over his shoulder and I did, too. Vierville was just a dot on the map. The new place he was pointing to was just dots and lines. I figured some German officer was doing the same thing with his maps. They would be waiting for us.

In the background there is always the sound of firing. Sometimes it is big guns, sometimes machine guns. Back in training I had a problem telling the difference between German guns and American guns. Here, I don't.

A major, his name is Bowie, or maybe Howie, told us he was going to get us a hot meal. I wasn't hungry.

Bobby Joe found me. God, I was glad to see him. He started talking to me about how his backpack had got shot up pretty bad. At first I couldn't even answer him.

"You doing all right?" he asked me.

"What kind of bullet did you take out of your backpack?" I asked.

He hadn't taken anything out of it and we went through it and found three ugly-looking pieces of lead.

"If I'd known I was that close to getting it I would have messed my pants," Bobby Joe said.

I told him I was afraid to check my backpack.

Bobby Joe started writing a letter to let his folks know he is alive. I feel discouraged and sad and alone as I sit here with all of these men around me, because now I know for sure that some of us are going to get killed. There's no question about it. I don't know why I'm alive now.

We're supposed to move out at daybreak. I'm so tired I don't want to move. When they tell us to get up from where we are lying, I just hope I can find the strength.

I am going to write down a copy of the letter I sent home. Just in case the real letter doesn't make it.

Dear Mom,

I am in Normandy. I can't tell you where. I am not wounded. We're doing all right so far. The Germans don't look like they're ready to give up, that's for sure. I've seen several French houses and a church. The houses are pock-marked from where shells have hit them. The church had only part of a steeple. There are civilians right here in the middle of this war. It doesn't seem fair. There are men, women, and children. The medics bandaged up a little girl today. She was about three, with dark brown hair and blue-gray eyes. Her leg was burned and her face was swollen real bad on one side.

Mom, I keep thinking about what the war would be

like if it was in Roanoke instead of here in France. It makes me almost choke up when I think about people in Roanoke, you and Dad and Danny and Ellen, having to worry about Nazis the way these people do.

One thing I wanted to tell you and Dad is that I love you both very much. Please tell Danny and Ellen that I love them, too.

Your son,
Scott

June 12

I have been over here forever.

Early this afternoon we were attacked by a German patrol. We were making our way from field to field at about two o'clock and got a little careless, I guess. The fields are separated by hedgerows. More or less they're just giant hedges that have been allowed to grow a long time without being cut back, so that the stems going into the ground are three or four inches thick. It's murder trying to get through them. The fields in Normandy go on forever, but they are not owned by one person or family. Instead they are divided up into smaller fields according to who owns them.

Anyway, we were trying to get through some hedgerows when we were attacked by a German company. They made a mistake, too, because they didn't know how many guys they were facing. Two of our guys got hit right away. As far as I could tell the Germans were not more than a hundred yards away, but they were on slightly higher ground than we were. I was one of the first to answer fire and I think I got the guy I was aiming at. He spun and his rifle spun, too, before it went out of his hands. They only got off one mortar round before our guys started laying down a blanket of fire. They threw a bunch of grenades at us, and we dug in close to the hedgerows. When they started moving out, we gave them enough respect to let them clear out before we moved up.

We got to the hedgerows and there were nine German soldiers wounded and two killed. I looked at the guy I thought I had shot. He was laying on his back looking like he was just taking a nap. It made me feel bad to think I had killed a man, but not as bad as I thought it would.

We took the weapons from the wounded soldiers and left them for the battalion medics.

We pushed down toward the Elle River. My left ankle hurt, and I asked a medic if he had anything to tape it up with. He said no, but gave me some APC tablets, which are aspirins. I asked him how he was doing. I didn't mean anything by it, it was just something to say.

The medic looked at me and shook his head. "If they're not hurt bad I don't do much," he said. "If they're hurt bad I don't do much, either."

I saw him helping a guy before. He was working hard to save him. I hope if I get hit he's around to help me.

We got to a place where we could see the river and were looking for a place to camp down for the night, when we started getting incoming artillery fire. I jumped into a ditch by the side of the road. There was water in the ditch, but I wasn't worried about getting wet. There was a sign on the road with an arrow that pointed in the direction we had been heading. It said St. Clair sur l'Elle. I keep reading these signs, wondering which town I'm going to die in. I don't want to think like that, but the thoughts come anyway.

"Three Squad! Move out!" The captain was pointing down the road, then curved his motion showing that Three Squad was going to move in from the left. Then he called out what One Squad and Two Squad were supposed to do. I forgot what squad I was in, so I went after Two Squad. Heads down, we ran along what looked like a cow path.

An old French woman was in one of the windows pointing at a two-story building with a steep roof. The shutters were green with white trim. They were closed. I looked around and saw that most of the windows had their shutters open. I aimed and shot through the shutters.

All the shutters opened and the Germans were firing back something furious. Some guys from One Squad saw what was happening and shot a couple of rifle grenades at the building. It was 10 minutes of heavy firing into the windows before we saw a white flag waving in front of one of them.

"Watch it!" the sergeant said.

We waited and after a while the door opened and a mess of Germans came out. I found out later that twenty-three came out with that crew. A lieutenant asked Brown, who speaks German, to question the prisoners.

The German officer's arm was already in a sling. He licked his lips before he spoke. Brown said that the officer told him there were three more Germans in the building.

"They're scared to come out," Brown said.

Which meant that somebody had to go in after them. All the other prisoners were made to sit out in the open while Three Squad went in. If they started firing from the windows again, they would hit their own men.

We waited for a while and we could hear our guys trying to get the Germans to give up. Then we heard shots and we got out of the clearing. One of the Germans who had given up tried to get up and move, and he was shot. I don't think he was trying to do anything, he was just scared. We zeroed in on the building, but shortly after that, our guys came out. They were okay. They didn't bring out any Germans and I didn't ask them what had happened in the house.

The Germans were knocked around a bit by our guys, but it wasn't too bad on them, just some bruises.

We dug in a little way from the Elle River. We had K rations and the guys who smoked lit up. I checked my gear and picked up some more ammo and some sulfa from the supply truck.

"You hurt?" It was the medic from before.

"No," I said. I was pissed at him for asking. I didn't want him to know that I was expecting to be hit any minute.

"Anybody got a map?" a tech sergeant asked.

I laid down and tried to get some sleep. Somebody had a radio with an English-speaking station. Not American-speaking, *English*-speaking, but they were talking about America. They thought some guy named Dewey was going to run against Roosevelt. I hope Roosevelt wins.

June 13

Early morning. It doesn't seem cold but my hands are shaking. Before we started off for the beach at Normandy,

I was excited and a little scared. I didn't know at the time what I was facing. Now, whenever we jump off to another battle, I am scared out of my mind. Today we're supposed to start to someplace called Couvains. The camp is quiet. It is also filled with smells. There is the smell of eggs and bacon cooking, the smell of the water we wash our mess kits in, and from somewhere, the smell of explosives drifts over us. There's not a lot of talking going on. I guess there's not a lot that anybody has to say.

We had a prayer service last night. The chaplain gathered all the guys who wanted to be there and we all either sat or knelt around the jeep he was using. The first prayer he started told everything about what was going on.

"Oh, Lord, look upon us this evening. . . ." Then he raised his head, looked at us, and said, "Don't bunch, guys."

He didn't want us to bunch up too close in case the Jerries sent in some artillery fire.

When the chaplain prayed for the dead, it touched us all. We had come over as an outfit of neighbors. Now there were spaces in our minds where friends used to be. I haven't wanted to write about the guys I was buddying around with before we hit the beach. I didn't even want to think about them. I knew Tommy Ward and Jerry Villency from back home. Tommy and I picked apples for a summer outside of Winchester. It was hard work, didn't pay much, but it was fun. I went to Jefferson High with Jerry.

We were going to double date if we ever managed to get dates. When we landed in Normandy, all the guys had been in the boat with me. I haven't seen any of them since.

Bill Darden and Dave Ewing I met at Camp A.P. Hill and we became pretty good friends. We hung out in the dayroom when we were in England, too, playing pool, whatever. Dave played the piano pretty good. He didn't know a lot of tunes by heart, but he could play "The Glow Worm" really good and also "Don't Sit Under the Apple Tree." That's the kind of song he liked. Bill, Dave, and I all agreed to go see *This Is the Army* when we got back to England and had a chance to get to London. I think Dave was from Bedford.

Another guy I sort of knew was Ellison. Back on D-Day, when I had made it to the wall, I looked back and I saw a guy I was pretty sure was Ellison. He had just reached the water's edge and was trying to crawl toward us. He had been hit already, and you could see the pain in his face. It was terrible and fascinating at the same time. We were all hoping he would make it, but none of us thought he would, and it was really like waiting for him to get nailed. When he got hit he just fell forward.

Sometimes it makes me feel guilty just being alive.

June 13, night

Couvains. I almost bought it today. The 115th was on the line and then they pulled back and we moved up. They made a path and we went right through them. They looked pitiful. Guys had bandages around their heads, around their arms and legs. And bodies. So many bodies.

"You think we'll ever get used to the killing?" I asked Bobby Joe.

"I don't know," he answered. "I hope it's over before we do. I don't want to get used to it."

We stopped on the edge of the city while the First Battalion got into position. Me and Bobby Joe got put into a new squad. They look like they're okay guys. They told me they had lost five guys from their old squad. Half the squad. I wished they hadn't told me that.

We were moving along the road when all of a sudden we're being fired on by the Germans. I guess I had been daydreaming for a minute. It was like half daydreaming and half night dreaming. What's really going on is that I'm so tired I can't even think straight most of the time. I'm doing stuff more because I was trained to than anything else.

The captain was telling us to watch out for mines, so I was walking with my head down. Anyway, we got fired on and we ran into some buildings, which was scary by itself because you never know if there are Germans in there waiting for you.

The building I ran into was a warehouse of some kind. When I saw the people in it, I fired.

The guy started yelling something like Mayday. Another soldier came into the room and dove to the floor. I saw the old man clearly now. He was sixty, maybe seventy. So were the woman and the priest who flattened themselves against the wall.

I had my rifle pointed at them, and they stared at it. Then the old woman raised her hand like she was greeting me and I calmed down a little. McCormack, a guy I just met from Martinsburg, West Virginia, was the guy who had come into the house with me. We checked out the place real quick to make sure it was safe.

We didn't know how many Germans were out there. Through the window I saw a squad of men edging toward where the shooting had come from. Then the shelling began.

You could hear the German shells coming in and they were coming in fast. When they hit, I was ducking and trying to get under something. If a shell actually hit close enough to me I wouldn't have stood a chance of living. Anyway, when you hear the *boom* it means that the shell missed you and you don't have to duck. Nothing I could do but sit there with the three old French people and McCormack and take it.

The shelling went on and on. When shells hit close by, the building shook and parts of the wall crumbled. I wanted to shoot back, but there was nothing to see to shoot at. I just kept my head down as much as possible.

Once, when I looked up, I saw that the old people hadn't taken shelter. The guy was sitting on a wooden chair, kind of hunched over into himself, and rocking back and forth. The priest had his hands folded across his chest and his head bowed. The woman was peeling an onion. She was small and wrinkled with dark black eyes. The shelling, even when it missed, shook the earth and sent small wisps of dust into the air. It was through the dust and sunlight that I was looking at her when she smiled. I thought that maybe she had once been a young and beautiful woman.

"I think they're afraid to get down," McCormack said.

I looked at them, and motioned for them to get on the ground. The priest flattened himself at once but the old man went to the woman and helped her down first.

After what seemed like forever we got the word to move out toward the main part of town. The shells were still coming in, but we were moving out anyway.

"They've got this place zeroed in!" a lieutenant said.

We ran in groups of two and three back to where we had come from. There wasn't any small-arms fire. When I got back to the road there were two dead guys lying in the middle of it.

We crept in toward Couvains. Our artillery was sending in a barrage of fire, and you could see the smoke building up. When the artillery stopped, we started into the city again. By noon the fight was over.

Me and Bobby Joe and two other guys were assigned to guard some wounded Germans. The Germans looked terrible. One had a huge wound in his side, and he kept his hand over it. One had a head wound, and he was moaning and shaking. Our medics took care of our guys first.

Bobby Joe gave one of the wounded Germans a cigarette and he took it and just stared at it.

"It's a Chesterfield," Bobby Joe said.

The German's hands were shaking when he lit the cigarette. I thought he was just scared, but it must have been his wounds. He took a few deep puffs, then fell over dead.

I found out later that there wasn't any way of getting the Germans back safely. We couldn't afford the men. I asked an officer if we were going to let them go. He didn't say anything, just looked away.

McCormack is okay, only maybe not too smart. He says he's got a girlfriend in Roanoke who teaches school.

I think he wants to buddy up with me and Bobby Joe. He looks like a good soldier.

June 14

We're on reserve. The captain says not to get too frisky because the Germans don't know we're on reserve. McCormack said he'd send them a telegram.

I had bugs in my socks and a tick under my skin. McCormack burned it out with a cigarette. I took my first bath in Normandy. Actually, I took two baths. First, I got my steel pot filled with hot water and washed everything from my waist up because I was kind of nervous about taking my pants off in case we got shelled. The water felt so good I went back and got another pot of water and washed from my waist down.

"You getting to be a real pretty boy," Crockett said.

Crockett is from Wheeling, West Virginia. He's a big guy with half his teeth missing. He has false teeth, but he only wears them once in a while. He works in supply. I was thinking about how much I liked him and was wondering why. Then I realized that he's left over from the guys that I trained with back in the States. I don't know how many of us are left. I don't want to know.

I slept for almost nine hours. I had bad dreams that I don't want to write about now. Maybe later.

June 15

Crap. My squad has to go back to pick up some replace-ments. I swear somebody must have volunteered us. I asked McCormack, but he swears up and down that it wasn't him. The new guys are back in St. Clair. We took off at 0500 and reached St. Clair by 0730. Traveling with a squad instead of the platoon or even a company is scary. I keep thinking about how many Germans there might be around. Never, in all my life, do I think I'll get to be brave.

The guys we picked up are radio operators. One of them is a big-mouth gung-ho dude named Hightower, just out of Fort Gordon Signal School down in Georgia. He thinks he knows everything but he hasn't been in any fights yet.

"Where Hitler made his big mistake," Hightower said, "was when he thought he could walk over the United States the way he walked over Poland and the Nether-lands."

Then he went on about how the Nazis have taken over all these countries in Europe and how they think they are the master race and all. It all sounded like stuff you hear back home on the newsreels. As a matter of fact, Hightower reminds me of that chicken that comes on when they start the news.

When we got back to camp we had our first mail call,

but I didn't get anything. I don't know how they expect to find me when I've been in about three different companies in the last week. By the time you get settled in one company, it could be so chewed up they have to reform you into another company. Let Hightower deal with that.

Dear Mom,

I read in the papers (from Ohio) that Dolph Camilli is probably going to win the slugging award for the year. I think Uncle Richie has his autograph, but I'm not sure. Tell Danny to ask him about it.

I also read a lot of stuff about how the Russians are attacking Hitler on the eastern front. I hope that we are the ones who get him in the end. That will make all the sacrifices worthwhile.

I am doing fine so far. Fine means something different over here than it does in Roanoke, though.

There are plenty of rumors going around. One is that we have only three more objectives and then we get to go home. That makes sense to me. I don't know if you got my last letter. Do you think it would be all right for me to write to Angie? I have her address in my book (my little black book, ha ha) but I don't want to write to her if she is seeing somebody steady.

Your son,
Scott

June 16

Mail call. Some guy from the adjutant general's office came around and told everybody to destroy their letters after they read them. Two guys told him to take a flying leap. Right to his face. He started explaining that it was in case we got captured. I knew he wouldn't like me carrying around this notebook, writing down everything that's happening to me. But sometimes I feel that this is the only thing I have to leave behind. Some guys worry about their wives and children and here I am wishing I had a wife and some children.

We are still near Couvains. We're massing for an attack. My stomach feels queasy. I know it's because I am scared out of my mind. All I can think about is the day we landed. I told Bobby Joe and he came out with this big grin and I felt bad having told him that I was scared.

"Scotty," he said, "I'm so scared that if I ran right into myself I'd shoot me two or three times before I said hello. Only thing that keeps me from running is I don't know which way to run and I'm too tired to get up and look around."

I'm bone tired, too. Sleep over here is different than even back in England. I dream about dead guys looking up at me, hoping I'll do something, hoping I'll give them a hand and get them up on their feet.

Lt. Rowe is leading my platoon. He's a little over six feet and thin. I remember him being a good ballplayer back in Virginia and a pretty fair guy. He said nothing can be as bad as what we've already been through. Maybe. My mind says that what he says is true but I didn't know how it was going to be then. I know now.

A plane came by and dropped some leaflets. Some flew toward us and we got a few of them. They were in German, and somebody said they were leaflets we were dropping to tell the Germans to surrender. I hope the Germans listen

ALLIIERTES · OBERKOMMANDO

(Supreme Headquarters, Allied Expeditionary Force)

BEKANNTMACHUNG

1. In dem unter meinem Oberkommando stehenden Kriegsschauplatz wird hiermit eine Militärregierung für die besetzten deutschen Gebiete errichtet. Die Militärregierung verfügt über die Vollmachten für Verwaltung sowie Gesetzgebung und Rechtssprechung, die in meiner Person als Oberbefehlshaber der Alliierten Streitkräfte und Militär-Gouverneur vereinigt sind.

2. Die erste Aufgabe der Militärregierung während des Fortgangs militärischer Operationen wird es sein, die rückwärtigen Verbindungen der alliierten Heere sicherzustellen und rücksichtslos alle Umtriebe in den besetzten Gebieten zu unterdrücken, die der baldigen Beendigung des Krieges entgegenwirken.

3. Zugleich wird die Militärregierung die Ausrottung des nationalsozialistischen Systems in Angriff nehmen. Die Militärregierung wird alle Mitglieder der NSDAP und der SS von verantwortlichen Stellen entfernen, ebenso andere Personen, die an führender Stelle am nationalsozialistischen System beteiligt sind. Diese Schritte werden sofort nach Eintreffen der alliierten Armeen und Einsetzung der Militärregierung in Angriff genommen.

4. Die Zivilbevölkerung hat nach Möglichkeit ihren normalen Beschäftigungen nachzugehen. Eingehende Bestimmungen werden für sie von den zuständigen Militärbehörden jedes betreffenden Gebietes erlassen werden.

DWIGHT D. EISENHOWER

General,
Oberster Befehlshaber der Alliierten Streitkräfte

ZG 64

A patrol went out to look for a minefield. They got jumped by a platoon of Germans. The sergeant in charge of the patrol said that they beat the Germans off and only lost two men.

"If we go back that way we can get them," he said.

"Who were they?" I asked.

"Nichols. Nichols and Weeks, you know them?"

I knew them.

June 17

We pushed off early. In the distance I could hear the booming of the artillery. Noise is death. Noise is the crackle of a machine gun from somewhere you can't see, or the explosion at the mouth of a German artillery piece four miles away, or a grenade or mortar landing close enough to send some jagged steel through your body. Bobby Joe said that if you hear the sound it means they missed. No, after a while even the noise wounds you.

When it comes from the ships offshore, it sounds different, a deeper sound like an animal exhaling. When it's smaller stuff, it sounds a little bit like a bear cub hissing when it's mad. It's all meant to kill you. That's why everybody is over here: they want to kill me. There are others they want to kill, too, I know, but it's me I'm beginning to feel pity for.

As we get closer to our target, stumbling in the early darkness to someplace named St. Lô, the air gets heavy with the mist and stink of the fighting. The sun catches wisps of smoke rising from the fires where the shells were hitting. It looks almost beautiful.

McCormack said he heard that they were shelling Carentan. "They're hitting it hard," he said.

"I thought they took it already," I answered.

He shrugged. We had heard that they had taken Carentan, but I guess the report was wrong.

June 18

It is an incredibly cold day. My fingers were almost numb this morning. By the time the sun was up, there was fighting all around us. I don't know where the Germans are and I don't know if they know where we are.

We started across a field when a plane strafed us. It didn't get anyone, but it shook us all up. Planes are scary.

We're spread out about two hundred yards, maybe two fifty, depending on the lay of the land. This morning I was closer to the enemy than I have ever been, except for some German prisoners. We went through a little village, St. Andre de l'Epine. A woman was putting her wash out of the windows on the second floor. Lt. Rowe pointed her out to us. It was so normal that we all had to turn and look.

We came up on a half-track that looked out of commission but it opened up on us.

I could hear it. I could hear the bullets hit them. The first two guys in the column went down, one quietly and one screaming. All the guys were firing toward the half-track. I was screaming, and then I saw Bobby Joe running and I went after him. I didn't know what Bobby Joe was going to do. Then I saw him get behind a tree. I was right with him and I saw him pulling the pin on a grenade. I did the same and we threw together as the half-track sent a burst into the tree.

The half-track was spinning around crazily on one track. Two Germans came out of the top. Maybe they were trying to surrender. I don't know. They were hit right away. One fell over the side and the other fell back inside the half-track. Two guys ran over and dropped grenades inside.

I got myself over to the road and saw the first German. He was dead. Then there was more firing and I saw the guys taking cover.

"Scotty! Scotty!"

Bobby Joe was screaming at me. I looked down the road and saw a bunch of Jerries spreading out, taking positions. They were on the road with another half-track. The corporal took a shot at the half-track with a bazooka. He missed, and the half-track's guns turned on him and fired. The corporal jumped into a ditch.

It took three mortar rounds before the half-track was knocked out. The German soldiers kept coming. There were about eighteen or nineteen of them. Then, suddenly, they stopped and started to hightail it.

"Stay down! Stay down!" Lt. Rowe signaled for us to spread out and stay down.

I was on the ground and shooting toward the knot of German soldiers running back toward the trees. About half of them were on the ground, wounded.

We exchanged fire for a while without actually seeing the Germans but knowing they must be there. Then we saw one of them coming forward waving a piece of cloth. They were giving up.

Sgt. Draper, a tough son of a gun, stood up and waved the Germans to come in. They came in, hands raised above their heads, and Sgt. Draper made them sit in a small circle. They weren't too far from me so I went over and took a look at them.

One of them, a bigheaded guy with a gold tooth, was wounded in the side of the face. It looked terrible and he kept wanting to put his hand on it. Sgt. Draper wouldn't let him.

Gearhart, a guy from Martinsburg who speaks German, questioned them. He said that they thought there were only four or five of us, or they wouldn't have come out.

There were seven German soldiers who were healthy enough to keep on walking. The rest were wounded pretty bad or dead. The German corporal told Gearhart that there were thirty guys originally, but the others had either been killed or captured. From where I was, I could see him looking around, wondering what was going to happen to him. Donalds, a heavyset guy with deep set eyes, took the German corporal by the sleeve. He pulled him over to the side of the road where one of our guys lay dead. Lt. Rowe went over to them and stood next to Donalds. I didn't see him saying anything but Donalds just turned and walked away.

Why am I alive? Bullets had flown around me. There were dead Americans lying on the ground. Why am I alive?

One of our wounded guys was calling for his mama. Nobody wanted to hear him or deal with the panic we knew was filling his chest.

"Move out!" Lt. Rowe, who carried a carbine, cradled it in his arms and started down the road.

McCormack got a letter from his folks. He read part of it about how President Roosevelt had told everyone that we were doing a good job and teaching the Germans a lesson.

June 19

It's raining. I am miserable. I am cold and sore all over. I picked up a French direction sign. I carried it for about a half-hour before I threw it away. I had been thinking about taking it home, but then it didn't matter anymore. Things that matter in the morning somehow don't matter in the afternoon. By the time the night arrives all that matters is that I am alive. We fought all day yesterday. First we called in artillery and blasted the crap out of the Germans. When we figured it was safe we started toward St. Lô again. I don't know how the Germans lived through the shelling, but they were firing from the rubble. Webster and Kesler got it. I know Kesler's family and feel sorry for them.

All around there are dead animals. They lie in the road and bloat up. I saw a calf lying near a dead cow that was probably its mother.

I know I shot a German today. He was in a window and I shot through the shutter. Maybe I didn't kill him. It's not something I want to think about.

I have to think about it. I was covering the squad as we moved through a circle of buildings. In the middle of the circle was a statue and I was behind it. That's when I looked up and saw the German in the window. I emptied a clip I had just put in. That's eight shots in maybe two or three seconds. The Germans have machine guns. McCormack said they even have machine pistols.

I am afraid of being killed. It's not something I think about all the time, but it's always there. Some guys make jokes about it; some don't even want to mention it.

A tank battalion came by. They stink of grease and oil. Lt. Rowe talked with one of the officers and somehow bummed a radio. We went past the center of the town, past the dead, listening to Glenn Miller.

There are people in these towns, men, women, and children. They are thin, with dark shadows around their eyes. They all look as if they have seen too much, that they can't take any more in. When we pass they stare at us. Sometimes they come out and kiss our hands. I think that somehow they believe that we will end the war for them.

Tomorrow we're going to head back toward St. Andre. It looks like we gain a few hundred yards and then we get pushed back. I wonder if anybody has figured out if we're winning or losing.

Today is my parents' anniversary. I'm glad I didn't die today; it would have messed things up for them.

June 20

Don't sit under the apple tree
With anyone else but me
Anyone else but me
Anyone else but me
No! No! No!
Don't sit under the apple tree
With anyone else but me
Till I come marching home

We're camping in an orchard grove. The trees are all shot up, but if I put my head back and look through the branches I can almost be home. I remember when my Boy Scout troop went on a camping trip with a Scout troop from Salem and we spent the night in an apple orchard. It was a glorious feeling to get out in the open and look up at the stars. It's a glorious memory now.

We had a lecture from a chaplain today who wanted to explain why we are over here. Some of the guys started kidding around, saying they had got on the wrong bus — stuff like that. The chaplain (a Catholic, but I didn't mind) started telling us about Hitler and his rise to power. I wrote down some notes.

Hitler — Born in April 1889, became chancellor in 1933, hooked up with Mussolini in 1936, got a bunch of land in the Munich Agreement in 1938, and started the World War in 1939. Then the chaplain gave us the five steps that he said led to us being over here.

"First, people tolerate evil because they see some benefit to themselves," he said. "Then, they feed it in hope that it will turn into something else. Then, they appease it in hope that it will not turn against them. Then, they respect it because they fear it. Finally, someone has to step up and stamp it out! That's the assignment we've been given, to stop this evil that Hitler and his Nazis represent."

I was taking notes, and later Bobby Joe asked me if he could copy the part about the five steps leading to us being in the war.

"One day when I get to explaining all this to my kids, I'm going to need to know what to say," he said.

I wanted to ask the chaplain just how the Nazis had got started and all but he had to get leave and go to the next outfit.

I didn't really know anything about the Nazis before I got into the war. Back when I was a kid I remember Joe Louis beating a German that somebody said was probably a Nazi.

Jerry Villency is alive! Some guys from the Second Battalion came into our outfit, and he was with them. I didn't recognize him at first. He looks so much older. He came over to where I was sitting against the wall of the church grounds and put his hand on my shoulder. Even when he called my name, it took me a while to remember who he was.

"I thought it was you," he said. "It was either you or a pile of rags with a rifle."

"Do I look that bad?"

"You look a lot worse," he said, grinning. He sat down next to me and put his arm around me.

Jerry's about my size and was always a good guy. He had taped his glasses and there was a scab on his forehead.

"You see anybody else we know?" I asked.

"Everybody's dead," he said sadly. "Cliff Lee, Jimmy Wright, so many guys."

"I'm glad you're alive, man," I said.

We hugged each other and I was near to crying just to see him alive. He was sad and tired. We talked for a while, and then some of his guys started moving out and he said he had to go.

"But the Second's not your battalion," I said.

"It is now," he said.

He started away, then stopped and came back. He took off his pack and went through it until he found what he was looking for. Then he gave it to me, waved, and started down the road.

What Jerry had given me was a copy of the *The Roanoke World-News*. It was a paper from right after

D-Day and there was a lot of stuff in it about the landing. None of it made much sense. They had maps showing us landing all over France, from Calais down to the south of France.

What I looked at most was the sports stuff and the advertisements. Jefferson had won a game. I saw names I knew, kids I had left behind who were too young to be in the war. They were still back there, being kids and living well.

There was an article about George Burns and Gracie Allen, who are comedians. When somebody asked them if they were funny when they were home, Gracie said she didn't think so, because she didn't hear anybody laughing.

St. Andre isn't too bad off. There's a really big church right in the center of it. Behind the church there's a cemetery. Some guys went into it and just walked around. There's a few craters where bombs hit, and most of the buildings have some pockmarks from shells.

There's talk about German paratroopers being dropped just past St. Lô. Maj. Howie (I think that's his name, but I don't know why I can't remember it that well) said the Germans are getting set for an all-out counteroffensive. All-out counteroffensive? If they haven't been fighting all-out, what have they been doing? Him saying that really pissed me off. He always gets me mad.

Bobby Joe likes him, though. He says he's really a stand-up kind of guy.

I'm taking a chance on writing to Angie. This is a copy of the letter.

Dear Angie,

In a way you know me and in a way you don't. Being in the war and everything has made me different. What I would like is to have somebody back home to write to, if you don't mind. If you have a steady boyfriend then I will find somebody else, but if you don't I would like to write to you. Even more than that I would like for you to write to me. Sometimes you get so tired and feel so low you need something or someone to bring you back to a point where you are even normal.

Angie, I can't say that I love you but I can say that I have always liked you and hope that you can find it in your heart to like me.

Yours truly,
Scott

The letter isn't strictly true because I am *thatclose* to being in love with Angie Gardiner. If anybody was to ask me how I came to fall in love with her, I would say I don't know, but in my heart I think I just need somebody to be in love with back home.

Two replacement guys joined our unit. Doug Kerlin is from Max Meadows, and J. J. Dandridge is from Winchester. They're scared. They came in on an LST, and when they got to the beach a company of Negro soldiers was loading coffins to take back to the States. That got them scared, but I tried to tell them that it was a good sign.

"Most of the guys that were killed on the first day are buried here," I told them. "We're just mopping up now."

They asked me how many guys were killed during the invasion and I told them that I didn't know, but it was a lot.

They were talking about us sticking together. I don't know if I want any friends over here, but I said okay.

June 21

Everyone was sitting around when a plane came overhead. We all ducked into whatever shelter we could find. The plane — I thought it was a German plane — was in trouble. We watched it stall out, go into a dive, then bank sharply to its left. Soldiers have been trained to stay out of the open; civilians haven't. When the plane came down, I moved a step into the house I was in. The plane first headed for a field and then turned sharply and, because its engines had stopped, silently. It came down like that, catching the sun on its wings, smoke pouring from its fuselage, until it crashed a few feet from a house at the corner of the town square. A small group of civilians tried to get away at the last moment, but it was too late.

June 23

There is fighting every day. You can hear it down the road, or in the distance. Sometimes, when it is cloudy, you can't tell where the sounds of the fighting are coming from. But they are always there. The artillery booms, booms, booms, and then is answered by the echoes in the distant valleys, all sounding like heartbeats coming from the earth. Sometimes, I'd swear that war is a living thing, huge and ugly, that eats up lives.

Squads go out and you don't look at them because you know they might not come back. When the sergeant looks around for volunteers you don't look away, but you don't look at him. Today, me and Billy Joe and Kerlin had to go out and look at a house near the far corner of the village.

"We're moving out tonight and we don't want anybody giving away our position," Lt. Rowe said. "But somebody thought he saw a light in that house and it's not supposed to be occupied. Check it out, and be alert."

Crockett said he was going to go with us.

Checking out a house for enemy soldiers is always hairy. Kerlin said we didn't even have to check it out since we were moving out anyway. Crockett told him if he didn't want to be a soldier he should turn in his M-1 and put on a dress. I was thinking the same thing as Kerlin, and I was glad that I hadn't opened my mouth first.

It was 2010 and still light out as we got near the building. Two kids, about six or seven, were playing on the stairs, and Bobby Joe told them to go away. At first they didn't understand, but then he made a mean face at them and they ran. I watched them run about twenty yards and then the little girl turned and made a face at Bobby Joe.

"I'll go upstairs," Crockett said. "You guys cover me."

"I'll go with you," I said.

"You see anything funny you just hightail it on out of there," Bobby Joe said.

Crockett went stomping up the stairs. If there were any Germans up there, they would have plenty of time to hide. A German with his head down was a lot better than a German with his head up and his sights on us.

There were three stories to the building. Crockett went up the first flight and stopped at the top of the stairs. He looked around and then started to move through the rooms. The floorboards creaked something terrible.

"Bitte?"

That was what Crockett was calling out. It means something in German like — hello? or What did you say? We were taught that back in England.

"Bitte?"

Crockett pushed into rooms while I covered the halls. Nothing. We checked every room slowly, and I wondered if there was an attic. Some of these old houses don't have regular American attics, but instead something like a half room, almost a crawl space that you could get a cot into if you had to.

There were three rooms on the second floor, and after Crockett had checked all of them, I started up the stairs to the third floor. He stopped me and went past me.

"Get the other guys up here," he said.

I went to the top of the stairs and was about to call Billy Joe when I thought I saw something move in the room at the end of the hall. I turned and saw Crockett, who was almost to the next floor.

My skin went real cold and I could feel my balls shrivel up into a knot. I whistled to let Crockett know I saw something, or thought I did. He whistled back. He didn't know what I meant. At the bottom of the stairs, Bobby Joe looked at me and shrugged.

I wasn't sure. Maybe I hadn't seen anything. Still, I

pointed toward the room. Bobby Joe came up the stairs quickly.

"I'm not sure, but I'll try to flush them out if they're there," I said.

I went up to the next landing where Crockett was.

"It's clear up here," he said.

"I think I might have seen something down below," I said.

I took a grenade and went into the room over the one I thought I had seen a movement in. It was a bedroom, and I pulled the mattress off the bed. I put the mattress on the floor, took two grenades off my belt, and pulled the pins. I held them for a second, then put them on the floor and put the mattress over them. I knew the grenades would bring down the ceiling below us. Me and Crockett moved out of the room.

"Bobby Joe! I'm blowing the ceiling!" I called out a split second before the grenades blew.

A huge puff of smoke came out of the room the grenades were in and Crockett went by me and sprayed some shots toward the walls. From the floor below I heard a series of shots and ran to the stairs.

Bobby Joe was firing into the room and Kerlin had come up and he was firing into the cloud of dust that poured through the doors.

I reached the landing and fired while Bobby Joe reloaded.

When the smoke cleared we saw two Germans. One was lying on the floor; the other, badly wounded, was on his knees and draped across the seat of the overstuffed couch. The couch had been pushed away from the wall and we moved it out more. There was a hole in the wall where the Germans had been. In the hole there was a radio and a pack of French cigarettes.

"They were shooting at the ceiling," Bobby Joe said.

"They won't be shooting at any more ceilings," Kerlin said.

I thought about Crockett. He hadn't come downstairs. I took the stairs two at a time.

Crockett was stretched out on his back.

"Right through the floor," he said.

"You okay?" I asked.

"I'm going home," he said. "I got to be okay, Jimbo."

Then he groaned. Then he died. That was the way the day ended.

June 24

I am so down over Crockett. I do have to admit that I am thankful it was not me who got killed. A feeling of shame comes over me when I think like that, but that's what's really going through my mind. It's terrible to see guys wounded and killed, but I don't want it to be me that's laying on the side of the road.

Today is Saturday, as if the day of the week had any meaning. The noncoms and officers had a meeting. We could see that something big was going on. After they had their meeting, each company had a meeting. I sat next to Bobby Joe as Col. Dallas talked to us. It was a little gung ho, but all right. He said the Germans are discovering who we are and they don't like it a bit.

"When they were running over the Netherlands and France, they thought we were too weak to fight," he said. "They thought that because we have all kinds of people in our society, whites, blacks, Asians, and Indians, that we didn't have the moral fiber to fight.

"When we entered the war, they thought we wouldn't have the guts of the German soldier. Then they thought they could stop us at the beaches and throw us back into the sea. They had their best at Omaha Beach, and they didn't think that we had the will to make the sacrifices that we have made to carry off the invasion. Now they're desperate. They know who we are, brave and determined men. They know how well we are trained and they know that we're not going to walk away from this fight. They're bringing everything they have to try and hold us here in Normandy. For some reason, they think they can still win this war. Maybe that's the way you think when you consider yourself a master race. I don't know. I do know they will not win because you will not let them win. Soon, very soon, the world will know that, too."

After Col. Dallas finished talking, we got another talk about how we were going to take St. Lô. Well, that was nothing new.

June 25

Went to a badly damaged church. It was beautiful except for the wall behind the altar being blown out. It had a nice effect with the cross silhouetted against the blue sky. Maj. Donovan delivered the sermon and I got to thinking about how things are back home.

"It's five hours earlier here than it is at home," Bobby Joe said after the service. A quartermaster truck had brought up supplies and he was putting on new socks. "Just about now, my mom is making breakfast and my dad is shaving."

"You think they'll pray for us?" I asked.

Soon as I said that, I was sorry I had opened my mouth. Bobby Joe saw me getting sad and threw his old socks at me.

In the afternoon some guys set up a radio and were dancing to Glenn Miller. Some French girls came out to watch them, but they wouldn't dance. J. J. Dandridge came over and told me and Bobby Joe that he had an invite to have dinner with a French family.

"Kerlin's got the crud and can't come," he said.

What Kerlin has is an infection between his toes. After we questioned J. J. about being sure the Frenchies were okay, me, him, and Bobby Joe went to this house. It was a nice place with two women and a girl. One of the women was small, or maybe just thin, and about forty or forty-five years old. She had dark hair and eyes and a sharp, kind of pointy nose. The other one was maybe seventy. She had white hair that she kept touching, pushing it into place. I think she was just nervous. She also had a pointy nose, so I figured that she was the mother of the first woman. The girl was eight years old.

Only the younger woman spoke English and so when we sat down she was the one to say how much she liked Americans. We sat around for a while and then Bobby Joe said he didn't think they had anything to eat.

"They invited me to dinner and said I could bring my friends," J. J. said.

I asked the woman who spoke English if they had any food and she just shrugged.

Bobby Joe told us to wait while he went to get some food. He came back with two five-in-ones. The five-in-ones are what the tankers and truck drivers eat. Each package has five meals in it. We opened one, and the French woman cooked it and we all ate it. We talked a little bit but she didn't speak enough English to make it a real conversation and none of us speak French. We left the other five-in-one with them.

The little girl was younger than Ellen, but she reminded me of my sister. Ellen is older in years, but this little girl was older in a different way. The fighting is taking away the little girl in her and making her old before her time. We soldiers are fighting for our lives. The French, already beaten down by the Germans, are fighting for their souls.

We are on reserve again and it feels good just to rest. We can still hear the sounds of fighting off in the distance, and every once in a while a plane buzzes us and we're diving under something or into a ditch. The scary thing is that the fighting is all around, not just in one direction. Rumor has it that the 101st Airborne is fighting against the Sixth Nazi Parachute Division and a panzer tank outfit. A guy who calls himself a "leftenant" from the English army says they're fighting against tanks east of us.

"The whole line has to hold or we're going to catch it," a sergeant said. "If their tanks break through, then they can swing around and start cutting off individual units."

"Thanks for letting us know the good news," J. J. said. "We were worried the Germans had run out of ideas."

I asked Lt. Rowe if I could see his maps and he let me.

What I saw was that the distance from the beach we landed on to St. Lô is just about the same distance between Roanoke and Bedford. On a good day I can make the trip to Bedford in thirty minutes. We have been fighting like crazy and we haven't taken twenty five miles yet.

June 26

Some units from the 115th are moving toward St. Lô. They look ready for a good fight. I have to admit they look sharper than we do.

I am getting used to being relaxed. Bobby Joe said that he thinks the Germans are retreating. I said that I agreed with him, but I don't really. I am hoping they are retreating more than thinking it.

Got a letter! Yes!

Mom said that everything is fine at home. Danny got a job at Furbursh's drugstore for the summer and Ellen got a two-week pass to the movies for collecting the most newspapers for the war effort. She said everybody is proud of us and praying for us. She wants me to write if I have a chance, but not to worry about it if I am too busy.

That probably means that she hasn't received my letters. I spoke to Lt. Hanken, and he said that as far as he knows, the mail is getting through. He is worried that his letters aren't getting through, too.

June 27

A guy stepped on a mine today just twenty feet behind the mess truck, so they made us look for more mines. The Germans have their minefields marked, but naturally they take up the signs when they go. There are three kinds of mines over here. The biggest is the tank mine which is not that bad because it won't go off if just a person steps on it. The small ones, the anti-personnel mines, are scary.

"I'd rather be looking for tank mines," J. J. said.

I don't think J. J. is all that bright. *Anybody* would rather look for a tank mine. All you have to do is stick your bayonet in the ground and you can find them. Then you need to dig under them carefully to make sure the Germans haven't booby-trapped them by putting an anti-personnel mine under the tank mine. The anti-personnel mines go off too easy. The Germans have one mine that will go off as soon as you step on it. It'll either blow off part of your leg or kill you outright. Another one they have doesn't go off right away — it shoots up in the air when you take your foot off it. Then it blows up so it gets you in your body. They call them Bouncing Bettys.

I was probing around for a half-hour when I hit something I thought was a mine. What I wanted to do was to shoot it, but I had to dig it out. It turned out to be a rock. Still scared me to death.

June 28

Three new guys showed up. Their fatigues are nice and shiny. They said they were over from Fort Dix and had been with the First Army. We got into an argument about whether the King Sisters or the Andrews Sisters sing the best. The new guys were saying that we didn't know what we were talking about when me and Bobby Joe said the King Sisters sing the best. Everybody got mad at them. They haven't been around long enough to make a lot of noise about anything.

Kerlin is going back to England. We heard him being chewed out and then saw him packing up his gear.

"What happened?" J. J. asked him.

"My crud got worse," he said.

He took off his shoes and we looked at his feet. The infections between his toes had gotten worse. It looked pretty bad. The skin between the toes was cracked and he couldn't walk without limping.

"When I get rid of the crud I'll be back," he said.

When he left on a truck with two other guys who had been wounded, I think we all had mixed feelings. One thing for sure, he isn't going to be in the fighting for a while.

Naturally we had an inspection of all our feet and socks. Everybody who had dirty socks on or sores on their feet got chewed out, same as back in the States.

June 29

A stream of guys from the 115th, the same that passed through a few days ago, came back from fighting at St. Lô.

"We got chewed up and spit out!" a guy with his head bandaged said. "They were dug in and waiting for us. They got 88s, mortars, panzers, everything. One of their panzers knocked out two of our tanks like they were toys."

Bobby Joe asked how many guys they had lost, and this guy said he didn't know. He was in a ten-man squad, with two machine guns instead of one, and five guys were killed and him and another guy wounded.

"They waited until we were in the town, then they attacked our flank with panzers that were in the buildings," the guy said. He took a lit cigarette somebody offered him. "They attacked the right flank and then started firing down on us from the buildings. We were shooting back, but we couldn't see what we were shooting at. Finally, we spotted some infantry guys coming toward us. They looked like paratroopers, maybe a company of them, trying to cut us off. I don't think anybody would have made it if our machine gunner hadn't stayed back to cover us."

"He get out?"

"No."

St. Lô is a railroad town and a communications center for the Germans. The longer they hold it, the better the chance they can get enough reinforcements to start pushing us back toward the beaches. Some of the guys from the 115th said the Germans have placed their guns to cover all the main streets so you can't get more than a squad involved in a firefight on a particular street.

"You can't send a whole company down a narrow city street," a sergeant said. "You have to fight them doorway to doorway, building by building."

The guys from the 115th looked beat-up. It didn't make us feel good to see them like that.

A captain just told us to get our gear together. We're moving out.

June 30

We moved toward St. Lô last night. Halfway there we got hit by artillery. Two trucks got knocked out in the first barrage and at first everybody thought it was mortars, but it wasn't. We moved forward to change the range of the artillery in case they had a spotter who saw us on the road. That looked like it worked because they were walking their artillery back the other way. But then we got hit by a new barrage and got into a firefight with what looked like a battalion. We pulled back fast, and for a while it took all the nerve we had not to panic. The Germans are good at what they do.

For some reason I was thinking that we should win all the fights because we're the good guys. It doesn't work that way. I don't want to question God or anything, but this fighting against the Germans doesn't work the way I thought it would.

The days off did me a little good but now that we're back into it I think I have to get used to the fighting again. No, I won't get used to it. I just hope I live through it.

When we got out of range, we picked up some more tank support. Some of the officers are saying that their tanks are better than ours. When we get into big tank fights our tanks get knocked out quick. But our infantry guys need tank support of some kind when we go up against the panzers. You don't shoot an M-1 at a German panzer and live to tell about it.

Found out that Col. Metcalf was wounded. Hope he'll be okay. Dallas is taking his place.

I'm sorry I wrote to Angie. Maybe she's going to think I'm stupid because I don't really know her. Maybe she won't get the letter.

July 1

Lt. Hanken was making a list of the wounded and dead and Paul Huntington's name was on it. I think he did some yardwork for Angie's family once. Also, Kerlin's name was listed on it as being dead, but I told Hanken that he only came down with the crud.

Bobby Joe has a terrible bruise on one side of his face.

"I was behind a tank when it got hit," he said. "When the shell hit the tank it knocked it back three feet. I was just lucky it didn't roll over me."

If I once thought I would make it home safe, that thought is gone now. They keep replacing guys, and sooner or later they're going to have to replace me. No use worrying about it.

Also, found out that Kerlin *is* dead. The truck they were taking him back on got wiped out. I'm glad I didn't know him better.

July 3

More replacements arrived. They seem like nice guys. They're coming in already scared. I wonder what they're being told. We're being allowed to sleep late, but then we do training maneuvers, weapon drills, and target practice. Bobby Joe thinks that they want the new men to get used to the noise. Lt. Rowe says that we have to get accustomed to working with each other.

"What we do depends largely on how we make out as a team," he said. "If we work together we'll be all right."

This is not my idea of work. What he really means is if we fight together we'll be all right.

Off in the distance the constant *boom-boom-boom* of artillery never stops. I think that if I make it back home I will always hear it. I'm tired today. I can't sleep soundly over here. Sometimes I dream, but most of what I dream about is fighting. In every dream I find a dead guy who just looks up at me. Sometimes I think I recognize the dead guy. Mikey . . . Wojo . . . Crockett . . . Kerlin. I'm forgetting some of the names already. Back home I never dreamed.

The officers are getting closer to the men. They're not friendlier or anything like that. They just know that we all know the same thing that they know about the last few weeks. The officers went over the plans to take St. Lô and tried to show us just what we have to do. All the towns in France are in valleys, and there are hills that overlook them. What we are going to do is to take the hills around St. Lô. On the maps, the hills are named according to how high they are. The higher the hill, the tougher it's going to be to take it. The Germans dig in and shoot down on you and it's just terrible. There aren't any easy battles, just fights that I somehow make it through.

We found a shallow grave in the back of a building. The way we found it was the rain had washed away some of the dirt and there were boots sticking up from the ground. The company commander had some of the new guys dig up enough to figure out that the bodies were Germans. Then we covered them back up.

July 4

Woke up feeling pretty gung ho because of the Fourth of July. We passed a French house and a young boy waved at us and called out, "Hey, Yanks!" That made me feel good.

I wonder if there were any parades going on back home. I know there must have been plenty. Picnics, too. Heard on the radio that the Russians took Minsk. It must be really good to take back your own city.

July 5

Went on a patrol last night to capture a German. Me, Lt. Rowe, and two sergeants jumped off at 2300.

"We want to get one guy and bring him back alive to headquarters," Lt. Rowe said. "The best way to do this is to find one or two guys off by themselves and snatch them. If we see a target, we'll split into two-man teams. Collins, you stick with me. The team that gets the prisoner will secure him and move out. The other team will cover."

We taped our dog tags to our chests so they wouldn't

make noise and put leaves and twigs in the webbing over our helmets to break up the outline. I put black grease on my cheekbones and chin.

There were Germans moving in the vicinity of Cerisy Forest and we headed there. One of the sergeants said that he knew there was American infantry in the northern part of the woods.

"That's why the Germans send patrols," he said.

So we were going to look for a German patrol that might be looking for American prisoners. I was carrying six grenades along with my rifle and a small carbine bayonet I had picked up from supply. I had my regular M-1 bayonet on my cartridge belt as well.

The night was warm, even though it was raining lightly as we moved along the hedgerows toward the road that led to Cerisy. There was a moon, and every so often it found a hole in the clouds and lit up the fields. At 2400 we saw a light coming from what looked like a small hut. We got down on the ground and started crawling along a ridge toward the light, with the two sergeants about 25 yards to our right. When Lt. Rowe and I got within ten yards of where the light was, it went out. I froze, thinking they must have spotted us.

We heard a noise and saw the outline of a figure coming toward us. He had something in his hands and I thought it was a machine gun. I pushed the safety of my rifle. It was already off. A cold trickle of sweat ran under my chin strap and down my neck.

The figure stopped just as the moonlight broke through the trees. It was just light enough to see a German soldier standing about fifteen feet away from me. I glanced over at where I thought Lt. Rowe was and couldn't see him. I looked back at the German and saw that he was fumbling with his belt. My mind said "grenade," and I aimed my rifle the best I could. Then I saw him dropping his pants.

When he squatted down I saw Lt. Rowe lift his hand and signal me.

Fifteen feet is one hash mark on a football field. I made it in a hot second. I grabbed the German around the neck and pulled him backward. Lt. Rowe got over him and put both his hands over the guy's face. I thought for a while he was going to kill him but then he let him go.

The German was gasping when Lt. Rowe released his face. Then Lt. Rowe put his hands over his face again. It was like choking down a wild horse.

I could feel the German's heart throbbing in his throat. His eyes were wild, and he was trying to bring his hands together, trying to pray.

Lt. Rowe pulled a hood from his shirt and put it over the guy's face.

"Heinreich?" A voice came from the hut. Another German. "Heinreich?"

Lt. Rowe had his hands over the face of the German we had down and I had the small bayonet pressed into his neck.

The German calling to him listened for a while, shrugged, and went back into the hut.

We dragged away the German we had captured and met up with the two sergeants. The German still had the hood over his face and I think he was kind of whimpering.

When I got back to camp Lt. Rowe said I had done a good job. Two officers took the hood off the German, searched him, then put him against a wall and started questioning him. His hands were shaking and he was stuttering. He tried to wipe the snot off his face, but the American officers wouldn't let him lift his hands. I couldn't understand anything being said, so I went to look for my squad and bunked down for the rest of the night.

July 6

Woke up early this morning and felt strange. Don't know why, but I did. Got some coffee. Mom is going to be surprised to find out I drink coffee, because I never did like it back home. I was thinking about Danny and Ellen and Dad and drinking the coffee when I saw some planes in the distance. They weren't more than a few miles away.

The sun hadn't burned off the haze yet so you couldn't see anything too clearly, but you could hear the angry buzz of the plane engines. They were strafing some ground position, going high in the sky, and then swooping down through the early-morning mist. From where I sat at the base of a tree, I could see the dark puffs of smoke, like black flowers, fill the sky around the planes.

"Would you rather be up there or down here?" J. J. asked me.

I hadn't seen him coming and jumped a little.

"It doesn't make a difference to me," I said, "Long as I don't miss the party."

Lt. Hanken asked me to take the casualty list to battalion headquarters. I said okay (as if I had a choice) and asked him if I could requisition some extra socks.

"Can't hurt trying," he said with a big grin.

I like Lt. Hanken and the thought came to me that I hope he doesn't get killed.

The jeep we took into battalion headquarters stayed in the tracks of another truck that had gone along the same path.

"That way," the driver said, "I know I won't hit any mines."

When I got to battalion I turned in the casualty list and the major said that he was relieved to see that we didn't take many casualties. We only had two wounded in action and one guy, somebody named Maddox, listed as killed in action.

"We weren't in any battles," I said. "He was just out on patrol."

I didn't get any extra socks.

On the way back I wondered about Maddox, and if somebody would be saying that it was a light day if I was the only one killed from my company. I told myself to think positive thoughts.

The officers got a movie, but they couldn't get the projector to work. The tech sergeant who was supposed to show it got upset, but nobody really cared. After two hours they finally got the thing working and started the movie right in the middle. It didn't matter. There were pretty girls and some guys speaking American. That's all I needed.

Maj. Howie came to the movie. Most of the guys who know him like him. They say he makes things simple. Something is either the right thing to do or it's not the right thing.

Some guys found some French wine and some soap. I got two (count 'em) bars of the soap and gave one to Bobby Joe.

"If I can't find nobody cuter than you, will you marry me?" he said when I gave him the soap.

He doesn't know it, but I am trying to get the can of Spam his mother sent him. I have given him a roll of toilet paper and the soap. After a while I think he will feel guilty and give me the Spam. Anyway, I hope so.

July 8

All week long we have been training, even marching some. I feel stupid marching. I hope the Germans don't see us. There were some tracks that looked as if a German patrol had come through our perimeter. That freaked everybody out. Not only that, but we got an order over the radio to move 500 yards down to the road. Guys were packing up to move out when we got the word that the order was false. They've got Germans who speak perfect English giving fake orders. Scary.

Bobby Joe brought over a cartoon that he got from *Stars and Stripes* or *Yank*. He thought it was the funniest cartoon in the world. It showed two GIs in England, and one was saying that if anybody volunteered to go to France to get away from the buzz bombs, they were a coward.

That wasn't funny to me but I laughed anyway so Bobby Joe wouldn't feel bad.

July 9

Another rumor. The war is just about over! The Germans are just waiting for a good time to surrender. I believe this is the real deal. I'm sure about it. We're still on thirty-minute alert, which means that we have to be ready to fight with thirty minutes of notice. Bobby Joe said he doesn't need thirty minutes.

"I sleep with my rifle, I eat with my rifle, I go to the bathroom with my rifle," he said. "You know how they say some dogs look like their owners?"

"Yeah?"

"Well, my M-1 is getting to look like me," he said.

We're bivouacking in the woods. We still have patrols and I was stuck on one with a squad of replacements. We were about thirty minutes out, going along the edge of a clearing, when we spotted a German patrol. There were about fifteen of them and eight of us. I got everybody down and we opened fire on the Germans. On my second clip my M-1 jammed. I had to roll over on my back, open the bolt, and clear the breech by hand. It was my first jam.

When I got back from the patrol I took my rifle apart, piece by piece, and cleaned it. Bow-koo (that's "a lot" in French) scary.

July 10

Two signal corps guys got it today. One was in a tree stringing wire. He got hit and his gaffs, the hooks they used to climb trees, were still dug in and his belt was still on so he didn't fall. Terrible.

July 10, evening!

Got two letters from Mom and newspapers from Roanoke. Mom got my letters. She said everything was blacked out but that she thanked God that I'm alive. I'm so glad she knows I'm alive. I'm so excited over the letters I don't know what to do. Mom said they had services at Second Presbyterian and the Jefferson High School band played. Afterward my name was mentioned with all the guys serving in the armed forces. She said that the Russians were beating the Nazis back in the east and that she thought the war was soon going to be over. Yes! She sent me a picture of the whole family that made me cry just to see it. It is a studio picture, with her and Dad sitting on a kind of couch and Danny and Ellen standing up behind them. I can't believe how big Danny looks. Wow! I hope the war is over before he gets into it.

There was another picture, wrapped up in tissue paper, and I put it aside for later.

Mom went on to say that Ellen's school, Morningside, collected a bunch of fat for the war effort. They didn't collect as much as West End, but it was still a lot and I am proud of her.

J. J. came over with two guys from Christianburg and when they found out I had newspapers from home they asked me to read them out loud. They didn't want to read the news themselves. What they wanted was for all of us to sit around and hear what was going on back home. I read the papers and I couldn't help but get emotional. The papers are *The Roanoke World-News* from June 10th and June 12th and I read just about everything I could in them out loud.

They have a map of France and we found Saint-Lô on it. It is just a dot but at least they know where we are going to be fighting. There was a mention that in Italy the preachers were complaining that the Italian girls are fooling around with American soldiers and that got everybody excited. The St. Louis Cardinals are in first place in the National League and the St. Louis Browns are in first place in the American League. I had eaten in Norman's Restaurant in Salem a lot of times and we saw they are looking for people to work there. J. J. said that he was going to leave right away and go apply for a job.

When I got to the part where they were advertising for a colored man to work in a garage, Bobby Joe said he would apply for that job because he feels kind of colored. I guess he just wants to get back home and I don't blame him.

Then we got to a part where they were talking about us! They didn't say anything about the 116th or the 29th because of its being a secret, but they said that Americans were striking through the Cerisy Forest, headed toward St. Lô along the main road and cutting off the German supply lines. It said the Germans are packing troops and armor into St. Lô, which they want to hold at all costs.

We checked out some other jobs. Sears is hiring and there are jobs for experienced mechanics at $40 a week. One of the guys from Christianburg said that if he made $40 a week he would buy a Cadillac car and a portable Emerson radio and drive around Roanoke all day with a blonde on his arm

The last thing I read was about the movies. Nothing good was playing except a western with "Wild Bill" Elliott and Gabby Hayes. They got into an argument about who is best, "Wild Bill" Elliott or Gene Autry. I didn't say anything because they are all fellow soldiers and everything, but I never considered Gene Autry to be half the cowboy that "Wild Bill" Elliott is.

I put the picture of the family in my pocket. Then I took out the other picture. It was Angie. Angie has blue-gray eyes and dark blonde hair and she wears glasses but in the picture she sent she isn't wearing her glasses. She has on this little smile and her head is turned to one side like she is glad to be looking out of the picture at me. I started to put the picture back in the tissue when I saw there was something written on the back of it. I turned it over and it said, *Dear Scotty, would it sound too stupid if I said "I love you?" Angie.*

No, it wouldn't sound too stupid.

July 11

I have been awake since 0100 when I was awakened by incoming artillery. We were scrambling in the darkness as the Jerries pounded us with their artillery. It just kept coming and coming and coming. I got under a truck with Lt. Hanken, and he was praying the whole time.

Sometimes you can take a lot and sometimes it just gets to you. A light rain was falling, not enough to put out the fires from the shells, but enough to make the air so heavy the stink from the incoming didn't drift off. It was so thick some guys thought we were being gassed. Most of us have lost our gas masks, so it didn't matter. There wasn't anything we could do about it.

The shelling went on until almost three o'clock. It got to me good. My body was shaking with it. Soon as it stopped, we got orders to move out. I crawled out from under the truck and found a place to pee.

"Jerry's got to be coming in behind that barrage," Bobby Joe said.

"Could be." That's all I could say. My mouth was dry and I was spooked clear through.

As we formed up I could see a detail gathering up the wounded and tagging the dead. They were using flashlights because the main generators were out. A medic was going through treating minor wounds.

"Where you hit?" he asked me.

"You okay?" Bobby Joe looked at me.

I looked at where Bobby Joe was looking and saw that I had blood on my side. I wasn't hit. I ran back to where I had been under the truck and got down on my hands and knees. Lt. Hanken was lying there. He wasn't dead. He was kind of whimpering. The medic had come with me and he shined his light on Hanken. You could tell he was hurt bad. His face was drained white and his teeth were chattering.

We helped pull him out and got some blankets to put over him.

"Let's go! Let's go!" The orders came and me and Bobby Joe each gave Lt. Hanken a pat before we got back to our squad.

We formed skirmish lines and started along the ridge line toward St. Lô. I remembered what the newspaper had said about the Germans wanting to hold it at all costs.

We moved up and took positions on the ridge and dug in. Our artillery opened up at 0600. They were shooting over our heads, but they were doing it with a vengeance. I figured we would be moving out any minute to go in behind the artillery or the Germans would be coming after us. Lt. Rowe was in a foxhole near us and he told a sergeant that our tanks were moving out away from us.

"Where're they going?" the sergeant asked.

"Couvains."

It's the same towns over and over again. I wonder if the Germans are feeling as discouraged as I am.

The road and fields are littered with dead animals. The decaying flesh smells awful. We buried dead soldiers, even German soldiers, but no one buried the animals. The smell is something you can't get used to no matter what you tell yourself.

No sooner had we dug our foxholes than we received the order to move out. No sooner had we got out of our foxholes than we got attacked from our left flank. I think the guys that attacked us were as surprised to see us there as we were to see them. They hit us with mortars and machine-gun fire. We had them outnumbered, and they started retreating down into a gulley. When one of our squads got too close to them, they opened up with a flamethrower and our guys backed off long enough for them to get away.

If I die I don't want it to be with a flamethrower.

A squad went out and searched the bodies of the dead Germans. They took their papers, ID and stuff, and sent it in a dispatch to battalion.

At 1400 we moved into position along a front with the rest of the regiment.

July 13

Me and Bobby Joe are dug in good. I started the hole and Bobby Joe finished it. He was digging in real deep. The shelf we stand on is the right height but the grenade sump, where we hope a grenade will go in case one lands in our hole, is too deep, and I told him so.

"I'm going AWOL," he said. "Digging right to China."

July 13, evening

Nothing to eat but crackers and jelly.

When the First and Third Battalions dug in the Second was still moving forward. Capt. King took a patrol and went out to look for them. He came back and said that they were chewed up pretty bad. There's a German outfit, bigger than a battalion, between them and us, and another German outfit, maybe paratroopers, on their flank.

I'm thinking about Jerry Villency, but I don't want to. I hope God is taking care of him. I heard that Capt. Heffner made a deal with the Germans to let them get their wounded and get some of ours back. It's strange making deals like that.

"We're trying to hang on to being civilized," Lt. Rowe said.

July 14

Happy birthday, Mom! I hope you get to read this and know I was thinking of you on your birthday. It's pouring rain. Even the artillery is quiet. Two patrols went out with ammo and medical supplies to take to the Second Battalion. Lt. White led one patrol and Lt. Williams led the other one. The Germans have reinforced their position between us and the Second Battalion and things don't look good for our guys.

July 17

We control the ridge and the Germans want to take it back from us. Lt. Rowe came back from the battalion meeting and said that we were going to move out early to take Martinville.

"The objective is to take the road and hold it," Lt. Rowe said. "That's a clear shot into St. Lô."

"They got tanks up there?" J. J. asked.

Lt. Rowe didn't answer.

We moved out at 0430. It was still dark and most of us were hungry. I had eaten everything I carried and got some canned peaches from Bobby Joe, who had scrounged them from a medic. Maj. Howie had given the order to keep as quiet as possible. Rumor had it that the commander of the 29th had given the order for us to take Martinville and that it looked risky. Eventually we were supposed to hook up with the Second Battalion, which was still cut off.

We were on the high ground and moved in without artillery. Our first sighting of the Germans was when we saw their fires. They were making breakfast! We opened up and they came back with mortars and fire from tanks. From the ridge, we could see them through the smoke. The muzzle fire from their rifles twinkled from the hedgerows like thousands of angry fireflies. Their heavy weapons were firing to the top of the ridge and over it. We had caught them off guard, but they were fighting back hard. They did have some armor, but it was on the wrong side of the hedgerows, and when they tried to get them over, two were knocked out with bazooka fire.

They kept up the shelling at the top of the ridge. They were still shooting high, but it kept our heads down. We could recognize guys from their paratrooper units and we saw a batch of them. Some of them were carrying flamethrowers, and we tried to pin them down.

"Here they come!"

They came in a line just as the sun came up over the

fields south of the road. They were pouring across the road and concentrating their fire to our left on A Company. They were trying to get a front attack and a flank attack.

Maj. Howie was moving down the line with his radio man. Lt. Rowe got a corporal on the radio to find out if they wanted us to retreat up the ridge. But we could see the guys down the road from us and we knew what they were doing. Lt. Rowe got on the radio, listened for a minute, then nodded.

"Fix bayonets!" he called out.

That said it all. We weren't going anywhere. Maj. Howie was going to have us hold the ridge if we had to fight the Germans hand to hand. I got out my bayonet and put it on the end of my rifle. In the early-morning sunlight, I saw Bobby Joe's profile. His lips were tight, pulled back. I couldn't see his eyes under his helmet.

The Germans started up the ridge and we began throwing grenades at them. Their first wave slowed as they hit the bushes and the grenades tore into them. They made a short run up the ridge but started falling back as more grenades came down on them. We were throwing everything we had and they were coming with everything they had. One of their flamethrowers got hit, and some of their own guys got it. They started retreating across the road, and our mortar guys gave them more to worry about.

We started digging in, but before we had our holes dug, they came at us again. The guys who had taken their bayonets off their rifles put them back on again.

This time their rush was even stronger, fanatical. But they were coming uphill, and we were shooting down at them and throwing whatever grenades we had left. We beat them back again, and this time we could see them moving out across the fields. We had held.

Maj. Howie came down the line, stopping and telling everybody how good they had done.

"If we had gone over the ridge they would have been shooting down at us," Lt. Rowe said afterward. "We might have been cut off, too."

The way things worked out was that since the Germans were retreating, we were able to hook up with the Second Battalion. Trucks from headquarters company came up and started taking out the dead and wounded.

They needed a lot of trucks.

July 19

We are in reserve, which means we're not fighting for the moment but are on thirty-minute alert again. Maj. Howie was killed. I never got to talk to him and I didn't really know that much about him except for the fact that he was one of those guys who made things simple. He figured out what was the right thing to do and then he did it. At first my not knowing him didn't stop me from thinking bad things about him. The truth was that he was the kind of brave soldier and brave man that I don't think I can ever be, and that bothers me. I wonder if his soul was just bigger than mine or if somehow I am incomplete.

We took St. Lô yesterday. I watched as guys from the 115th moved down the Martinville road into the city. It was a road I helped take. Bobby Joe and J. J. went into the city to get some food from the 115th. Bobby Joe brought back some K rations and some real eggs. We cooked them in his pot and they tasted almost as good as my mom's eggs. I asked J. J. what St. Lô looked like and he said he didn't know.

"It's nothing but a big pile of rubble," Bobby Joe said. "Ain't nothing standing in that town. Every building is shot or bombed down, every street is filled with stones from what used to be buildings or broken-down vehicles.

"They took Maj. Howie's body into the town," Bobby Joe said. "It's right in the main square on a pile of stones and covered by a flag."

July 23

North of St. Lô. We moved out of the area in style, riding on tanks and antitank tracked vehicles. Got to ride in a tank. No way I would want to be cooped up in one of those things for long.

We rode through the city, although we didn't have to, so the guys could see what they had been fighting for. The convoy stopped and we looked around for maybe fifteen minutes. The whole town is in ruins. A Frenchman, he was an old guy with dark shiny eyes that made his face look younger than his stooped body, took Bobby Joe by the hand. Bobby Joe towered over the guy, but he went with him as he took him halfway down the street and pointed out what had once been a church.

"Notre Dame," he said.

Bobby Joe started telling the old guy that we had a college called Notre Dame in our country. From where I stood I could see that the old man wasn't listening. He kept repeating "Notre Dame" over and over as tears ran down his wrinkled face. I walked back to the troop carrier I had been riding on.

Two letters from home. One from Mom and the other one from Ellen. Mom read some stuff by some guy named Walter Cronkite and wants to know if I saw him over here. She said she just found out Mrs. Lucado's son is missing in action. I don't know who that is. She said she hasn't been getting mail from me but thinks in her heart that I'm all right.

The letter from Ellen is about how she was playing

softball in the park and got two home runs. She wants to know if there are colored soldiers fighting over here.

No letter from Angie, which got me down a little. But since we're in reserve again I can't get too down. I was lying down the other night when I started thinking about St. Lô. I feel bad about the piles of stones that all those lives paid for. Then I think about Roanoke, and I know what the old man was crying about.

July 24

The story going around is that Hitler's own guys tried to kill him last Thursday! He's wounded and might have to give up command of the Nazi army! This thing has got to be over soon. I bet they know back home if any of this is real or just another stupid rumor. I hope it's real. Hitler is a creep and doesn't deserve to live.

We're on thirty-minute alert. All day long our planes are overhead flying toward wherever the Germans think they can hide.

I don't know if I can get rested even though that's what we're supposed to be doing here. You can't really rest when you're on thirty-minute alert and might have to move out any minute. Wrote another letter to Mom to let her know I'm all right. Couldn't think of a lot to say, though.

Dear Mom,

We're in a rest area. The churches in this town are really old and you can tell that before the war they were really something. The French people are worse off, a lot worse off, than we are. I was speaking to a French woman and she told me her entire family was killed by shelling. I hope it was German artillery and not ours. But at St. Lô I know that the French were caught between us and the Nazis and a lot of them died.

The French try to live normal lives, which is strange in a way and in another way it's all they can do. This morning they were clearing away some rubble and found three bodies under a pile of wooden beams. Awful.

Tell Ellen that there are some colored soldiers over here. Most of them are driving trucks, or with the engineers or grave registration. Back at the beach, the guys who brought in the barrage balloons were colored.

Your loving son,
Scott

I told Bobby Joe about the colored guys bringing in the barrage balloons and he said that when he becomes president he's going to let all the colored guys fight right up front.

"Just to show them I'm a good guy," he said.

July 26

Okay, I can't believe this. Col. Dwyer comes around and starts talking to Lt. Rowe and some other officers. Then they call me and a guy from headquarters company over and Col. Dwyer says we're both going to be sergeants!

"We need some men leading this thing that have experience," he said. "You men are old-timers."

When Col. Dwyer left, Lt. Rowe told me I looked pretty stupid standing there with my mouth open.

"If I didn't think you could handle the job I wouldn't have recommended you for it," he said.

"I never made corporal," I said.

"If we run into any more engagements like we did at St. Lô," he said, "you're liable to make lieutenant before you make corporal."

When I told Bobby Joe he said that they must be scraping the bottom of the barrel, but then he said he would rather follow me than some guy fresh off the boat. That made me feel good. Also, I made a mental note to call a fight an "engagement" the way Lt. Rowe had.

July 27

We're still on thirty-minute alert. I haven't fired my rifle in an entire week. Cleaned it three times and also sharpened my bayonet, which I hope I will never have to use.

Two guys were hit by sniper fire. One died. Our guys killed the sniper. He was a kid. A Nazi kid.

I think the war is just about over. We'll probably stay here for another week or so and then start withdrawing and going home. The Germans have had it.

July 28

At 0530 we were up, and were on the move by 0800. Moved generally south to St. Samson. Lots of grumbling because the rumor was that we were headed home. Then there was some grumbling that we had to do all the dirty work because we were experienced or, as Col. Dwyer put it, old-timers.

I saw guys getting careless. A couple of guys got hit because they weren't alert. We also ran into a bunch of 115th guys and some Brits. I like the Brits. Back in England, the regular English people seemed a little soft and schoolmarmish, but the guys over here doing the fighting are a bunch of rough-and-ready guys. Our guys are getting down because they're so tired. The officers are running drills to keep us sharp. I guess being mad at them is better than relaxing too much.

"The next time America has a war we should have one with Delaware," J. J. said.

"Delaware is American!" Bobby Joe said.

"Well, won't they be surprised when we attack them?" J. J. said.

July 31

Fourteen days before my eighteenth birthday. I'm never going to make it. We attacked Moyon. It looked like a regular firefight at first, then we got hit on the flank by a panzer unit. Lord, there is nothing scarier than a German tank. The tanks stirred up a lot of dust as they came at us. Their infantry followed the tanks, and we were beat back. There was one block where four of our guys fell in the middle of the street. I could see the tanks coming toward them as we moved out.

"Bazooka! Bazooka!"

Lt. Rowe was calling for a bazooka, anything that would stop the tanks from running over those men. But it was too late. We fired at them with our rifles, but it wasn't any use.

The panzers didn't want to come away from the buildings, where our antitank guns could get a clear shot at them. We got away, but not before losing a lot of men. We attacked again and called in artillery.

It took four tries and a lot of wounded and killed

before we got the Germans to retreat from Moyon. Then we moved in and they shelled us all night long as usual.

Lt. Rowe broke a tooth from grinding his teeth together. Talk about tense!

August 1

Everything is messed up. We've been fighting on the outskirts of Moyon for days. We push the Germans out and then they push us out. It's another town that's going to be blown to bits.

The radio talks about buzz bombs in London and in the surrounding countryside. They say that there's no warning. All of a sudden they're just there — *Ka-boom!* The radio announcer said that the bombs are "not an effective way of fighting a war." Tell that to the people who are killed.

The units are mixed up again. It's like the days following the landing where you had to go around looking for your unit. The officers can't give orders because they can't find their men.

August 4

Where are they getting their artillery from? Wherever we are they seem to have us zeroed in. The pounding keeps coming and coming. It rolls around and grumbles as you are crouched against some tree or some rock or some truck, hoping that you're safe. But you are never safe. The Jerries are shooting from three to five miles away. They can't see you. They just send out their shells and hope that the shells will somehow find you. They are finding so many men.

The number of dead animals, stiff and bloated in the streets and along the paths to the city, is as many as it was at St. Lô. The stink is the same, too.

I can tell the difference between the smell of a dead cow and a dead man. The things you learn in war.

August 5

Meeting. My first as sergeant. Lt. Rowe and the other junior officers and noncoms, including me, were given our objectives for an attack on Vire. We're leapfrogging like crazy. One unit attacks, establishes a foothold, and the next unit goes through them and attacks the next objective.

I found Vire on the map. The coordinates are 632317.

"As per usual the town is in a valley and it's surrounded by hills," Col. Dwyer said. "And as usual we're going to fight our way up those hills and take them from the Jerries. From what we've been told, they're digging in to stay and they intend to fight to the last man. Since the attempt on Hitler's life, all their officers are trying to prove they're loyal. Keep that in mind. Good luck."

The latest rumor, which means that we got it within the last twenty-four hours, is that the attack on Hitler never happened. Col. Dwyer wouldn't have said that if it hadn't. But every time I hear about the Nazis it's something about them digging in and fighting hard, which means there are more tough days ahead.

"We're responsible for this small section, right here." Lt. Rowe pointed to a spot on the line drawing he had made of Hill 203, our battalion's objective. "We're going to send two squads and try to secure this little path right here. According to the Resistance in this area, the path leads all the way up the hill.

"Once we take this path we secure it and hold it while the next two squads move up and secure the next level area. Then we move up while Charlie Company secures the base. At that point we're going to be relieved by the Ninth Infantry. We move out at 2300. Any questions?"

I thought about making a smart remark about that being past my bedtime, but decided against it. When I got back to our platoon, Bobby Joe and J. J. were waiting for me. They wanted to know what we were going to be doing. If I ever get to be an officer I will always tell my men what they will be doing and what dangers they will face.

"How does it look?" Bobby Joe asked.

"We can get it done," I said.

August 7

I'm out of food and toilet paper. I must have left my rations somewhere. Don't know where. Our battalion took the lead. We found a stream and started up it. The water flowed against us as we went along at a quick pace. A light rain started at 1500 and I reversed my rifle, turning it butt up as I walked. We weren't getting any incoming artillery, and I figured either the Jerries didn't know where we were or didn't care.

They had to know we were coming. The same way they knew we were coming when the invasion started. I wondered what they thought of us. A couple of guys who speak German read us the surrender leaflets the Ninth Air Force planes had dropped on the Jerries. The leaflets said that they thought we couldn't beat them, but we were beating them, and that everything they had been told about how invincible they were wasn't true.

But they were still in the hills and in the cities of France and leaving a trail of bodies behind. A lot more were giving up than when we first landed, but a lot were still fighting hard.

Lt. Col. Cassell was leading the march in the stream.

"What are you going to do when this is all over?" Lt. Rowe asked me. I knew he meant the war.

"Get married, have a family, maybe work for the railroad back home," I said. "Or maybe work in television. That's a new field and there should be plenty of jobs there. How about you?"

"I got a house in Bristol," he said. "When I get home I'm going to build a porch on the back of it and sit on that porch and drink Tennessee moonshine and smile. And if anybody asks me why I'm smiling I'm going to say it's because I ain't in France."

When we reached Hill 203 we started spreading out around it. A reconnaissance patrol went out to see how it looked while everybody else double-checked their assignments. From where I was, I thought I could see the path we were supposed to secure, but I wasn't sure.

There weren't any hedgerows, but the paths were fairly narrow and twisted up the steep hill. The Jerries waited until the first platoon had climbed nearly thirty yards before they opened up.

We couldn't see them but figured they could see us. Lt. Col. Cassell got the officers together again. When Lt. Rowe came back he was pale.

"There's going to be a big push on Vire in an hour," he said. "If we don't take this hill overlooking the city it's going to be a massacre. Omaha Beach all over again. Charlie Company's going first; they're over there in that stand of woods. We're up next."

"We getting any artillery support?" a corporal asked.

"One bombing run," Lt. Rowe said. "If we're lucky."

August 9

On Hill 203. I'm exhausted and feeling sick. We didn't get the air support we wanted on the 7th and had to slug it out. Just as well, heard that a lot of men were killed when our planes dropped bombs on the wrong area near Colombelles.

August 10

We're dug in on Hill 203 over Vire. From what I can see of the city, it's pretty messed up already, and will probably be more so by the time we clear it out. Dwyer says we're on two-hour alert, not thirty-minute. I hope he told the Germans.

On the 7th, Charlie Company led the attack and got hurt pretty bad. A lot of their men were replacements, and when the guys on point were hit, the men behind them turned and headed back. According to their company commander, there was a moment of confusion, and when the shell hit there were body parts blown everywhere. Awful, just awful.

When men are wounded you can smell the blood and the gases coming from them. We got the order to move out and we had to run through the smoke and the bodies of the men from Charlie Company. Men were begging for help as they lay dying, and you couldn't stop to help them. Something heavy hit about thirty yards behind me, close enough for me to feel the heat from it, and close enough for the blast to shove me forward and onto the ground.

All I could think of was the beach, being pinned against the seawall and watching guys get torn up by Jerry fire. I scrambled to my feet and flattened out against a building. Behind, I saw more bodies and the guys scrambling back to the far side of the road.

"Scotty!" It was Bobby Joe. He was trying to pull somebody out of the line of fire. I grabbed the fallen guy by the shoulder straps and we dragged him to the base of the hill as two other guys fired over us, trying to cover us while we got to safety.

On our side of the road, built into the side of the hill, was a small house and we dragged the wounded guy into it.

J. J. and a soldier I didn't know were with me. The guy was lugging an automatic rifle. He was thin and pale, with wide shoulders.

"We're cut off!" Bobby Joe said. "I hope they don't start lobbing grenades down here."

I looked out and saw a knot of bodies lying in the road. The Germans had a concentration of automatic weapons covering the road that led to the path up the hill. Bobby Joe was right: the company couldn't get across, and we couldn't get back to them without running through a hail of bullets.

"Don't leave me . . . please don't leave me," the wounded guy we had dragged in was saying. He was looking at us, searching our faces for someone to say he was going to be all right. His right side under his arm was soaked with blood, and I figured he would go into shock pretty soon.

We propped him against a wall and J. J. covered the window. I asked the guy I didn't know what his name was, and he told me it was Henderson.

"Henderson, I'm Sgt. Collins," I said. "You cover the other window, and don't get yourself framed in it."

Bobby Joe was checking the small house and came back to say that there were only three rooms.

I tried to figure out how we were going to get the wounded guy back across the road. Even though I didn't think he was going to make it, I didn't want to leave him.

The place we had run into consisted of two tiny rooms, a toilet, and a big kitchen. The first room looked like a sitting room and the second one had a small bed in it. There was a door at the back of the kitchen, and Bobby Joe covered me as I opened it. Inside there was an empty wine rack. It reminded me of a house I had seen back in Virginia.

"Bobby Joe, you ever go to Monticello?" I asked.

"No," he answered.

I had been to Monticello, Thomas Jefferson's mansion, and I remembered that the servants cooked in a big kitchen and they had an underground passage to the main house.

I was about to close the doors when Bobby Joe looked up and saw a trapdoor in the ceiling. It wasn't more than six feet up and I could reach it with a chair. I held my breath as I pushed it open. It was a dark, narrow passageway with a dim light at the top. The wooden ladder that went up one side didn't look too safe, but I knew going out the front door wasn't a good idea.

"The servants can take wine up through there if they need to," I said. "You think the Jerries know about it?" Bobby Joe asked.

I shrugged and asked J. J. what was going on outside, and he said a few guys had tried to get across the road and hadn't made it.

"They must have a concrete bunker built up there," he said.

I thought that wasn't likely.

The passageway was too narrow to get up with a pack on, so I took mine off. I told Bobby Joe to wait until I got up and gave him a signal.

I climbed onto the chair and then into the hole. I had the sling of my M-1 draped over my right hand. It would be useless while I was climbing.

Near the top I stopped to listen. I could hear the sounds of battle, but they seemed far off. Slowly I eased the rest of the way up and out of the hole into a small closet. There wasn't any noise coming from the outside of the closet, and I opened the door and found myself in a dining room. The firing was more distinct now, and I made my way to a window and eased back the curtain. There was a German machine-gun nest, made out of sandbags and what looked like the door off a truck. They were under a rock formation that gave them shelter from the air, and looked pretty cozy.

I went back to the hole and signaled for Bobby Joe and the others to come up.

It took them five minutes to get up into the house. I got Henderson to set up the automatic rifle on a table that Bobby Joe and J. J. eased up to the window.

The Germans never knew what hit them. They were protected from the fire coming up at them, but their flank was open. When we knocked out their gun, Bobby Joe went to the front window. From there he could see the whole road, and he signaled down. Some guys pointed down the side of the mountain. We went up to the next floor, and saw they were pointing to what sounded like a fifty-caliber machine gun. J. J. tossed down a grenade as me, Henderson, and Bobby Joe opened up from the windows.

Soon as we opened up, the German gun went quiet, and moments later our guys were pouring onto the mountain.

Lt. Rowe made a lot of us get into the house and up into the main house. He said he was going to make sure it made it into the battle reports. The wounded guy, the one we had dragged into the house, died before the medics could get to him.

August 11

0800. Hot food. Powdered eggs and fried Spam (from Bobby Joe) tasted as good as anything I have eaten. There are still pockets of Germans to be cleared out, but it looks good. We watched from Hill 203 as guys from the Ninth Infantry slogged through the mud headed toward Vire. They gave us the thumbs-up sign and we flashed the V for victory.

Lt. Rowe told me what Vire had cost. We lost 107 men Killed in Action, 862 Wounded in Action, 151 Missing in

Action. It was another city taken, another list of guys down, and hopefully another step toward ending the war.

August 14

We got over a thousand replacements!

"Not a good sign," Bobby Joe said.

We didn't want to see replacements; we wanted to see us going home. I went into Vire with Lt. Rowe to get some training in map reading. We were headed toward the town square and had stopped to ask directions when we came under fire. I grabbed my rifle and jumped out of the jeep to run for cover.

I thought I had banged my knee into the side of the jeep. There was an incredible pain in my leg, and it went numb as my rifle clattered to the ground. There was firing all around me, and I turned onto my stomach to get a good prone firing position. It turned out to be just sniper fire, and they flushed out two German noncoms dressed in civilian clothing from a building over a restaurant.

"Medic!" Lt. Rowe was calling out.

At first I didn't know what was wrong with him, because he looked okay, and then I realized he was calling the medics for me. I had been shot just above the knee.

There was pain. A lot of pain. But more than that I felt panicky. All of a sudden I was afraid of being left alone.

Lt. Rowe kept reassuring me, saying that I was going to be all right.

When I got to the field hospital, a doctor said I would be as good as new in a few months.

"English food is good for leg wounds," he said.

Bobby Joe came to see me. He told me that our outfit is going to get some rest and is now assigned to First United States Army Reserve.

August 16

Bobby Joe came back to say good-bye and to tell me that we are attached to the 29th again, and on the move.

"We're too good to be out of the fighting," he said. "We're headed toward Brest."

"Bobby Joe, watch your intervals," I told him. "Don't let the new guys bunch up on you."

"Hey, don't be getting soft on me," he said with a grin. "Bobby Joe ain't no rookie."

I said good-bye to him again and when I took his hand I didn't want to let it go.

August 24, Omaha Beach

I can't believe how organized the beach was. It didn't seem like the same place I landed on a little more than two months ago. There were guys unloading LSTs, mountains of equipment pouring in a steady stream up over the beach. There were also coffins, neatly stacked, with an honor guard arranged around them and an American flag flying over them. I thought about the guy we had dragged into the house at Hill 203, and about Kerlin, and Wojo, and Mikey and all the guys who had started out with me in Virginia.

I was on a stretcher with the wounded. A navy officer came and told us we would be loaded up soon. The officer, his name was McFarland, checked my dog tags against his list.

"Hey, you were wounded on your birthday!" he said.

"Yeah."

I guess he saw I was having a bad time and he asked me if I needed anything for pain. I told him no. I didn't want to tell him I was worrying about Bobby Joe and J. J. and Lt. Rowe, my guys pushing on toward Brest.

"I think the delay is because the water is so choppy," McFarland said. "They don't want the trip to be bad."

I sat up and looked out over the beach teeming with men, almost covered with equipment. Beyond the loose dirt and sand was the English Channel. I had seen it choppier.

Epilogue

The 116th Infantry Regiment was made up of young Americans, many from central Virginia, who offered up their lives for a cause in which they believed. Beginning with the horrendous D-Day landing, they fought in some of the most brutal battles of World War II. Hundreds died on Omaha Beach, many without ever reaching the shore. Once onshore in Normandy, every foot of ground taken by the regiment from the determined and often desperate German army was paid for with blood.

The landing on Omaha Beach took 341 lives from the 116th. The first company to leave the boats lost close to 90 percent of its personnel, either killed or wounded.

The battle for St. Lô resulted in 87 men listed as Killed in Action, including Major Howie, 648 men Wounded in Action, and 113 men Missing in Action.

And so on it went, as the regiment moved on to Brest, and then into Holland, and finally Germany. Each city, each hamlet, would be marked by the falling of more young men. They fought in Europe until the end of the war in May and finally began the journey home by ship on Christmas Eve, 1945.

Lieutenant Arthur Rowe, wounded at Brest, opened a sporting-goods store in Roanoke and coached high school basketball for twenty-five years. He died in the Veterans' Hospital in Martinsburg, West Virginia, in June 1986.

J. J. Dandridge stayed in the army and was stationed in White Sands, New Mexico, in 1956, during the atomic bomb tests. He left the army in 1960. At loose ends in civilian life, J. J. had a series of jobs and began drinking heavily. He was homeless in 1963 and was arrested for petty theft. After his release he entered a Veterans of Foreign Wars-sponsored rehabilitation program. He met and married Ellen Custis, a nurse whose husband had been killed in the Korean War. J. J. did volunteer counseling for the Salvation Army in Roanoke until the summer of 1990, when he died of leukemia.

Bobby Joe Hunter went to William and Mary College under the GI Bill, earning a bachelor's degree in history. For thirty years he worked as a teacher in the Winchester, Virginia, school system. On retirement he and his wife, the former Sylvia Cooke, opened a used bookshop in Fredericksburg, Virginia. Each year, on Memorial Day, the Hunters, along with other area veterans, give a party for children in the local hospital.

Angie Gardiner moved with her parents to Anniston,

Alabama, in the summer of 1945, shortly before the end of the war in Europe. She wrote to Scott for a few months, but then met and married John Bryan Gadsen, a naval officer. She went with him to the San Diego Naval Station. The couple had six children. After her husband's death, Angie Gardiner Gadsen became a school crossing guard. She still lives in San Diego.

Scott Pendleton Collins came back to Roanoke after the war and lived with his parents. The wounds he received in Vire left him with a permanent limp. He started college under the GI Bill, but dropped out after a year to work. He found a job as a short-order cook in a restaurant, where he met Julia Bennett. They were married in 1952 and had three children: Nancy, Joseph, and Michael Collins.

Scott kept in touch with J. J. Dandridge for a while but then lost contact with him when he and Julia opened their own restaurant in Christianburg. The restaurant was successful, but Scott, whose wounded leg was amputated in 1973, had to retire early. He spent the rest of his life working with troubled youngsters in the Roanoke area.

Scott's son Joseph, a pilot, was killed in aerial combat in Vietnam in 1968, during the Tet Offensive. Nancy runs the restaurant and Michael is a minister in Duluth, Minnesota.

Scott and Julia stayed in touch with his best friend,

Bobby Joe Hunter, and his wife for the remainder of their lives.

Scott Pendleton Collins died on March 19, 1992, at the age of 65. Julia now lives in a small apartment just outside Roanoke. The house she had lived in is being used as a group home for youngsters. In the living room over the couch, there are four pictures. Besides the two pictures of Scott's great-grandfather and father, there is also a picture of Scott Pendleton Collins and one of his sons, Joseph.

The central player in this story is the war itself. It lives on.

Life in America
in 1944

Historical Note

The events leading to the invasion of Normandy began at the end of the First World War. Germany, defeated on the battlefield and forced to sign a humiliating peace treaty, was in a state of confusion. German currency was practically worthless and many people were close to starvation. Thousands of jobless veterans roamed the streets, feeling betrayed by their government and looking for some way to redeem themselves. These conditions, bordering on social and political chaos, created a unique opportunity for anyone shrewd enough and ruthless enough to take advantage of them. Such a person was Adolf Hitler.

Hitler was born in Austria, on April 20, 1889. As a young man he studied art, but was not successful in his wish to become an architect. He fought in World War I, and after the war became involved in the *Nationalsozialistische Deutsche Arbeiterpartei*, popularly known as the Nazi party.

The late twenties and early thirties were the years of a global economic depression. In the United States, a man named Franklin Roosevelt promised, with hard work and government help, to bring America out of the Depression. In Germany, Adolf Hitler built up the Nazi party with promises to bring his nation to a position of worldwide dominance. The German people, anxious to at last escape the crippling depression, first tolerated this charismatic man, but then grew to fear him. Hitler surrounded himself with men who were loyal and as willing to use terror and violence to achieve their ends as Hitler was. Hitler's vision was of a master race expanding to fulfill what he considered to be the destiny of the German people.

One way of establishing power is to create a strong and loyal army. Hitler worked hard to build such an army even as he worked to create the myth of himself as a superman sent to lead his people to greatness. Part of his idea of the pureness of the German race required the extermination of what he considered to be non-pure people, such as Jews, Gypsies, homosexuals, and non-whites.

By 1938, Hitler felt ready to begin his quest for world domination. He began to claim territories that he announced as being German in character. German armies rolled into Austria and occupied large areas without firing a shot. In 1939, Hitler's armies occupied Czechoslovakia and Poland, killing thousands of civilians while overwhelming the armies of those countries. It was clear to the rest of the world that Hitler and the Nazis were intending to dominate, by force, all of Europe.

France and England declared war against Germany, but a confident Hitler moved on, ordering his armies first into Denmark and Norway, and then France. By the end of June 1940, the Germans' *blitzkrieg,* the lightning attacks of planes and armored vehicles used by the German army, had forced the French to submit to a peace treaty.

England presented a different problem to the aggressive Nazi army. Bringing an army across the natural barrier of the English Channel depended on essentially subduing the British by air attacks. In the fall of 1940 the Battle of Britain began with German bombers invading England. But British fighters and antiaircraft guns, more sophisticated than any the Germans had faced before, exacted a heavy toll on the German bombers. The British people, although badly shaken by the destruction from the skies, had the resolve to withstand the bombing. They would not surrender.

Winston Churchill, the prime minister of Great Britain, appealed to the United States for funds and material to fight off the Nazi aggression. Roosevelt agreed to the request and tons of equipment began to cross the Atlantic. German submarines sank some American ships but enough got through to help England fight back. Then, on a bright Sunday morning, December 7,

1941, the Japanese attacked Pearl Harbor, an American naval base in Hawaii. Thousands were killed in this vicious raid by a Japanese war machine intent on expanding its small island territory in the Pacific. Two days later, Germany, which was allied with Japan, declared war on the United States.

Hitler, his confidence bolstered by his victories in Europe, thought it was just a matter of time before he would be capable of launching a successful attack on England. His vision of world domination seemed within his grasp. But he had made mistakes that would cost him dearly.

Hitler badly underestimated the ability of the United States to produce war materials that would equal those of Germany. He occupied France but he needed time to build the ships and boats required for an attack across the English Channel. By 1944, American bombers, flying from bases in North Africa, were bombing German cities. On the eastern front the Russians were taking back their cities. In England, there was a great buildup of English and American troops. The Germans knew these troops were meant to be an invasion force.

Thousands of men were being drafted to fight in the war. National Guard units were activated, and thousands of men and women volunteered to help rid the world of Nazi aggression in Europe and Japanese war-making in the Far East.

The Germans knew the invasion of France was coming. A leading German general, field marshal Erwin Rommel, had supervised the building of the defenses along the coasts of France. They seemed virtually impregnable. The English and Americans, led by American general Dwight D. Eisenhower and field marshal Bernard Law Montgomery, who was Commander-in-Chief, Ground Forces, understood the price in human lives that would be paid by the invasion. But the evil that Hitler represented had to be destroyed. On D-Day, June 6, 1944, the beginning of that effort began with the landings in Normandy.

The battle of Normandy was difficult. It took weeks against a determined Nazi army for the Americans and British to break out of the Normandy area. But break out they did, in battles at places such as Saint-Lô, Vire, Cherbourg, Brest, and the Ardennes. The invasion found men who would become heroes, and heroes who would save the world.

Hitler, the man responsible for the deaths through warfare of millions of soldiers and civilians, as well as the planned deaths of millions of Jews, Gypsies, homosexuals, and other political enemies of the Nazis, committed suicide in April, 1945.

Dwight Eisenhower, a four-star general in the U.S. Army, was the Supreme Commander of Operation Overlord, the Allied assault on Nazi-occupied western Europe. On June 5, 1944, three days before the invasion would take place, Eisenhower talks to the 101st Airborne, stationed in England.

On D-Day, when Operation Overlord was set in motion, Eisenhower commanded 39 land assault divisions, each with approximately 20,000 troops, 5,000 ships and smaller craft, and 50,000 vehicles, with 11,000 aircraft overhead. When American troops hit the beaches of Normandy on June 6, 1944, they faced obstacles in the surf, land mines, barbed wire, antitank ditches, and a barrage of fire from German guns.

The Nazi troops erected their fortifications against the Allied forces' attack long before D-Day. These obstacles were veiled at high tide, imperiling ships and landing craft; they forced the Allies to land at low tide, when the killing zone was at its greatest. Along with the casualties in the foreground are several Allied vehicles destroyed during the attack.

After scrambling across the beach, these troops sought protection behind a concrete wall. In the center and lower right corner, a censor has blotted out the regiment's insignia on the left shoulder of two soldiers' uniforms.

As D-Day wore on, many soldiers were killed, wounded, or captured. This group of wounded American assault troops sought the safety of a bluff after storming Omaha Beach. A total of 675,000 American soldiers were wounded in World War II, and 292,000 were killed or missing in action.

After his landing craft is sunk off the coast of Normandy on D-Day, a wounded U.S. soldier receives a plasma transfusion.

The Roanoke World-News *announces the Allied forces' landing at Normandy. Though the headline indicates that there was only slight opposition, casualties among the first wave of troops to arrive were horrendous, and the success of the landing was in doubt for several hours.*

Allied forces are amassed offshore at Omaha Beach as support equipment is unloaded. Backing up the initial troops who landed at Normandy were almost three million troops who assembled in England before the invasion. Barrage balloons were anchored to many ships to discourage low-flying enemy planes.

The US Army Air Force dropped men and supplies over a new beachhead as part of Operation Uppercut. *Above, parachutes fill the sky over southern France, somewhere between Nice and Marseilles.*

Adolf Hitler, leader of the Nazi Party, salutes his troops. Hitler became Chancellor of the Reich in January 1933, inaugurating a reign of violence that lasted for twelve years. Within three months of his taking power, all German clubs for boys and girls between the ages of ten and eighteen were consolidated into the Hitler Youth, which had a membership of 8.9 million when war came in 1939.

In 1937, the first year of the Hitler Youth's rifle school, more than 1.5 million boys were taught to shoot. Here, a young German soldier surrenders. He is wearing an Iron Cross, one of many medals and insignia meant to enhance the self-esteem and sense of authority of the Nazi Party.

Sherman tanks were an important part of the Allied invasion force. The Sherman had a motor designed to run for three thousand miles without a major overhaul and was known for its durability in the throes of war. Here, a Sherman tank rumbles through the ruins of Flere, France, in August of 1944.

St. Lô, France, was demolished during the Normandy Invasion. Above, U.S. soldiers patrol the ruins of St. Lô on July 25, 1944. In the background is the Notre Dame Cathedral.

An American soldier adjusts the elevation of a mortar, a short-barreled cannon used to hurl shells at the enemy. Germany suffered more than six million civilian and military casualties during and immediately after World War II.

The battle-wise Infantryman...

...*is* **CAREFUL** of what he says or writes **HOW ABOUT YOU?**

Soldiers' letters to friends and family were closely monitored by censors in order to maintain secrecy about the invasion and subsequent movements. This World War II poster emphasizes the importance of using discretion in regard to dates and troop locations.

A French girl presents flowers to members of an American tank crew in appreciation for the liberation of the town of Avranches, France. As they made their way farther and farther into Europe, American soldiers often mingled with European civilians, who were thankful for the Allied forces' presence.

Since Nazi attacks were unpredictable, soldiers had to grab a bite to eat whenever they could. Above, three American soldiers down their rations in a foxhole in Normandy, France.

The hedgerows in Normandy provided protection for the German soldiers defending the area, but Allied forces took advantage of them as well. Here, a line of 411th Infantrymen of the U.S. Seventh Army take positions along a hedgerow in Alsace, France. Geese wander by, seemingly unaware of the danger that surrounds them.

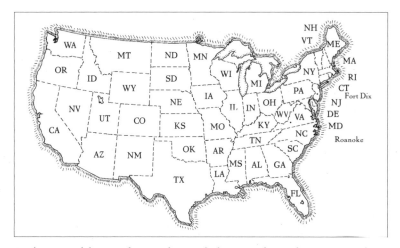

Modern map of the United States, showing the locations of Roanoke, Virginia, and Fort Dix, New Jersey.

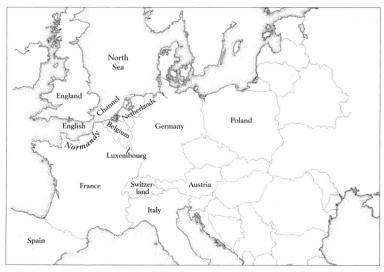

Map of Western Europe, showing the location of Normandy.

About the Author

Walter Dean Myers says, "There is no more dramatic event in a country's history than the occurrence of a war. We have a tendency to talk about war in larger than life terms — invasions, battle plans, and grand campaigns. But all wars, in my mind, depend ultimately on individual soldiers like Scotty. Talk about 'smart bombs' and 'saturation bombing' tends to let us forget about the families of the soldiers, the dreams, beliefs, and aspirations which personalize the sacrifices endured. It's important to me to write about this intensely personal concept of war. The losses suffered on D-Day and during all of the war should be remembered forever and should always be a restraint when we think about military actions to solve international problems. I can think of no better way to prevent war than to present a true picture of its horrors."

Walter Dean Myers is an award-winning writer of fiction, nonfiction, and poetry for young people. His many books include *The Journal of Joshua Loper, A Black Cowboy*, in the My Name Is America series; *Slam!; Somewhere in the Darkness; Fallen Angels,* winner of the Coretta Scott King Award; *Malcolm X: By Any Means Necessary,* a Coretta Scott King Honor Book and ALA Notable Children's Book; and *The Glory Field,* an ALA Best Book for Young Adults and a Notable Children's Trade Book in the Field of Social Studies. Mr. Myers is the recipient of two awards for the body of his work: the Margaret A. Edwards Award for Outstanding Literature for Young Adults and the ALAN Award. He lives in Jersey City, New Jersey.

For Nancy Larrick,
whose concerns helped bring me into
the field of children's literature

Acknowledgments

✳ ✳ ✳

The author would like to thank Henry B. McFarland, a naval officer during the war, who shared his experiences of the Normandy Invasion, and Joan Trew of the Roanoke City Library for her help in background research.

Grateful acknowledgment is made for permission to reprint the following:

Cover portrait: Photograph of soldier, Culver Pictures.

Cover background: Photograph of U.S. troops landing at Normandy, France, National Archives.

"Don't Sit Under the Apple Tree" by Lou Brown, Sam Stept, and Charles Tobias. Published by EMI/Robbins and Shed Music. All rights reserved.

Page 124 (top): Dwight Eisenhower, National Archives.
Page 124 (bottom): Troops landing at Normandy, France, ibid.
Page 125 (top): Obstacles, AP/Wide World Photos.
Page 125 (bottom): Troops at seawall, UPI/Corbis.

Page 126: Wounded soldiers, National Archives.

Page 127 (top): Soldier receiving medical care, Archive Photos.

Page 127 (bottom): *The Roanoke World-News.*

Page 128: Barrage balloons, National Archives.

Page 129: Paratroopers, AP/Wide World Photos.

Page 130 (top): Adolf Hitler, Archive Photos.

Page 130 (bottom): German soldier, The Trustees of the Imperial War Museum, London.

Page 131 (top): Sherman tank, Archive Photos.

Page 131 (bottom): St. Lô, ibid.

Page 132: Soldier with mortar, ibid.

Page 133 (top): *Battle-Wise Infantryman*, West Point Museum Collection, United States Military Academy.

Page 133 (bottom): French girl, AP/Wide World Photos.

Page 134 (top): Soldiers in foxhole, ibid.

Page 134 (bottom): Soldiers behind hedgerows, ibid.

Page 135: Maps by Heather Saunders.

Other books in the My Name Is America series

The Journal of William Thomas Emerson
A Revolutionary War Patriot
by Barry Denenberg

The Journal of James Edmond Pease
A Civil War Union Soldier
by Jim Murphy

The Journal of Joshua Loper
A Black Cowboy
by Walter Dean Myers

Copyright © 1999 by Walter Dean Myers.

❋ ❋ ❋

All rights reserved. Published by Scholastic Inc.
557 Broadway, New York, New York 10012.
MY NAME IS AMERICA®, SCHOLASTIC, and associated logos
are trademarks and/or registered trademarks of Scholastic Inc.

Library of Congress Cataloging-in-Publication Data available.

ISBN 0-439-05013-8;
ISBN 0-439-44576-0 (pbk.)

10 9 8 7 6 5 4 3 2 1   02 03 04 05 06

The display type was set in Old Typewriter Regular.
The text type was set in Berling.
Book design by Elizabeth B. Parisi
Photo research by Zoe Moffitt

Printed in the U.S.A. 23
First paperback printing, October 2002

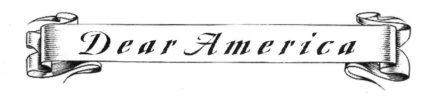

MY SECRET WAR

THE WORLD WAR II DIARY
OF MADELINE BECK

BY MARY POPE OSBORNE

Scholastic Inc. New York

LONG ISLAND, NEW YORK

1941

SEPTEMBER 26, 1941

Dear Diary,

A cold rain is falling. The wind blows hard from the Atlantic Ocean, rattling our windowpane.

Mom and I have been living here in Mrs. Hawkins's Mansion-by-the-Sea for a week now. The name's misleading. Really, it's just a run-down old boardinghouse. Mom and I share a drafty room with heavy wooden beds, dusty oil paintings, and a ratty Chinese rug.

The other people living here are positively grim. Tonight Mom left me to have supper alone with them in the dining room while she volunteered at the Presbyterian Church, knitting sweaters for people bombed out in Britain.

Mom is good at making new friends. Unfortunately I'm not. All week the girls at my new school have shown no interest in me at all. I don't know what to do to break the ice.

SEPTEMBER 29, 1941

Dear Diary,

Good news! We got a letter from Dad today. The minute he received our new address, he wrote back. He says his ship will be leaving San Francisco any day now to safeguard the Pacific.

Mom's asleep, and I'm gazing at the framed picture of him between our beds: Dad's got a cigarette in one hand as he leans against a ship railing. His pale blue eyes seem to stare right at me, though I wasn't even born when the picture was taken.

I just wrote him a letter. I tried to sound cheerful. I kept my fingers crossed as I wrote that we're living in a wonderful place, and I have lots of new friends.

OCTOBER 8, 1941

Dear Diary,

The radio's on. Freddy Martin and his orchestra are playing "To Each His Own."

A keen thing happened today: On the way home from school, Johnny Vecchio and Bert Lyman caught up with me on their bikes. Bert is real nice. And Johnny is just about the most admired boy in the eighth grade. He has black curly hair and sparkly brown eyes. He always knows the answers in class, but never acts conceited.

They wanted to know if it was true my dad was an officer in the navy.

I told them Dad was a lieutenant commander and had been trained to be a navy dive-bomber.

"Jeepers," Johnny said. Bert said my dad sounded swell.

I told them he was on a ship safeguarding the Pacific right now, but we didn't know exactly where. I explained that we send all his mail to the U.S. Army Post Office in San Francisco; then they get it to him wherever he is in the world.

From the looks on Johnny's and Bert's faces I could tell I'd grown about a foot taller in their eyes. I expect after this conversation, things might turn around for me at school.

OCTOBER 9, 1941

Dear Diary,

I guess Bert and Johnny didn't tell anyone about my swell dad because today, as usual, the girls left me out completely.

Maxine Stone, the prettiest girl in our class, wears her hems at least two inches shorter than mine. Tonight, when Mom was heading out to her knitting circle, I begged her to help me raise my hemline. I told her I thought that the girls might be leaving me out because I don't have any style.

Mom disagreed. She said it was only because I was new and they'd all known one another for years. But she promised to pin up my skirts this weekend if I promised to stop worrying about my lack of style. "It's a deal," I said.

OCTOBER 11, 1941

Dear Diary,

This afternoon, as Mom pinned up my blue circle skirt, the lights kept blinking on and off, sending me into a tirade against Mrs. Hawkins's Mansion-by-the-Sea.

I carried on about all the strange people living here: Mrs. Hawkins, the landlady, who's nearly deaf and cooks nothing but boiled fish and watery cabbage dishes; her twenty-year-old son, Theo, a fisherman with a bad limp and a deep, gruff voice, who for some reason didn't go to school past the seventh grade; Miss Burke, a retired schoolteacher who talks all the time; and Mrs. Rosenthal and her nineteen-year-old daughter, Clara, refugees from Germany.

The Rosenthals are a bit spooky. Clara has a soft, whispery voice, and Mrs. Rosenthal seems lost in another world. She never looks directly at anybody and sometimes she talks to herself in German.

When I finished my ranting, Mom sighed impatiently. "Listen, young lady," she muttered, gripping straight pins between her lips, "I'd like you to be a little more charitable toward your fellow humans. We have no idea of the suffering others might have gone through in their lives."

She also said there's a housing shortage because so many coast guardsmen have been moved to this area. So we should thank our lucky stars we found a place to live at all.

I lifted my hands heavenward, thanking my lucky stars, and Mom laughed, all the pins falling out of her mouth.

OCTOBER 13, 1941

Dear Diary,

My shorter skirt seemed to have had no positive effect on the girls. In fact, today was my worst day at school so far. During lunch, Maxine formed a little group she named the "Star Points." She chose the five prettiest girls (including herself, of course) to be "Points."

Needless to say, I'm not one of them. I have a gap between my front teeth. I desperately need a new hairdo. And doggone it, I've got to stop biting my nails!

I suppose it should comfort me that Eleanor Roosevelt is not very attractive, either — especially around the teeth — and she's one of the finest women alive. But somehow that doesn't help. Oddly, right now I'd rather be a Star Point than Eleanor Roosevelt.

OCTOBER 14, 1941

Dear Diary,

Today Johnny Vecchio shared the front-page news with the class: The U.S. Navy is ready to arm the American merchant ships that deliver war materials to Russia and Great Britain.

This information seemed a total bore to the Star Points. But I jumped on it right away and explained to the class that German submarines have been attacking our merchant ships, so it was necessary to protect them. Protecting the ships, however, does *not* mean that we're entering into any war with the Germans — though there's still a chance we might. (Luckily, I'd heard all this on the radio last night.)

Mr. O'Malley seemed impressed. Johnny Vecchio just stared at me, his eyes shining, like he thought I was amazing.

OCTOBER 18, 1941

Dear Diary,

Mom trimmed my hair last night and put it in pin curls. Before I went to bed, I looked in the mirror and practiced smiling without showing my teeth.

This morning, I had nice, bouncy curls. I borrowed Mom's blue sweater, then set out on my bike, looking for Maxine and the Star Points. Knowing they often attend the Saturday matinee, I posted myself in front of the ten-cent store, next to the movie theater where *Citizen Kane* is playing.

They never showed up. Just as well. By the time I got back, my hair was as stringy as spaghetti.

I passed Theo and Clara sitting on the porch. Theo was saying that Adolf Hitler was a deadly microbe. Clara was silent as she shelled peas. I have no idea what she thinks of Hitler. I do know that she and her mother came here from Germany two years ago. Miss Burke told me that Clara works for Mrs. Hawkins to help pay for their room and board. I wonder what the rest of Clara's story is.

OCTOBER 19, 1941

Dear Diary,

Amazing news: This afternoon, after church, Johnny Vecchio came to see me!

As we sat on the porch steps and talked, I was so nervous, I couldn't look him in the eye. I did, however, remember to smile without showing my teeth.

Johnny himself seemed completely at ease. He asked if Dad was serving on an aircraft carrier, a battleship, a cruiser, a destroyer, or a submarine.

I told him an aircraft carrier right now, but we didn't know which one. For security reasons, the navy makes him keep that a secret.

Johnny nodded with a big grin.

He's got a great grin. It spreads slowly from ear to ear and makes his eyes shine even more. Before he left, he asked if I wanted to come over to his house tomorrow and see his war map.

Come see his war map? As Johnny says: "Jeepers."

OCTOBER 20, 1941

Dear Diary,

Johnny's war map *is* a jeepers. It's a huge colorful map of the whole world. Tiny black flags are stuck in the countries that have fallen before Hitler's army: Austria, Poland, Czechoslovakia, Denmark, Norway, Belgium, the Netherlands, and France.

Johnny and I talked about how the Nazis are now smashing through Russia.

His parents were both at work down at the cannery, but his grandmother and six-year-old brother, Bill, were home with us. After we talked about the war in Europe, I bragged a little by showing them on the map the various naval bases where we've been stationed: California, New Hampshire, Virginia, Florida, Panama, and Far Rockaway.

Every time I pointed to a different place, little Bill said, "Holy smokes!" which made Johnny and me laugh.

When Bill asked where my "hometown" was, I shrugged and said, "I guess it's everywhere."

"Gee, that's something," Johnny said.

On the way home, I realized I'd forgotten to smile

without showing my teeth. But it didn't seem to matter. I think Johnny likes me a lot — whether I have a gap between my front teeth or not.

OCTOBER 21, 1941

Dear Diary,

A terrible day today. Before the bell rang, the Star Points linked arms in the schoolyard and drifted around, singing, "I Dream of Jeanie with the Light Brown Hair." Though I was standing off to the side by myself, I made the hideous mistake of singing along with them. Maxine pointed at me, and they all giggled like I was a goon.

I can't even tell Mom about this experience. It was so humiliating. It's hard to even write about it in my diary.

OCTOBER 22, 1941

Dear Diary,

Right now I hear Clara Rosenthal singing in her room. She sings in a high, beautiful soprano, ten times better than any Star Point.

I think Theo likes her singing, too. The other night I

heard her playing the old piano in the parlor and singing for him. He stares at her quite tenderly now. Is romance in the air?

OCTOBER 25, 1941

Dear Diary,

The Rosenthals are Jewish. I learned this at an awkward scene at dinner tonight.

Miss Burke asked Clara how she and her mother were able to come to America from Germany. (Though Mrs. Rosenthal knows little English, Clara seems to know quite a bit.)

In her soft, whispery voice, Clara answered that they had come to live with an uncle on Long Island, but he had died unexpectedly of a heart attack last spring.

Did they have other friends or relatives in the states, Miss Burke wanted to know.

Clara shook her head.

Miss Burke said it was a good thing they got out of Germany when they did.

She said she'd read that the Nazis had recently given out pamphlets to thousands of Germans saying that every Jew is Germany's enemy. Any German who helps a Jew for any reason, even by showing a friendly attitude toward a Jew, commits treason against the German people. And Hitler has ordered all German Jews to wear a yellow star with the inscription *Jude*, the German word for "Jew."

"Isn't that awful?" Miss Burke said.

Clara sat there, looking ill.

Theo Hawkins glared at Miss Burke. "That's enough," he said.

Miss Burke looked surprised and hurt.

Clara said something to her mother in German. Mrs. Rosenthal started wringing her hands and rapidly asking questions, her voice rising.

"*Nein, nein,*" said Clara.

But Mrs. Rosenthal seemed very upset. Clara had to lead her out of the room.

Theo left, too, banging out the back door.

"Oh, my goodness, what happened? What did I do?" Miss Burke asked Mom.

Mom explained that she thought it was difficult for the Rosenthals to hear Miss Burke's information. "They're Jewish, you know," Mom said.

Miss Burke replied that of course she knew. She said that's why she was talking about the Jews in Germany. She thought they'd be interested in hearing about their people.

When we got up to our room, I whirled on Mom and asked why on earth she hadn't told me that Clara and her mother were Jewish. I had no idea they were Jewish. I don't think I've ever met any Jews before. If I have, I wasn't aware of it.

"It's not polite to talk about people's religion," Mom said. "It's also not polite to make Clara and her mother talk about things they don't want to talk about. So don't pry, like Miss Burke does."

I don't want to be like Miss Burke, but I am dying to know Clara's story. Did the Nazis persecute her and her family? What happened to her dad? Did he stay behind in Germany, and is that why Miss Burke's news upset them?

OCTOBER 27, 1941

Dear Diary,

Interesting news today: Maxine Stone has a crush on Johnny Vecchio. When I passed her desk, I saw she'd written something on the inside of her notebook:

M. S. + J. V.

Maxine Stone plus Johnny Vecchio?

She must be dreaming.

NOVEMBER 2, 1941

Dear Diary,

After church today, I made a point of being nice to Clara. I invited her to come up and listen to the Benny Goodman Orchestra on our radio. She surprised me by saying yes.

As we sat together in my room, I asked if she knew how to jitterbug. She didn't. I asked her if she liked Frank Sinatra. She doesn't even know who he is. Imagine!

I'm afraid I then crossed the line a little — Mom's prying line. I asked Clara if she liked living in the

United States better than in Germany. She looked at me with a strange expression. Just as I was about to apologize, she gave me a surprising answer: She said she liked Germany better — but only the Germany she had known when she was very small. She said it had once been lovely, and her family used to have many friends. But then everything changed.

"In what way?" I whispered, feeling guilty for prying.

"Every way," she said.

Just then Mom came in the room. I clammed up, feeling like an old snoop. Clara excused herself to go help Mrs. Hawkins with dinner. On her way out of my room, though, she looked back and gave me a warm smile.

Her smile made me think she didn't mind my prying too much. Maybe Clara and I can do something fun together sometime. Normally a nineteen-year-old wouldn't want to be pals with a thirteen-year-old. But maybe Clara is desperate for a girlfriend.

I know I am.

NOVEMBER 9, 1941

Dear Diary,

Before sleep, Mom and I lay in our beds and listened to the news on the radio. The announcer said that out in the Pacific, our navy was ready to move at a moment's notice. America had a striking force of battleships, their guns at the ready.

I sat straight up and nearly yelled at Mom: "What is that guy talking about? A 'striking force'? What's he mean — 'guns at the ready'? Is Dad going to *fight* in the Pacific?"

"No, no, no," Mom said. "Dad has simply gone to safeguard the Pacific. That's what he wrote us — 'safeguard.' Now go to sleep."

I tried to sleep. But it was hard. I kept tossing and turning, worrying that Dad's ship *might* end up in dangerous waters.

NOVEMBER 13, 1941

Dear Diary,

I feel better tonight. We got a letter from Dad. He said he was fine. He loves all the letters he gets from us. He reads and *re*reads them. He said he was glad I loved where we were living, and he was glad I was having so much fun at school. (Ha.) He said there was no news with him, and no news was good news.

Mom and I always feel happy after we hear from Dad. We took a walk on the beach. In the cold sunlight, we identified three falcons and two sparrow hawks migrating south. We collected some lovely shells. When fog moved in and it grew dark, we came home and made hot chocolate.

NOVEMBER 14, 1941

Dear Diary,

This morning before the bell rang, I found Johnny and Bert talking with Maxine. I interrupted them to tell Johnny we'd gotten a letter from Dad.

When he asked me what Dad had said, I couldn't help but fib a little and say, "It's sort of a secret."

Johnny immediately left Maxine's side to walk off with me. So I was forced to keep up the lie and throw out phrases like "special maneuvers" and "top secret exploratory operations." I *had* to say these things, to keep him from going back to Maxine.

NOVEMBER 20, 1941

Dear Diary,

At sunset, I saw Theo give Clara a falcon feather. She was setting the dinner table, and he came in, still wearing his waders. He handed her the feather, and in his gruff, deep voice, said, "I thought you might like this."

"Ah, it's so beautiful," breathed Clara.

Theo smiled at her — a shy smile, the sort of smile you might not think Theo had in him.

I think romance *is* in the air.

NOVEMBER 24, 1941

Dear Diary,

Mom worked at the church again tonight, so I was on my own with the others, eating Mrs. Hawkins's boiled fish and cabbage.

As usual, Miss Burke was the main one who talked. She said she thought we would soon be at war with Germany.

Theo shook his head and muttered, "No, no. It's all about to boil over in the Pacific. Keep your eye on Tojo."

"Tojo?" Miss Burke said.

"The premier of Japan," Theo said.

"I know who Tojo is," Miss Burke retorted. "But I think you're wrong about his being dangerous." She shook her head, as if she thought Theo was too uneducated to have a serious opinion on the matter.

Boil over in the Pacific?

Dad is in the Pacific.

I'd better keep *my* eye on Tojo.

NOVEMBER 27, 1941

Dear Diary,

I never thought I'd have a Thanksgiving dinner that didn't taste good. Mrs. Hawkins and Clara served us duck — duck! — instead of turkey. Lumpy sweet potatoes, kale, and of course, fish chowder. No stuffing, no cranberry sauce, no pumpkin pie.

Theo, Mrs. Hawkins, Mrs. Rosenthal, and Clara didn't mind, because they don't seem to know the difference. Mom didn't mind, because she's too nice and kind. Miss Burke didn't mind, because she was eating at her sister's in Far Rockaway.

So that just left me to mind — selfish, ungrateful, bratty me, who minded so terribly that when we all silently gave thanks before the meal, I prayed that next Thanksgiving, we'd be somewhere — anywhere — but here.

NOVEMBER 28, 1941

Dear Diary,

For days, Theo's warning — "Keep your eye on Tojo" — has been running through my mind. This afternoon I rode my bike to the newspaper stand and scanned the front page of *The New York Times* for information about Tojo. All I saw was a small article saying the Japanese have rejected conditions for negotiations with the United States.

I don't know what that means, but it doesn't sound good. I think I'd better share my concerns with Johnny.

NOVEMBER 29, 1941

Dear Diary,

I rode by Johnny's house this morning and told him what Theo had said about Tojo. He got really interested, so we took off together for the newspaper stand in town.

As we parked our bikes, I saw Maxine and the other Star Points heading into the Saturday matinee. I know they saw me with Johnny. It's wicked of me, but I enjoy being the object of Maxine's envy for a change. Give her a dose of her own medicine. Doggone it, if she were smart, she'd get interested in these war matters herself.

Anyway, on the front page of *The New York Times* was a big picture of the Japanese ambassador. It said, "Envoy in pleasant mood."

Johnny thought that was a good sign. He then read aloud a part that said President Roosevelt was taking a personal hand in the negotiations over Japanese soldiers being sent into Indochina.

I'm not sure what that means. But Johnny said it was a good sign, too, and I shouldn't worry about my dad.

Johnny's turning out to be a great friend. Could he ever be *more* than just a friend?

J. V. + M. B.?

Sometimes I wonder.

DECEMBER 1, 1941

Dear Diary,

We heard from Dad! He said our letters are the only thing that brightens his boring days. I'm glad he has boring days. I hope they stay very boring until we see him again.

DECEMBER 2, 1941

Dear Diary,

I desperately need some brown penny loafers. All the Star Points wear them. I need a wide white belt to make my waistline look slimmer, too. And I wonder if there is some kind of nail polish that tastes so disgusting, I won't bite my nails anymore.

DECEMBER 3, 1941

Dear Diary,

Mom and I walked on the empty, windblown beach this afternoon. I wanted to discuss my shoe, belt, and nail problems with her, but I didn't think it was a good time. She seemed sad.

I figure she's always missing Dad. He's been gone a whole lot during our lives, being a career navy officer. But for some reason, this time feels different from the other times. It feels ominous. Is that the right word? Ominous.

DECEMBER 5, 1941

Dear Diary,

During social studies Mr. O'Malley quoted from a newspaper column written by Eleanor Roosevelt. Mrs.

Roosevelt wants all Americans to "pledge to be a little thoughtful every day about the meaning of freedom."

Mr. O'Malley asked us each to tell the class what freedom means to us. Johnny said it meant he could read the newspaper and listen to the radio.

I said freedom meant that if I chose, I could be friends with a German Jew named Clara and no one would mind. I added that as a true friend, I would be kind and accepting and if I had a group, I would let her be part of it. I got a little carried away, I guess, trying to send a message to the Star Points.

When Maxine's turn came, she froze. She had no idea what freedom meant to her. She giggled, and like a bunch of nuts, all the Points giggled with her, changing the exercise into something silly. I thought Johnny would finally see that Maxine was an idiot. But when I looked over at him, he was laughing, too.

DECEMBER 7, 1941

Dear Diary,
The Japanese have attacked us!

Theo was right — things boiled over in the Pacific!

At about 2:30 this afternoon, Mom was writing to Dad, and I was dancing to the Benny Goodman Orchestra on the radio when the announcer broke in:

"Flash! The White House has reported a Japanese attack on Pearl Harbor. Japanese Imperial headquarters announces a state of war with the United States! Stay tuned for further developments!"

"Oh, my gosh!" Mom cried.

I threw open our door and shrieked to the household, "The Japanese have bombed Pearl Harbor!"

Miss Burke came out of her door, exclaiming, "What? What?" as she ran into our room, clumping in her big black shoes. "Where's Pearl Harbor?" she asked frantically.

"I don't know!" Mom said. "Maddie, find out where it is!"

I ran back into the hall and shouted over the banister, "Theo! Where's Pearl Harbor?"

Theo didn't seem to be home. As I started back to our room, I saw Clara and her mother standing in their doorway. They look scared, so I tried to speak calmly. "The Japanese have attacked a place called Pearl Harbor," I said. "We don't know where it is. But don't worry."

Mrs. Rosenthal shook her head nervously and went back into their room. Clara stayed in the hall.

I asked her if she wanted to listen to our radio. She said she'd better not leave her mother. I told her I'd come give her reports.

At that moment, Theo came through the front door, and I hollered the news to him.

When Theo joined Mom, Miss Burke, and me, he told us that Pearl Harbor was in Hawaii. Miss Burke didn't believe him until the radio confirmed that Pearl Harbor was on the Hawaiian island of Oahu.

Mom and I were nearly hysterical, worrying that Dad's ship might have been at Pearl Harbor. It was a relief when the announcer finally said that hundreds of ships were destroyed or damaged, but none of them were aircraft carriers. Mom grabbed me and hugged me, and we both laughed. It was terrible of us, but we were momentarily so happy — one thing we know for sure is that Dad is on an aircraft carrier.

For the rest of the day, Theo, Miss Burke, Mrs.

Hawkins, Mom, and I all listened to the radio, and I kept delivering the news to Clara:

"Early this morning, mustard-colored warplanes with red suns on their wings attacked the U.S. naval base.

"Thousands were killed.

"Invasion of the West Coast of the United States is possible.

"Men of all military services are being summoned back to duty at once.

"Now the entire world is at war."

All the time we listened to the news, I kept thinking about Dad. He's not on assignment just to "safeguard" the Pacific anymore. Now he's there to fight.

DECEMBER 8, 1941

Dear Diary,

At school today all the kids kept saying, "The Japs are coming! The Japs are coming!"

A lot of attention got focused on me because Johnny

told everyone that my dad is a navy fighter pilot who's serving in the Pacific. So far, I'm the only one in my class who has a dad in the military. But that probably won't be for long.

I explained that my dad was safe because no aircraft carriers were hit at Pearl Harbor.

Mr. O'Malley had brought in *The New York Times*, and he asked me to read it and make a report to the class after lunch. I worked on this assignment during recess (while the Star Points linked arms and strolled around the school grounds, singing "I Got It Bad and That Ain't Good" as if they didn't have a care in the world).

In my report, I told everyone that the mayor of New York City had urged the public to be on alert. He said the city was an extreme danger zone and should take every possible safeguard against sabotage. He also said the FBI had rounded up over two thousand Japanese people in New York City, and that he was putting extra guards at the tunnels, on the waterfront, and in important public buildings.

I read the Japanese Declaration of War to the class because it sounded like something from a fairy-tale book:

"We, by the grace of Heaven, Emperor of Japan and seated on the throne of a line unbroken for ages eternal, enjoin upon thee, our loyal and brave subjects. We hereby declare war on the United States of America and the British Empire."

I also read an inspirational message from Eleanor Roosevelt to America's women, and a message from her to America's young people.

You could have heard a pin drop while I gave my report to the class. I felt important, as if I myself were playing a role in history.

As soon as school was out, I hurried home on my bike and found Mom and Miss Burke in the parlor, knitting scarves for the British. I read them Mrs. Roosevelt's words to women:

"You cannot escape anxiety, you cannot escape the clutch of fear at your heart, and yet, I hope that the certainty of what we have to meet will make you rise above these fears."

For myself, I saved Mrs. Roosevelt's words to America's young people, and tonight copied them onto a piece of blue stationery and taped it to my wall:

"You are going to have a great opportunity. There will be high moments in which your strength and ability will be tested. I have faith in you."

Mom's already gone to bed. She's exhausted, I think, from worrying about a war with the Japanese and what it all might mean for Dad. I'm worried, too. I'm shivering so hard, I don't know if I'll be able to sleep tonight.

"I have faith in you," Mrs. Roosevelt said.

I want desperately to rise to her challenge. I feel like saying my prayers to Mrs. Roosevelt tonight, instead of to God.

DECEMBER 9, 1941

Dear Diary,

I copied down more information for the class today from Mr. O'Malley's *New York Times*.

During recess, while the Star Points yapped about a

Christmas dance sponsored by the women's auxiliary, I wrote out parts of the speech President Roosevelt gave to Congress on Monday:

"Yesterday, December 7, 1941 — a date which will live in infamy — the United States of America was suddenly and deliberately attacked by naval and air forces of the Empire of Japan . . . No matter how long it may take us to overcome this premeditated invasion, the American people in their righteous might will win through to absolute victory . . . I ask that the Congress declare that since the unprovoked and dastardly attack by Japan on Sunday, December 7, 1941, a state of war has existed between the United States and the Japanese Empire."

When I read the declaration to the class, Johnny stared at me like I was made of gold.

I was bushed at the end of the day and went home and crawled into bed. I feel like I'm in a fever, a war fever. What can I do? How can I help? Mom's working at the church. I wish she'd asked me to go with her. I wish we would hear from Dad soon. Please write us, Dad, as soon as you can.

DECEMBER 11, 1941

Dear Diary,

Tonight Miss Burke told us the radio had announced that Hitler and Mussolini have declared war on the United States.

"What's going on?" Mrs. Hawkins asked, cupping her hand around her ear.

"The Germans and Italians have declared war against us!" Miss Burke yelled. "War! *War!*"

Mrs. Rosenthal stood up from the table as if she were going to run out the front door.

Theo grabbed her. Then he and Clara led Mrs. Rosenthal out of the room.

I myself wasn't all that shocked to hear about Hitler's declaration of war. Ever since Pearl Harbor got bombed, the enemy has all blended together. I just pray we hear from Dad soon.

DECEMBER 12, 1941

Dear Diary,

Today, Johnny asked Mr. O'Malley if he and I could make a sign for the class. He wanted to write a quote he'd seen in an advertisement: VICTORY DOES NOT COME WITHOUT A PRICE.

A super idea, Mr. O'Malley said. So Johnny and I got to work. While we lettered the sign during recess, we discussed the evils of Hitler and Mussolini. (I borrowed Theo's description of Hitler as a "deadly microbe.") While we talked, I could feel Maxine's eyes on us. I have to confess once again, I didn't mind making her jealous.

DECEMBER 13, 1941

Dear Diary,

We heard from Dad! He told us not to worry about him. Since we are now at war with Japan, his place of duty will be even more secret than before, he said. But he's sure he won't be seeing any combat soon.

Thank goodness!

The weirdest thing was that some words in his letter were blacked out. Mom explained that the words had been censored by the military for fear they might give the enemy information if the letter fell into their hands. She said all letters from servicemen were being censored now.

At least the censors didn't black out the last words he wrote: "Please, my Sweetheart and my Doodlebug, do not worry. I am not (underlined three times) in harm's way."

DECEMBER 15, 1941

Dear Diary,

I couldn't wait to tell Johnny about our letter from Dad. I caught up with him on the way to school and told him that Dad's letter was so secret, the military had censored parts of it. I confess I didn't tell him Dad said he wouldn't be seeing any combat. I might have even made it sound a little like Dad *would* be seeing combat. But I kept my fingers crossed while I said this. Fortunately, the subject moved quickly to aircraft carriers, and I could honestly tell Johnny that I'd been on one before.

DECEMBER 16, 1941

Dear Diary,

Mom and I put together a great Christmas box for Dad and sent it to the military post office in San Francisco. Military mail is the priority mail in the country now.

We made brownies and oatmeal cookies and packed them along with some handkerchiefs and socks, and books by Damon Runyon and James M. Cain, and a sprig of mistletoe. Plus, of course, a love note from both of us, signed, your Sweetheart and your Doodlebug.

DECEMBER 17, 1941

Dear Diary,

Another letter from Dad with whole sentences censored. He told us to be brave and do all we can to help the country. We must preserve our freedom at all costs. He said, "Doodlebug, take good care of Mom and yourself. Give thanks each day that you are an American. Keep the home fires burning."

I'm aching to do something for the war effort. Aching

so bad, I feel crazy. Right now I'd do *anything* for Dad and for America.

DECEMBER 18, 1941

Dear Diary,

In the girls' room before class, all Maxine could talk about was the dress her mother is making for her to wear to the women's auxiliary Christmas dance. Apparently it's a green velvet jumper with a peppermint-pink striped blouse. For crying out loud, doesn't that girl know there's a war on? When is she going to start doing her part?

DECEMBER 19, 1941

Dear Diary,

Today I learned that life is definitely not fair.

It was our last day of school before the holidays. On our way out of the building, Maxine called to Johnny, "Hey, silly! You didn't tell me what time your dad is picking me up!"

I froze, wondering what she meant. I pretended to

fiddle with the belt on my coat, waiting to hear his answer.

"What time is that dance?" he said.

Then I understood completely. It was as clear as a bell. My face got so red, I felt as if I were about to explode. I could hardly find my bike in the bike rack. When I did, I jumped on it and pedaled fast for home, trying to get there before the dam broke.

So Johnny's taking Maxine to the Christmas dance sponsored by the women's auxiliary. I've been a dope. All this time I was sure he preferred me over Maxine. I thought I had so much more to offer than her — brains, war knowledge, a military dad. But now I realize winning someone like Johnny is about being beautiful and having a slim waistline and penny loafers. It doesn't matter if you have rocks in your head.

Before I was even in the house, the tears started down my cheeks. I got up to our room as fast as I could. Thank goodness Mom wasn't here, so I could cry.

I guess I am more fond of Johnny Vecchio than I realized. *I* should be the one singing that stupid Star Point song: "I Got It Bad and That Ain't Good."

DECEMBER 21, 1941

Dear Diary,

I brought up my shoe and belt problem with Mom today. She said I couldn't get new penny loafers this Christmas because we had to live on peanuts now. Any extra money we have, she wants us to contribute to the Red Cross War Fund. I yelled at her, saying I didn't think I could wait till the war was over. I need friends *now!* She told me I was being crazy. We had a big fight. She said shoes and belts don't make friends. I said in this town they do. She said the girls here were just being snooty and infantile, and I shouldn't take it all so seriously. I shouted, "Yes, I know they are, but I still want them to like me!" I was all wound up. I cried as I told her I hated the gap between my teeth and I needed a slimmer waistline. All she said was, "Phooey." That sent me around the bend. "It's not phooey! It's not!" I said. Again she accused me of being crazy, and I know I am, but I can't help it.

DECEMBER 22, 1941

Dear Diary,

It was a lonely afternoon with Mom volunteering at the church all day.

After supper, all I could think about was that the stupid Christmas dance was taking place at that very moment. I made hot chocolate for myself in the kitchen. Clara was finishing the dishes, so I offered her a cup, too. She accepted, and we sat together in front of the fire in the parlor.

I found myself telling her all about Maxine and the Star Points, and Johnny and the dance tonight, and about how I felt left out of everything.

She listened gravely. She said she knew just what I meant. She said that when she was twelve, the German government wouldn't allow her to go to school with German children anymore because she was Jewish. She said all her neighbors stopped speaking to her family.

I was shocked. What a horrible thing to happen to somebody! I felt worse than ever, so spoiled and selfish.

All I could think to say was something stupid like, "My problems are so tiny compared with yours."

I wanted to ask her more questions about what had happened to her in Germany, but just then her mother called her.

After she went upstairs, I sat alone, listening to the distant waves and the whistling wind. I shivered as I tried to imagine Clara's life in Germany.

The sound of the ocean pounding at night on a dark shore gives me such a sad feeling, like I'm listening to the very heart of loneliness.

DECEMBER 23, 1941

Dear Diary,

I told Mom what Clara had told me, and she was very touched. Even though she's trying to save money, she gave me fifty cents so Clara and I could see *Citizen Kane* and have sodas after.

I loved *Citizen Kane*. Over our vanilla sodas at the drugstore, I tried to explain to her why Mr. Kane, one of the richest men on earth, longed for his childhood sled on his deathbed. I said it was because little things often mean so much more than big things.

Clara shook her head. "Sometimes evil people can kill even the beauty in little things," she said.

"Did evil people ever try to hurt you?" I asked her.

She nodded, then said evil people had once come into her house.

I figured she wanted to tell me her story. So I casually asked, "What did the evil people do?"

Clara just stared at me, looking terribly sad. I felt like I'd opened the door to her worst memories.

"I'm sorry," I said, feeling guilty and remembering Mom's warning not to pry. If Clara wanted to tell me something this personal she would tell me in her own way and in her own time.

I tried to blow away the clouds by changing the subject to Theo. I said I thought he might like seeing *Citizen Kane*, too.

Clara's face brightened at once. "No, that crazy man likes only to work," she said. She told me Theo has been working since he was twelve years old, when his father died. Even though he hurt his leg a few years ago in a fishing accident, he still works night and day to help out his mother.

Clara's eyes were shining the whole time she talked about Theo. You can tell she's crazy about him. I'm glad there is something in her life now that makes her happy.

DECEMBER 24, 1941

Dear Diary,

Christmas Eve. After Mom and I went to a candle-light service at church, she gave me my Christmas gifts: a white belt and pair of penny loafers. I was shocked. I told her that I thought we weren't supposed to give presents this year and that I didn't have a thing for her. She hugged me and said that just having me with her was the greatest gift. Her kindness made me burst into tears.

DECEMBER 25, 1941

Dear Diary,

Merry Christmas.

Mrs. Hawkins and Mrs. Rosenthal are both in bed

with bad colds, and Miss Burke spent the day at her sister's. So Theo, Clara, Mom, and I were the only ones at dinner. With just the four of us, I took notice of how gently Theo speaks to Clara, and how she stares at him with loving eyes.

After dinner, I went into the kitchen and caught them kissing!

It makes me happy to see Theo and Clara together. They're quite alike in some ways. They both were forced to grow up fast.

DECEMBER 27, 1941

Dear Diary,

Clara tapped on my door after lunch today and asked if I wanted to go to the ten-cent store with her and Theo.

"Whoopee," I said. I had been feeling bored stiff.

The three of us walked through a wet, windy snow. As soon as we stepped inside the store, we ran into the Vecchio family — Johnny, Bill, and their parents!

Johnny was all smiles. "This is Maddie Beck, Dad," he said. "The girl with the dad in the navy. She knows all about war stuff."

I nodded. Suddenly Clara took my arm and said, "Maddie, you must hurry now and prepare for your date!"

"Oh, yes! Bye!" I called to Johnny.

We grabbed Theo and hurried out of the store. On the street, Clara and I cracked up laughing.

"That was good, no?" she said — except she says "good" like "goooot."

"Very goooot!" I said, making Theo laugh, too.

DECEMBER 29, 1941

Dear Diary,

A storm's coming. A hard, cold wind is blowing, making the windows rattle. Clara and Mom both have colds now, so they stayed away from dinner, along with Mrs. Rosenthal and Mrs. Hawkins. That left just me, Miss Burke, and Theo to slurp our cod soup together.

While we were at the table, Miss Burke wondered aloud why the newspapers no longer print daily weather reports.

"They don't want to aid the enemy," Theo muttered.

I asked him what he meant, and he said that our weather reports would let any German U-boats close to our shore know when the sea was going to be calm or stormy, helping them make their plans.

Theo's words seemed to roll right off Miss Burke, but they gave me a jolt. German U-boats close to our shore? I have to talk to him about this, as soon as I can catch him alone.

DECEMBER 30, 1941

Dear Diary,

The wind's still blowing hard. It feels like it's blowing right through me as I sit here, feeling scared.

Theo came home from the harbor after dark, smelling of fog and fish. I followed him out into the laundry room. As he pulled off his ice-caked mitts and waders, I asked him if he thought there were any Nazi U-boats off the coast of Long Island.

He said yep, that the U-boats are creeping up and down the East Coast like water snakes.

I asked him how they got here from so far away. He explained that they can glide thousands of miles undersea without being seen. He knows some fishermen who work for the Coast Guard, and they told him they've been helping patrol the waters with minesweepers, looking for explosives planted by the Nazis.

I was dumbstruck. Theo asked me not to say anything about the U-boats around Mrs. Rosenthal, because she's scared enough of the Germans as it is.

I told him of course I wouldn't. Why, I won't even tell Mom, for that matter. It might worry the heck out of her, too.

There's only one person I'd like to share this information with. But he doesn't deserve to know it.

JANUARY 1, 1942

Dear Diary,
I have two New Year's resolutions:

1. Write to Dad a lot and let him know how much I love him.
2. Be a friend to Clara Rosenthal and other persecuted peoples wherever I find them.

President Roosevelt proclaimed today a national day of prayer, to ask for God's help in the days to come. He also signed the Declaration of United Nations, which affirms the alliance of the United States and twenty-five Allied nations to fight Germany and Axis countries.

Time magazine has named President Roosevelt "Man of the Year." The magazine said that Roosevelt once told the people of this country their generation would have a "rendezvous with destiny." He was right, the magazine says. The United States now stands for the hopes of the world.

A rendezvous with destiny — those might be the most beautiful, dramatic words I've ever heard put together. I'd like to personally have a rendezvous with destiny. I'd like to meet destiny alone on a dark path and fight for the good. I only wish I had someone to share my fight with me.

JANUARY 5, 1942

Dear Diary,

First day back at school. I managed to be calm and cool. Johnny spoke to me a couple of times but I barely answered him. When he waved at me from his lunch table, I ignored him completely.

Maxine and the Star Points seem as snooty in 1942 as they did in 1941.

JANUARY 6, 1942

Tonight, as Mom and I wrote letters to Dad, our radio show was interrupted by war news. The announcer said that Manila, the capital of the Philippines, fell to the Japs yesterday. Mom and I listened silently as Eleanor Roosevelt came on the air and said that the war was on a vaster scale than anything we had ever dreamed of before.

Mom and I didn't look at each other or say a word. I knew we were both wondering the same thing: What does all this mean for Dad?

JANUARY 7, 1942

Dear Diary,

Hard rain all day. Mr. O'Malley asked me to scan the newspaper and find something important to share with the class.

I reported that Mrs. Roosevelt had expressed concern about employers firing foreign-born citizens.

Mrs. Roosevelt warns us to beware of Nazi techniques: "Pit race against race, religion against religion, prejudice against prejudice. Divide and conquer! We must not let that happen here."

The class seemed impressed with Mrs. Roosevelt's words. Some kids had questions. I called on everyone who raised their hand, except Johnny, of course. I'm sure he's aware that I'm giving him the cold shoulder, but I don't think he's figured out why.

JANUARY 8, 1942

Dear Diary,

Every day now at 6 P.M., church bells ring all over town. They ring to remind people to stop what they're doing and pray for one minute for God's help to win the war.

When the bells ring, everyone at our table bows their heads. During our silent minute, I feel very close to Clara, Mrs. Rosenthal, Theo, Mrs. Hawkins, Miss Burke, and my mom. It's as if we're all sending up one prayer, a sort of family prayer to God.

JANUARY 9, 1942

Dear Diary,

Miracles happen.

On the way home from school, Johnny rode up alongside my bike. He didn't say a thing, and neither did I. It was awkward, but fascinating because he kept riding alongside me all the way home.

When I pulled into our driveway, he pulled in, too. "Hey, why are you sore at me?" he said.

"I'm not sore," I said.

"Oh, I thought you were sore," he said.

"Why should I be sore?" I asked.

He shrugged.

There was silence for a moment. Then he started to turn his bike around. I saw that I was about to lose my chance to speak my mind. Instead of pouring forth with a tirade, though, I simply said, "Did you have a good time at the Christmas dance?"

His face broke into one of his best grins. "Oh, is *that* why you're sore?" he asked.

I repeated that I wasn't sore, but doggone it, I could feel my face turning as red as an apple.

Johnny just kept grinning. He said he *had* to go to the dance with Maxine. His mom made him because his dad works for her uncle.

I laughed — I couldn't help it. I blurted out joyfully, "Did you know there are German U-boats off Long Island?"

His eyes got huge. I told him all about the Coast Guard and the minesweepers. He said we should ride along the shore together and check it out as soon as possible. He also said I should come over and see his map. He told me he's added red flags to the Pacific, showing the places the Japanese have taken over: Wake Island, Guam, Hong Kong, and Manila.

When I got inside, I tapped on Clara's door and told her Johnny and I were pals again.

"Whoopee," she said with a smile.

JANUARY 10, 1942

Dear Diary,

Good things happen in bunches. A letter from Dad today. He loved our Christmas package. He read one of the James M. Cain detective books in just a couple of hours. He'd blown his nose on the handkerchiefs, eaten our treats, memorized our love notes, and kissed nobody (underlined two times) under the mistletoe. He's a riot. He sounded real cheerful, and that made us cheerful. Mom and I even danced together as the Harry James Orchestra played "You Made Me Love You" on the radio.

JANUARY 13, 1942

Dear Diary,

I nearly had a heart attack today! Johnny and I took a bike ride along the beach after school. I didn't really expect to see anything. But then we *did* see something! We saw this huge black shiny thing in the water! It floated up above the surface and then disappeared.

We waited for it to reappear. My heart pounded like I was going to have a heart attack. But the black thing never came back.

I shouted above the wind that we should tell Theo. We rode home so fast, my bicycle chain popped off and I had to push my bike the rest of the way.

Fortunately we didn't have to search long for Theo. Just as we got to the house, we saw him coming down the street with his ice-fishing gear. Together we told him about what we'd seen, and he nodded, looking thoughtful. Then he said, "I think what you two saw was a whale. A humpback, maybe. One's been spotted near here lately."

"A whale. Jeepers," said Johnny.

"Just a whale?" I said.

I felt a little foolish. But Theo didn't act like I was a dope. The fact is, Theo always treats me with respect, like I'm his equal, actually, and not just a kid.

JANUARY 15, 1942

Dear Diary,

Today, in the library at school, I saw a photograph in *Newsweek* that made me gasp. It was a photo of six servicemen on the deck of an aircraft carrier in the Pacific.

Though the men were in dark silhouette, one of them looked just like Dad! He was leaning against the ship railing exactly the same way Dad is in the photo beside my bed. "I think that's my dad!" I said, and a group gathered around me, including Maxine.

She had a tender look in her eyes as she studied the

photo. She then looked at me with the same caring expression. "Tell your dad we're all rooting for him, Maddie," she said.

I have to admit that was a really nice thing for her to say — especially since it's been obvious lately that Johnny Vecchio is more mine than hers.

JANUARY 16, 1942

Dear Diary,

Unbelievable top secret information from Theo today! He told me and Johnny that one of his Coast Guard friends confided in him that the Coast Guard had picked up a German radio message. They heard a voice with an accent say, "You escape this time. Next time we sink you. *Heil* Hitler."

Theo explained that the voice must have come from a U-boat right off *our* shore! Probably the Germans had tried to torpedo a merchant ship traveling through the shipping lanes out of New York harbor.

Then Theo said the *most* shocking thing:

"Word is, a German invasion fleet might be coming to our coast at any time." Then he limped inside.

Johnny and I just stared at each other in shock. We couldn't even get out the word "jeepers."

Finally I took a deep breath and told Johnny we shouldn't tell anyone, not even his brother, Bill. We don't want people to panic.

Johnny agreed. He said we should start regular beach patrols. I said yeah, every day after school we should ride our bikes along the shore and look for periscopes sticking up out of the water.

We decided that when the two of us couldn't patrol together, we'd write our findings in a note and leave it in this hollow stump we pass on the way to school, like secret agents. In fact, we even have a code — we write two letters past the correct alphabet letter. Example: for "a," we write "c."

I'd better write a letter to Dad now. But you can bet I'm not going to worry him with this stuff. It's odd, but I may end up seeing more enemy action than he sees.

JANUARY 18, 1942

Dear Diary,

Johnny had to baby-sit today, so I patrolled the beach alone, looking for signs of an invasion fleet. I rode against the wind from the Coast Guard station all the way down to the three big dunes.

Once I screeched on my brakes because I thought I saw a periscope sticking up, but it turned out to be just a piece of wood. Another time, I saw something long and brown tumbling through the waves, but it turned out to be a piece of wood, too.

My hands were almost frozen by the time I left a note for Johnny in the hollow stump.

It said: Vyq cngtvu, hcnug cnctou, pq cevkqp vcmgp. (Two alerts, false alarms, no action taken.)

JANUARY 20, 1942

Dear Diary,

Still no sign of the invasion fleet. But today the local paper confirmed definite U-boat activity near here. It says on January 14, a Norwegian tanker was torpedoed and sank just sixty miles southeast of Montauk Point by a German U-boat! "The sinking has revealed the close presence of German submarines to the shoreline of the United States."

Now everybody knows. Not just me, Johnny, and Theo. Theo still doesn't want the Rosenthals to know, however. When he showed the article to me, he said I could borrow the paper, but I shouldn't let Clara and her mother see it.

I carried the paper over to Johnny's house to show him. He said our patrols are really important. I agreed. *Really* important. Heck, we might have prevented this if the U-boat had come a little closer to shore and we'd reported it in time. I wonder if the "false alarms" I saw yesterday were actually wreckage from the tanker.

JANUARY 23, 1942

Dear Diary,

Johnny and I were discussing the torpedoing of the tanker today when Clara stepped out onto the porch. I punched Johnny's arm and shook my head. He shut up like a clam. I'm sure Clara noticed, because she looked embarrassed and went right back inside.

Doggone it, what if she thought we were talking about Jews or something? I can't bear to think that we might have hurt Clara's feelings.

JANUARY 24, 1942

Dear Diary,

Tonight I knocked on Clara's door and invited her to come listen to Benny Goodman. She said she had to stay in because her mother wasn't well. I was afraid she might be telling a white lie, so I blurted out I was sorry if I hurt her feelings yesterday. I told her that Johnny and I were only playing a game. We didn't mean to shut her out.

She just smiled and said her feelings hadn't been hurt. She said she thought Johnny might have been saying sweet, romantic things to me.

I quickly told her that our relationship wasn't like that. He and I are just best pals, I told her. I love it that way.

Clara smiled as if she only half-believed me.

But it's true! When you're just best pals with someone,

you can be completely yourself. You don't need to wear green velvet jumpers and peppermint-pink blouses. You can smile without worrying about the gap between your teeth.

JANUARY 28, 1942

Dear Diary,

Mom and I have both been so busy lately, we hardly see each other. While I'm patrolling the shore with Johnny, she's raising money for the Red Cross War Fund, and helping organize their blood drive. She's also heading up the Free Library's book drive to gather books for servicemen.

I imagine next she'll try to get a job at a defense plant! I just read that thirty thousand women are already working in the plants, making parachutes and gas masks.

Sometimes I think Mom keeps herself extra busy so she won't worry so much about Dad. I don't know why she's so worried though. He's promised us he was not (underlined three times) in harm's way.

FEBRUARY 2, 1942

Dear Diary,

A letter from Dad today. He said he'd finished the rest of the books we'd sent him. He asked for more. What a coincidence! Now that Mom's running the book drive for servicemen, she can pick out the best books and send them straight to Dad. I can just hear what he'll say: "It pays to know people in high places."

FEBRUARY 9, 1942

Dear Diary,

Several times lately I've caught Mom staring anxiously out the window at the distant ocean. I know she's not thinking about a German invasion fleet. She's thinking about Dad. It's as if she's hoping his ship will appear over the horizon at any moment, bringing him home to us. If she catches me looking at her, she smiles sadly. I just smile back, afraid to pry.

A little while ago, Theo came back late from scouring the bay for scallops. In secret, he told me he saw a flare out at sea as he was walking home in the dark. He's afraid it might have been an enemy signal, and he's going to report it to the Coast Guard tomorrow.

I'm huddled in a blanket near our drafty window right now, watching the sky for strange lights. If it weren't so dark and cold, I'd dash to Johnny's house before Mom gets home and tell him about Theo's sighting.

Johnny's been calling me "Mad" lately. I like that. Mad Beck. Or how about Mad Vecchio? Gee, I'm crazy, I don't want to marry him. Like I told Clara, I love just being his best pal. I do, darn it.

FEBRUARY 10, 1942

Dear Diary,

Theo said the Coast Guard told him the flare he thought he saw last night was just a falling star. He doesn't know whether to believe them or not. The good news is that tomorrow Theo is going to start courses to be part of the county volunteer Civil Defense Force. He said it's sort of a "home front army" that protects Americans in case the enemy action reaches our shores.

"We'll lick those monsters," he said, putting his hand

over Clara's at dinner. I get the feeling Theo would fight the whole German army by himself for Clara's sake. It's a shame his bad leg keeps him out of the military.

FEBRUARY 11, 1942

Dear Diary,

When Theo came home this afternoon, he told us about his day at the Civil Defense Force's training course. At the fairgrounds, the New York State Troopers staged a demonstration of defense against chemical warfare. The volunteers even got to put on masks and enter a tent full of tear gas!

Once Theo has completed the training, he can choose to be an air-raid warden, a medical helper, a messenger, or a member of a road repair squad — or even a bomb squad!

He is so darn lucky. I wish they'd let kids join the Civil Defense Force and be a part of the home front army.

It's not fair.

FEBRUARY 13, 1942

Dear Diary,

A swell idea occurred to me when I woke up this morning. I started thinking that maybe Johnny and I should start a club, a club for kids to help on the home front. It wouldn't be like the Star Points club, where only a privileged few can belong. In my club, any kid who wants to work seriously for the war effort can join. By "kid" I mean six to thirteen years old, so a kid as young as Bill Vecchio could participate.

I can't wait to tell Johnny when I get to school.

LATER

Dear Diary,

Johnny loves, and I mean LOVES my idea of starting a club together. We discussed it all the way home, walking our bikes. Our motto will be: "Victory does not come without a price."

I suggested we use Mrs. Roosevelt's words as our guiding light, the words I have taped to my wall: *"You are going to have a great opportunity. There will be high moments in which your strength and ability will be tested. I have faith in you."*

We're thinking of calling the club Kids Fight for Freedom, or K3F.

We decided we'll announce the club idea at school on Friday after we've had a couple more planning meetings.

FEBRUARY 14, 1942

Dear Diary,

An amazing thing happened late this afternoon. After we coasted on our bikes along the shore, talking about our club, Johnny asked if I'd looked in the tree stump lately. I said no, and he didn't say anything more about it.

After he drove off toward home, I naturally went to look in the tree stump.

Guess what I found.

A piece of notebook paper with a heart drawn on it. Inside the heart, it said: Dg oa xcngpvkpg. (Be my valentine.)

Johnny Vecchio wants *me* to be his valentine?

I scribbled a little valentine note back. I drew a heart and, in the middle of it, I wrote: Qmca. (Okay.) Maybe he'll check the stump after church tomorrow.

What does all this mean? Will I have to change my way of acting around him? Change the way I look and dress?

FEBRUARY 16, 1942

Dear Diary,

Johnny must have found my note, because when he came up to me in the school yard this morning, he winked. Neither of us mentioned the valentines, though. We just leaped into a discussion about the K3F club. What a relief we have the club to talk about. It would have been embarrassing to talk about "us." I feel like Johnny and I have both silently agreed to keep our romantic feelings toward each other a secret. Not just from the world, but a little bit from ourselves, too.

Thank goodness. I don't want to start worrying about my appearance or my behavior when I'm with him. I want to just keep being my old self.

As for K3F club news, Johnny insisted that I should be the "colonel," since it was my idea in the first place. He said he'd be happy to be the "major." All the other kids can be enlisted persons, like "sergeants" or "corporals," depending on their age. But the enlisted kids can become officers by brave deeds and good works.

Tomorrow we're going to figure out just what we mean by "brave deeds" and "good works."

FEBRUARY 17, 1942

Dear Diary,

In my whole life I've never had so much fun. Johnny and I had a meeting today and decided that our K3F club will give kids points for doing these things:

1. Buying Defense Stamps with savings from allowance
2. Giving allowance to the Red Cross War Fund
3. Selling War Bonds to neighbors
4. Collecting used books for servicemen
5. Gathering scrap metal for the county's Salvage for Victory drive and women's silk stockings to be used for parachutes and medical supplies
6. Volunteering to help make first-aid kits for the Red Cross
7. Collecting newspapers and binding them into stacks

We decided not to include U-boat patrol in the list of activities because we don't want to create a panic about the situation. Just the two of us — "Colonel" and "Major" — will patrol the beach.

FEBRUARY 20, 1942

Dear Diary,

Today Johnny and I made our big announcement to the class. When we described the K3F club, kids seemed genuinely knocked out by the idea.

We wrote on the board: "Victory does not come without a price." Under that, we listed our seven ideas of what kids can do for the war effort. This led to a big discussion of what other things they could do.

Bert Lyman suggested that club members make signs to hang around town, inspiring *all* citizens to do the things on our list. (Bert's got a good brain and could easily become one of our first captains.)

Mr. O'Malley said he would talk to the principal about us announcing the club to the whole school in assembly next week. He said we could take a half hour every morning to record the "good works" that kids report to us.

After school, Johnny and I walked our bikes home together so we could talk. Again, neither of us said anything about our valentines. We only talked about the K3F club and a little about my dad. But sometimes Johnny stared at me in a way that made me feel sort of fluttery. I had to fight to feel like a colonel again.

FEBRUARY 22, 1942

Dear Diary,

All weekend, Johnny and I have kept up our planning. Today we sat on my front porch in the cold and made lists of all our ideas. Bill was with us because Johnny had to baby-sit. The little guy kept saying, "Holy smokes" whenever we said something keen.

Mom thinks our club idea is really swell. She served us cookies and hot chocolate while we worked.

We spent a lot of time trying to figure out what will happen when kids collect points for their war effort. We finally decided they should either get promoted or get special insignia. (In my experience, all kids love insignia.) I suggested we could make paper medals. Kids could pin them to their clothes.

When I suggested the idea of a "Medal of Honor" for a kid who makes a ton of points, I thought poor Bill would die. He actually collapsed on the ground and howled with joy.

After Johnny and Bill left, Theo came home with a scary piece of news: A couple of days ago, a Japanese submarine shelled the coast of California. No one was hurt, but it was the first direct attack on American soil in the war. The sub was only a half mile offshore. This is exactly the kind of thing Johnny and I have been trying to prevent from happening here on Long Island.

FEBRUARY 26, 1942

Dear Diary,

This morning, in the special half hour allotted to us, Johnny and I enrolled kids from our class into the K3F club. Maxine and all the Star Points stood in line, eagerly waiting to join up. It almost made me sad to see them acting so humble and eager. I guess my anger toward them is water under the bridge now. Two months ago, who would have ever thought *I'd* soon be running the best club in town?

I have to write Dad a long letter now, telling him all about the club. I can just see him sharing my letter with his buddies, so I'd better make it good.

FEBRUARY 27, 1942

Dear Diary,

Johnny and I gave our assembly presentation today. A funny thing happened before we went onstage. While we were standing in the wings, Johnny took hold of my hand. He gave it a big squeeze. Then he gave me a quick kiss on my cheek and said, "Good luck." The next thing I knew, we were introduced by the principal and went onstage.

I haven't had a real chance to think about that squeeze and kiss until now.

Is the truth starting to creep out into the open? That we're *more* than just best pals?

Stay tuned. . . .

MARCH 2, 1942

Dear Diary,

Quickly, first the Johnny-Maddie News of the Day: We got one check next to the "Best Pals" category, and one check next to the "Romantic" category.

In the "Best Pals" category, we planned more stuff for the club. In the "Romantic" category, he stared fondly at me a few times and, on one occasion, gently brushed a lock of hair off my forehead.

Now, for the War News of the Day:

The radio said that 112,000 Japanese Americans were being forced to move to "assembly centers." Japanese men, women, and children are being forced out of their homes here in the United States. Mom said she doesn't understand why this is necessary. She said it doesn't seem fair. After all, many of these Japanese people were actually born here.

I think she's right. Remember Eleanor Roosevelt's words? I have them written down. She said we should not pit race against race. Religion against religion. Prejudice against prejudice. Divide and conquer — we must not let that happen here, she said.

MARCH 3, 1942

Dear Diary,

This week, the cover of *Newsweek* shows a man wearing a helmet who has his fingers pressed to his lips. It says, "Shhhh. Fight Against Loose Talk . . ." Mom says it means that you're never supposed to talk about things concerning the military. Spies and Nazi sympathizers might be anywhere.

I asked her if that was the reason the government was making Japanese Americans live apart from other Americans.

Mom said she couldn't believe that all of those people were spies. She said little children aren't spies! She thinks it's a tragedy, and someday everyone will see it that way.

MARCH 4, 1942

Dear Diary,

Tonight at dinner, the whole group talked about the K3F club. Miss Burke actually had a very good idea. She said the Masonic Temple had recently started a servicemen's club and they might need furniture and stuff. She said Johnny and I should go by there and talk to them about helping out.

There was a good quote from President Roosevelt in the paper today:

"The months just ahead are the critical months of the war. Victory depends in large measure on the increased war production we are able to get from our factories and arsenals in the spring and summer of 1942. This is total war. We are all under fire — soldiers and civilians alike... We are all belligerents. To win we must fight."

Mom read this quote to me a little while ago. She's wondering seriously if she should get a job in a defense factory.

MARCH 5, 1942

Dear Diary,

Johnny, Bert, and I went to see the lady in charge of the servicemen's club today. She seemed delighted and asked us to please spread the word to the kids that they need all kinds of things. Just minutes ago, I finished making a sign that says:

KIDS FIGHTING FOR FREEDOM IS PUTTING OUT THE CALL! THE SERVICEMEN'S CLUB NEEDS YOUR HELP! CHAIRS AND CHINA! LAMPS AND RUGS! TABLES AND PLATES! FORKS AND SPOONS! PLEASE DELIVER YOUR CONTRIBUTIONS DIRECTLY TO THE MASONIC TEMPLE ON FULTON STREET.

MARCH 7, 1942

Dear Diary,

A heavy snowfall last night. Everything quiet today. Mom, Miss Burke, Clara, and I all knitted in front of the fire.

Mom had a great idea for the K3F club. She suggested we give information to kids on how to plant "Victory Gardens" this spring. That's a garden with everyday foods for a family, like cabbage, cauliflower, carrots, peppers, peas, potatoes, spinach, radishes, tomatoes, and squash.

Mom said Americans need to plant Victory Gardens

so transportation facilities won't have to be used to carry food to grocers and can be used for military purposes instead. Mom even offered to come to the school and talk about all this. I'm thinking that the K3F club should have a series of special guest speakers.

By the way, Miss Burke has come through in a swell way again. She's going to tell the local paper to write an article about us. She has a good connection there — a woman from her church who writes the garden column.

I can't wait to tell Johnny.

MARCH 9, 1942

Dear Diary,

Tonight Theo suggested that K3F members collect bacon grease from their mothers' kitchens so the Civil Defense Force can use the lard to make glycerine for explosives. And he said we should roll up little pieces of tinfoil for collection.

Theo seems impressed with my new leadership role. He calls me "Colonel" and says, "How's it going, Colonel? Win the war today?"

Even though he has a gruff manner, something about Theo is positively sweet. I love the way he brings Clara little gifts from the shore, like a pretty shell or a smooth stone.

I regret I haven't had much time to be a good friend to her lately. But I'm sure she understands.

I've also not written Dad very much lately, but I'm sure he'd understand, too, if he knew how busy I was with the club and all.

MARCH 10, 1942

Dear Diary,

On our U-boat bike patrol today, Johnny pointed at the ocean as if he'd just seen something suspicious. We both stopped our bikes and stood in the windy cold and stared at the whitecaps for a long time. Finally we shrugged and went on our way. It's amazing how Johnny and I can just silently beam our thoughts to each other sometimes.

Oh gee, is this anything like love?

MARCH 12, 1942

Dear Diary,

I had a great idea today. It was inspired by an announcement I read in the paper that said a Russian refugee is going to speak at the Presbyterian Church, giving a firsthand account of the Nazi invasion of Russia.

So my idea is: Clara Rosenthal can be one of K3F's special guest speakers and speak to our school, giving a firsthand account of the persecution of the Jews in Germany. I know she finds it sad to talk about the past. But this would be in service to a higher cause. I feel certain she'll see the importance of trying to educate kids about Hitler's evil.

(I hate to brag, but I think I'm the only one in our school who has a Jewish refugee for a friend.)

MARCH 13, 1942

Dear Diary,
I am such an idiot.

Today after school, I saw Clara and Theo on the porch. I bounded up to them and blurted out my idea about Clara being a special guest speaker and talking to the school about the Nazis and the Jews.

I knew at once I'd made a mistake. Clara looked upset, and Theo scowled at me.

I quickly muttered that it was a stupid idea and I was sorry. My face felt like it was on fire.

As I started to leave, Clara grabbed my hand. "I'm sorry, Maddie," she said in a soft, sad voice. She said she could not talk about these things yet. Especially in public to so many people. She said maybe someday she could, but not now.

I said I understood. I felt close to tears. I'd rather die than hurt Clara. Maybe her story is simply too sad for her to tell to anyone.

MARCH 14, 1942

Dear Diary,

Mrs. Hawkins was frying bacon tonight. So I brought her a clean, empty can and asked for some fat from the pan. She didn't understand. She said fat wasn't good to eat.

"Not for me! I'm giving fat to the club!" I said, nearly shouting. (Her deafness seems to be getting worse.)

Mrs. Hawkins shook her head in disapproval, but poured the fat into my can, anyway.

Later, at dinner, she told everyone she'd never in her life heard of a fat club. She wanted to know what kind of people joined a fat club.

I cracked up and explained to the others what had happened. They cracked up, too, and soon we were all laughing so hard, we couldn't stop. Though I think she still didn't understand, Mrs. Hawkins joined in because she's such a sweet sport. It was kind of crazy, the way we all howled over this misunderstanding. I think all of us needed a good laugh.

MARCH 16, 1942

Dear Diary,

A letter from Dad today. Big chunks were blacked out. (Where is he? I wonder this all the time.) But the censors didn't cross out the part that said he was so proud of me. He thinks the K3F club is a super idea. He says all his men think so, too. See? I predicted he would share my letter with his buddies. I know him. He also said he'd like to hear from me more often.

MARCH 20, 1942

Dear Diary,

Mom gave blood at the Red Cross today. I got the funniest feeling thinking about it. Her blood might be transfused into some soldier somewhere. He might be in a hospital recovering from a wound. He might be in a foxhole, in a plane, on a ship. Wherever he is, a part of Mom will be with him.

I shared these thoughts with Johnny, and he said it gave him the shivers. He said I should write them down and send them in to the newspaper. He said I was deep. "You're deep, Mad," he said.

I could only sigh and shake my head modestly. But I wonder, *Am* I deep?

MARCH 24, 1942

Dear Diary,

Johnny says Bill got into trouble the other night because he kept going around singing, "Praise the Lord and pass the ammunition," until his mom finally shouted, "Enough!"

Laughing about Bill is one of the things Johnny and I love to do most. We're both crazy about that little guy.

And each other? Today I'd have to say the thermometer reading was high on the sweetheart end. After we stopped laughing, Johnny ran his hand over my cheek. I got chills when he did that.

Oh brother, I want to stop this. Thinking about this kind of thing makes me feel less like a colonel and more like a silly Star Point.

MARCH 26, 1942

Dear Diary,

Japanese troops have attacked our forces in a place called Bataan. In cases like this, I'm glad Dad's on the sea, and not on land. If I had to worry about him fighting on land, I'd be in a state of constant anxiety.

APRIL 1, 1942

Dear Diary,

There's been so much to do, I haven't had time to write in my diary for almost a week. And now, there's more! Mr. O'Malley suggested to Johnny and me that K3F put together an extra calisthenics program (separate from gym) to encourage kids to build up their muscles so we'll have a "sturdier nation." It seems he saw something about this in a magazine.

For crying out loud! Johnny and I can't do everything! I'm thinking this might actually be a job we can give Maxine. She enjoys thinking about her looks so much. As a matter of fact, the other day she asked if she could design a uniform for members of K3F. Positively not, I told her, *this* club is not about clothes and shoes and looks! It's about helping win the war!

She just shrugged and accepted it. It pays to be the commanding officer sometimes.

APRIL 2, 1942

Dear Diary,

Maxine's excited about leading the girls in jumping jacks and sit-ups before school. Bert will lead the boys. Maxine hinted these jobs warranted promotions for her and Bert. "Jeepers, not so fast," said Johnny. "Let's see how you do first."

Theo said the Civil Defense Force is planning a blackout test for April 23. That means we'll have to turn out all our lights at night to protect the shipping lanes near the Long Island coastline from enemy submarines. Apparently when the lights are on, the Germans can spot our ships at a distance of up to forty-five miles from shore.

Johnny told me lately he's added more Japanese flags to his world map: Papua and New Guinea, the Solomon Islands, Burma, and all of Borneo. The biggest fight now is over the Philippines.

APRIL 4, 1942

Dear Diary,

We haven't heard from Dad in a while. But then I haven't written him in a while, either. I have to buckle down and give him a report on all our club activities.

Gee, I wonder where he is. Mom doesn't like even to speculate. She says the less we know, the better we'll sleep. As long as we don't get a telegram, we don't have to worry, she says.

Never has anything seemed so horrible and wretched

as getting a telegram. If I ever see a telegram boy at our door, I'm afraid I'll start screaming and never stop.

APRIL 6, 1942

Dear Diary,

Last night Theo told me the Civil Defense Force would be having a practice drill on the beach today. So Johnny and I snuck down there to watch. We hid behind a dune and, in the cold, gray weather, we saw a group of men creeping across the sand, pretending to be invaders from an enemy submarine. Suddenly another group dressed as armed police appeared on the beach and opened fire with blank bullets.

It was so scary, I have to confess I actually started to shake. What kind of colonel am I? I fear I'm a complete impostor.

APRIL 11, 1942

Dear Diary,

Something very romantic happened today.

It happened after Johnny and I had our meeting with

the chairman of the county war board. We'd gone to his house to discuss different ways kids can help with the scrap drive.

The chairman said mills are hungry for iron and steel scraps to make ships, tanks, and planes. They need more copper, brass, and other metals. They need rubber, too, from old tires.

"To win this war, the mills need all the scrap left lying around in people's yards — old tools and farm equipment!" he said. "Our war machine is starving for scrap to be melted down!"

The poor guy got so worked up, his face turned beet red. "Tell your friends! Collect scrap to slap a Jap!" he cried.

Johnny and I muffled our laughter until we left the house. Then we started laughing and couldn't stop. We were leaning against the back of the house in the twilight, shaking with laughter — when suddenly Johnny kissed me.

I was so surprised, I said, "Hey!"

"Sorry," he said.

"No, no, 'hey' means 'good,'" I said.

He asked if I was sore.

"Are you kidding?" I told him I was happy.

He said he was happy, too. Then, without another word, we got on our bikes and took off together.

That kiss must mean we are *officially* more than pals now.

J. V. + M. B.

Should I write that on my notebook?

APRIL 13, 1942

Dear Diary,

Miss Burke's connection at the paper seems to have paid off. A reporter wants to interview me and Johnny and take our picture a week from Wednesday. As Dad would say, "It pays to know people in high places."

Speaking of Dad, as soon as I get a copy of the paper with my picture, I'll send him one. The article will floor him. Plus, it'll help him understand why I've been too busy to write him lately.

(I won't say anything about Johnny being my boyfriend, of course. I don't want to make him jealous.)

APRIL 14, 1942

Dear Diary,

This week the paper said that there's a great shortage of ships right now. This shortage is making it very hard for the United States to deliver arms and munitions overseas.

For Mom, this article was the straw that broke the camel's back. She went and got a job as a welder in a defense plant about ten miles from here. She'll get picked up by a friend in the afternoon and return after midnight. She's asked Miss Burke and Mrs. Hawkins to keep an eye on me and make sure I eat a good supper and get my homework done.

The truth is, I'm so busy, I don't really mind. I have the feeling Mom and I are doing the same thing. We think if we work hard enough for the war effort, Dad will be safe and sound. In other words, everything we do, we do for him. He's our shining light. Our beloved. I guess people all over America are going through the same thing. For most people, the war comes down to one special serviceman you desperately love. A father, a brother, a son.

APRIL 18, 1942

Dear Diary,

Beautiful, warm day. Another Civil Defense drill to-morrow. Theo has invited me, Johnny, and Clara to participate. He told Clara he wants her to know that people here will fight the Germans if they ever try to invade us. We will never let the enemy hurt the Jews who live in America, he said.

When he said that, I got the chills. I can't imagine living in a country that would allow anyone to hurt Clara Rosenthal.

APRIL 19, 1942

Dear Diary,

It may sound strange, but Theo, Clara, Johnny, and I had a ball at the Civil Defense drill today.

At a fake bombing site, Clara and I were supposed to pretend to be casualties of a bombing. Theo and Johnny had to get us to the safety of the settlement house, where a fake emergency hospital had been set up.

At first, I was worried that Clara might find the whole

thing upsetting, but my fears were for nothing. Johnny and Theo were so funny trying to rescue us that Clara and I spent more time laughing than anything else. When they tried to carry us out of an old shack that was supposedly "bombed," they dropped me! Then Clara pretended to have a broken leg — and they put the splint on the wrong leg!

We laughed till tears came down our cheeks. I'll admit I never had so much fun.

Afterward, the four of us walked along the sunlit shore. It felt like a double date. Theo and Clara held hands as Theo talked about shad and bluefish. Johnny and I held hands, too, and kept our eyes pinned on the waves for periscopes. Several times we poked one another, but what we saw always turned out to be a seabird or piece of driftwood.

Gee, one thing's for sure: Life's never dull anymore. I'm having a great time. Can a person be in love with the excitement of war? Or is that too wicked?

APRIL 21, 1942

Dear Diary,

It might be time to promote Bill Vecchio from corporal to sergeant. Maybe even give him a medal. On Saturday, in a light spring rain, he drove his uncle's pony cart up and down his street, collecting flattened tin cans for the scrap drive. The tin will be melted down and reused for the war. All the time, he sang in his little high voice Bing Crosby's song "Junk Ain't No Junk No More." He threw his own tin soldiers and roller skates onto the heap.

Bill's already collected so many chewing gum wrappers that he's got a ball of aluminum the size of a baseball. Holy smokes, Bill!

He may be no bigger than a minute, but he's got the heart of a hero.

APRIL 22, 1942

Dear Diary,

Hey, Johnny and I had our picture taken today for the local paper! The photographer included Bill in the picture, too, with his pony cart and his scrap collection, as well as his aluminum baseball.

We're all famous! But I guess you could say there's still miles to go before we sleep.

In fact, Theo now thinks that K3F members should help the Aircraft Watch Service watch the sky for German planes. He's going to draw some pictures of the planes for us to pass around.

APRIL 23, 1942

Dear Diary,

Johnny and I worked as volunteer sky-watchers today, which means we watched the sky for two hours, detailing the number and kinds of planes we saw.

We didn't actually see any, but we did hold hands the whole time. I kept shivering, and I couldn't tell if it was from the cool ocean breeze or from my nerves.

We watched until twilight, when the Coast Guard told us to leave. The beach is strictly off-limits to all civilians after dark.

APRIL 24, 1942

Dear Diary,

Last night we had the first county blackout. It began at 9 P.M. with a five-minute blast of police sirens. Everyone on the road had to pull over and turn their lights out. House lights, streetlights, and traffic lights had to be turned off, too.

Mom stayed home from work because of the blackout. We all gathered in the parlor, except for Theo, who had to help patrol the area. Mom explained as best she could what was going on. Clara tried to translate for her mother. But when all the lights went out, we could hear Mrs. Rosenthal whimper with fear. Clara, Miss Burke, Mrs. Hawkins, Mom, and I all tried to comfort her, like we'd comfort a child afraid of the dark. We said silly things. We laughed. We sang. Mrs. Hawkins even lit a tiny candle and then brought out a surprise for us. A blueberry pie! It was actually delicious! By flickering candlelight, she cut big pieces for each of us, and we all greedily ate the berries and soft crust. Before our tiny light went out, I saw a childlike smile on Mrs. Rosenthal's tear-streaked face.

The blackout lasted three hours. During that time, Mrs. Rosenthal, Mrs. Hawkins, Clara, and Miss Burke all went to sleep sitting on chairs or on the sofa. In the end, only Mom and I were still awake.

Looking out the window, Mom said, "I've never seen such blackness before."

Not even the stars or moon were shining.

APRIL 29, 1942

Dear Diary,

Our picture came out in the paper today! Mr. O'Malley pinned it to the classroom wall. Mom bought ten copies to take to work and church. Of course, we also sent one to Dad right away. I can't wait to hear what he thinks about it.

APRIL 30, 1942

Dear Diary,

National registration for sugar rationing books took place at school today. Sugar has to be rationed now because the ships that deliver it from the Caribbean have to be used to fight the war.

Mom volunteered to register for everyone living in Mrs. Hawkins's Mansion-by-the-Sea. She had to tell the number of pounds of white or brown sugar already owned by our "family unit."

By this simple act of registration, me, Mom, Theo, Mrs. Hawkins, Clara, her mother, and Miss Burke all became members of a family unit. We do feel like a family these days. The war has a weird way of bringing strangers together.

MAY 5, 1942

Dear Diary,

Today Theo came home, wearing an official armband of the Civil Defense Force. Golly, it looks keen.

I'm thinking Johnny and I should consider making armbands for the officers of the K3F (which is still just the two of us). Maxine and Bert might get promoted soon, though. They're actually working quite hard leading the kids in calisthenics every morning. Maxine's invented a cheer that goes, "Pep! Pep! Pep up for the war!"

MAY 8, 1942

Dear Diary,

A great letter from Dad today.

He hasn't gotten my newspaper picture yet, of course. I'll be relieved when he gets it, because once again he mentioned that he'd like to hear more from me. He wondered how the K3F club was doing. He said President and Mrs. Roosevelt would be proud of us.

(Hey, an idea: I'll send one of the newspaper pictures to Mrs. Roosevelt! Our club's doing exactly what she wants kids to do.)

Dad teased Mom about working in the defense plant, but he said he admired her more than ever. He said she was working harder than he was.

He said he was still bored. (Good news.) He's gotten to be a darn good poker player, but he'd give up his poker winnings any day to see our faces. He said he dreams about us a lot.

Good night, sweet Dad.

MAY 9, 1942

Dear Diary

Great war news. A really long headline in *The New York Times* declared what happened yesterday:

JAPANESE REPULSED IN GREAT PACIFIC BATTLE WITH 17 TO 22 OF THEIR SHIPS SUNK OR CRIPPLED AND ENEMY IN FLIGHT PURSUED BY WARSHIPS

I read the article a bit anxiously, wondering if Dad might have been involved in the battle. But I breathed a sigh of relief when I came to "United Nations losses were said to have been comparatively light."

Later, when I showed the article to Johnny, I told him I thought Dad had probably been involved in this victorious Pacific battle. He looked at me in awe and said, "That's really keen, Mad." It's probably awful of me, but I liked getting credit for Dad's service and courage. (In other words, it pays to know people in high places.)

I can't wait to get a letter from Dad and find out what he thinks of my picture in the paper.

MAY 11, 1942

Dear Diary,

I have a terrible spring cold. I keep blowing my nose and can hardly breathe, so Mom wanted me to stay home from school today. I'll probably stay home again tomorrow, but I'm not loafing around. Today, when I had the strength, I worked on a design for a club uniform. I know I told Maxine "positively not," but I'm rethinking my position. Maybe it's not such a bad idea. What about just a simple white blouse or shirt and blue skirt or blue trousers? Any kid could come up with that, couldn't they? An armband would look really keen with that outfit. Maybe the Star Points could embroider a "V" for victory on all the shirt pockets.

MAY 13, 1942

Dear Diary,

Yesterday a telegram came.

Late in the afternoon. Mom was at work. I was sitting in the parlor designing our club uniform, when the front bell rang. I looked out the window and saw the telegram boy at the door.

I started to scream as I always thought I would. I screamed and screamed and I even tried to lock the front door.

Theo limped into the hall and grabbed me and held me, and Miss Burke opened the door and signed for the telegram. It was from the Department of the Navy.

I was shaking and crying as Theo held me. Clara, Mrs. Rosenthal, and Mrs. Hawkins all listened gravely as Miss Burke read the telegram aloud:

THE NAVY REGRETS TO INFORM YOU THAT YOUR HUSBAND LIEUTENANT COMMANDER DAVID BECK HAS BEEN CRITICALLY WOUNDED STOP WE WILL FURNISH MORE DETAILS WHEN AVAILABLE STOP

That's all it said.

They helped me up the stairs to my room, and Mrs. Hawkins and Miss Burke put cold cloths on my face and tried to calm me because I was shaking and sobbing uncontrollably.

Clara stayed and sat with me and, as I cried, she stroked my hair.

Theo drove his truck to Bridgetown to pick up Mom at the defense plant.

By the time they got home, Mom had known the news for some time, but had not spent all her tears. She got into bed with me, and we held each other for a long time, crying our hearts out. When you think you can't cry anymore, you always can.

MAY 14, 1942

Dear Diary,

I didn't go to school today. Miss Burke knows Mr. O'Malley, so she said she'd tell him my situation.

I don't feel like getting out of bed. I just keep staring at the wall, lost in my questions and worries. Clara brought me lunch and supper, but I don't feel like eating or talking. Mom went back to work because she said she doesn't know what else to do. It's better not to have her here, because every time I look at her, I see her sadness and it makes me feel worse. I just want to be alone.

I keep wondering, was Dad flying when he got

wounded? Was he in a battle? Did a torpedo hit his ship? Was he playing poker? Was he writing to us? Was he sleeping? Did he have time to think? Did he lose an eye or a leg? Is he already dead? What exactly did the telegram mean when it said he was "critically wounded"?

I looked up "critically" in the dictionary and all I could find was that it's the adverb of "critical," meaning "crisis" or "turning point."

MAY 16, 1942

Dear Diary,

Yesterday, Mr. O'Malley told the class about my dad. Johnny came by the house, but I told Clara to tell him that I didn't want to see anybody right now.

"Not even Johnny?" she asked in her soft voice.

I shook my head.

No, not Johnny. Especially not Johnny.

I can't be strong now or excited about the K3F club. I just want to be alone and think things through.

I can't get the picture out of my mind of the telegram boy at our door. I've relived that moment a hundred thousand times, as if by reliving it, I can change it, I can undo it, I can make the boy disappear and the day will stay simple and happy forever.

But I know that I'd have to reverse much more than just the boy's telegram. . . . I'd have to go back to some earlier day when Dad got wounded. A day and an hour I don't know a thing about. His last letter was sent May 3. Sometime between then and probably May 10 or 11, he was wounded. Was it May 8? In that victorious battle that made such huge headlines? I feel so guilty now about bragging to Johnny that Dad was probably in that battle.

When I looked at my last words in my May 8 diary entry, I burst into fresh tears. I'd written: "Good night, sweet Dad."

MAY 17, 1942

Dear Diary,

I took a walk on the beach with Mom today. Neither of us said much. I think we're both afraid to burden the other with our grief and worry.

We saw Johnny and Bill sitting on the pilings of the abandoned pier, watching for planes. Johnny saw me and shouted. But I just gave a little wave and kept walking.

When we got home, Mom prepared a covered dish for dinner at the church. She had to take a sugarless dessert, called a "war recipe." I went up to our room while she whipped up a fruit salad.

In spite of her sadness, she keeps going. I don't know how she does it. Just a week ago I would have loved to spot planes with Johnny and Bill. I would have gotten a kick out of helping Mom come up with a war recipe. But now I positively hate war. Everything about it makes me sick.

MAY 18, 1942

Dear Diary,

Mom said I have to go back to school tomorrow. She doesn't want me to sit by the window another day, just moping and biting my nails. I said I'd go, but if any more telegrams or letters, good or bad, arrive about Dad's condition, someone from the house has to come immediately to the school to get me.

It seems cruel beyond words that the navy doesn't tell families more. Loved ones could go insane trying to piece together the story on their own. I cut out a *New York Times* map about the Battle of the Coral Sea, that victorious battle on May 8.

The map shows where Japanese and American ships met near these islands in the Southwest Pacific. I also cut out a *Newsweek* cover concerning that same battle. It shows a stream of American ships and planes with the caption "Thunder at Sea: The Navy Meets the Enemy."

I feel if I stare long and hard enough at these puzzle pieces, maybe they'll reveal Dad's fate somehow.

MAY 19, 1942

Dear Diary,

Today when I went back to school, everyone was extra nice. Maxine and all the Star Points told me they were sorry. Johnny kept trying to catch my eye, but I wouldn't give it to him.

I'm mad at him. I'm not sure why, but it might be because while Dad was in mortal danger, Johnny and I were acting like we were having a ball. Flying around on our bikes, looking for U-boats, running the K3F club like it was all a fun game, holding hands while we plane-spotted. Playing war with Johnny kept me from worrying about Dad enough. It kept me from writing to him enough and praying for him enough.

MAY 20, 1942

Dear Diary,

I officially resigned from the club today. I left my resignation in the hollow stump. This time, my note was not written in code. It said simply:

Dear Johnny,

I have to resign as colonel of K3F. It's your job now. Sorry, Maddie

MAY 21, 1942

Dear Diary,

After school Johnny caught up with me on his bike and asked if we'd heard any more about Dad. I shook my head. He asked if I had any ideas about what had happened to Dad. I said no. I told him I was sorry about resigning my post. Then he surprised me by sounding a little angry.

"You should work harder than ever to help service-men like your dad," he said.

His tone made me lose my temper. "Are you trying to tell me what I should do?" I said.

"I just know you shouldn't turn into a chicken, Mad," he said.

"Oh yeah?" I said.

"Yeah!" he said. His usual sparkling eyes looked furious.

"Well, you don't know anything, Johnny Vecchio," I said coldly. I told him he thought that war was just a big game, but it wasn't a game at all. Then I pedaled away as fast as I could.

I know I was acting mean and crazy. But it made me feel good for a moment. It made me feel stronger — until I got home. Then I broke down and sobbed.

MAY 23, 1942

Dear Diary,

I listen to the sound of the ocean at night and I feel that same terrible loneliness I've always felt listening to the waves in the dark. Except now that terrible deep loneliness is connected to my grief about Dad.

MAY 26, 1942

Dear Diary,

It's been two weeks since we got the telegram. Not another word from the navy since. I keep a constant lookout for another telegram. I never stray far from the front porch. I keep watching out the window for that boy on his bike. I'm obsessed with getting another telegram to find out what's happened to Dad.

MAY 27, 1942

Dear Diary,

Theo peeked inside my room tonight. "How ya doin', Colonel?" he asked.

I was just lying on my bed, with a knot in my stomach, staring at the ceiling. I murmured, "Okay," without bothering to tell him I wasn't a colonel anymore.

Theo said his mother was worried because I hadn't come down for dinner. He said my mom would get mad at all of them if I didn't eat.

I just kept looking at the ceiling and told him I wasn't hungry.

He sat on the edge of Mom's bed and said, "Colonel, I got a gut feeling your pop is going to pull through."

He said he had feelings that were seldom wrong . . . he could predict storms, he could predict the amount of fish that the boats would bring in on a summer day.

I asked him if he had predicted that Dad would get wounded in the first place.

He squinted and slowly nodded. "I predicted to myself that you and your ma might run into a hard time, Colonel."

Good prediction, I thought.

He told me other folks in the house had suffered bad times, too. He said Clara and Mrs. Rosenthal had seen things we couldn't imagine in America. He said that four years ago Nazi storm troopers had broken into their house. They beat Clara's father to death right in front of her eyes.

I felt a jolt of horror go through me when Theo said this. Tears started down my face. But he went on calmly. He said Mrs. Rosenthal had not been right in the head ever since, but somehow Clara had found the strength to go on. She had gotten them out of Germany and over to America, where an uncle lived. When the uncle died, they had no more relatives or friends, and very little money. But once again, Clara found the courage to survive. She'd searched everywhere for a place to live, until she'd come upon Theo and his mother. With them, she had made an arrangement to help in the kitchen in exchange for room and board.

Theo said Clara had faced the darkness and she had won the war. The only thing that worries him, though, is that Clara seems to have lost the ability to cry.

As Theo told me all these things, the knot in my stomach tied itself tighter, and I could hardly breathe. Finally I know Clara's story.

Before Theo left, he patted my hair. "Colonel," he said, "you're a tough officer. I know you're going to make it. Before this is all over, you'll know a lot more about yourself, too."

All I know now is that I'm not like Clara. I don't have the courage to face the darkness like her. All I want to do is run away from the darkness.

MAY 29, 1942

Dear Diary,

Every day after school I still sit on the front porch, waiting for either a telegram or a letter.

My worst fear is that the navy has forgotten all about us. They'll never get in touch with us again, and we'll never know what happened to Dad.

JUNE 2, 1942

Dear Diary,

I cry every night when I'm lying in the dark, trying to sleep. I try to cry into my pillow. Usually I've cried myself to sleep before Mom gets home. But sometimes I'm still awake when she comes in and I know she can hear me sniffing, but she doesn't say anything. I know she doesn't want to pry. But sometimes I wish she would.

JUNE 4, 1942

Dear Diary,

It's been over three weeks since we got the telegram. We've had no more word from the navy. And not one word from Dad himself. If he was recovering, he would write us. I know him. If he was conscious at all, he would write. No news is terrible news, and it makes me feel emptier every day.

I remember in third grade I was in a ballet recital and Mom was hosting a luncheon at the officers' wives' club, so Dad had to come see me alone. He sat in the front row, wearing his white navy uniform, and when I came out in a rose-colored tutu for my solo dance, I caught sight of him beaming at me and all the steps my teacher had taught me went right out of my head. So I made up a dance on the spot. I turned and turned and turned and miraculously I never got dizzy. I danced the best I'd ever danced. I felt like a wind chime, and Dad's smile was the wind making me whirl.

All my life I've felt strong under my dad's gaze. Without him on earth, I imagine I'd feel so completely empty, I'd collapse in on myself and die.

JUNE 5, 1942

Dear Diary,

Tonight I did something against the law: I walked on the beach after dark. For security reasons, all persons, except the Coast Guard, are supposed to keep off the beaches from sunset to sunrise. But at about ten o'clock, while Mom was still at work and everyone had gone to their rooms, I heard Clara singing. The sound of her sweet voice nearly tore my heart out of my chest. I remembered Theo's words: Clara had faced the darkness and won the war.

Suddenly *I* wanted to face the darkness. And the darkest place I know is the beach at night.

I threw on my dungarees and a sweater, then snuck out of the house and ran all the way to the dunes, to the very heart of loneliness.

It was low tide. There was no sign of the Coast Guard beach patrol, so I sat on the sand and stared at the moonlight shimmering on the black water. It actually wasn't as lonely and frightening as I always imagined the beach to be at night. Somehow I found it a little comforting . . . the dark shapes of crabs scavenging the seaweed, the swell of the waves rising and washing over the shore.

I sat there shivering until I thought I saw a flashlight at the end of the beach. Then I ran for home.

Now I'm a little worried that I might be losing my mind. I mean, was I crazy to go to the beach tonight?

JUNE 9, 1942

Dear Diary,

Last day of school. What a relief. I won't have to bear the sad looks that come my way whenever the war's discussed. Or listen to Bert and Johnny talk about K3F plans. (Johnny's the colonel now. Bert's the major.)

Today near the bike stand, they were all talking about New York City's war parade. The Civil Defense Force has invited club members to march with them.

Johnny caught me listening and walked over to me. I tried to move away, but he caught my arm and asked if I wanted to go to the parade with them.

I told him no thanks, I hate war parades (not that I've ever been to one before).

But Johnny wouldn't take no for an answer. He said

we could go together on the train and I should just tell my mom we'd be home before dark.

The way he said "home before dark" suddenly made me feel like a little kid and made me miss my dad so terribly that I snapped, "No," again and started off on my bike.

"Chicken!" Johnny called softly behind me.

"You are!" I retorted, and drove off without looking back.

I can't go to a dumb parade when Dad might be dying or already dead somewhere in the Pacific.

JUNE 10, 1942

Dear Diary,

Johnny's wrong. I'm not a chicken. To prove it, I faced the darkness again tonight. After the house grew quiet, I headed down to the lonely beach. I hid behind a dune while a Coast Guard cutter moved along the foggy shore. When it was gone, I wandered down to the edge of the waves. Soon, clouds covered the moon and a thin rain began to fall. So I went home.

JUNE 11, 1942

Dear Diary,

Mom had the night off tonight. After dinner, she and Clara and I sat on the porch together. We talked about the lilacs blooming and about movies and the jitterbug. We never pried into each other's sorrows. We talked as if nothing were wrong in our lives. We talked like normal people, as if none of us had been shredded to pieces by grief.

JUNE 12, 1942

Dear Diary,

Tonight I got caught.

I'm still shaking. I don't understand what happened, really. I was walking on the foggy beach and when I got close to the abandoned pier, I heard voices and saw the shapes of two men near the dunes. I turned back to go home, but one of the men called out and shined a flashlight on me, and I froze like a rabbit.

The man angrily told me to halt and he asked who I

was and where I lived. I told him my name was Madeline Beck and gave him my address. He ordered me to turn around. I did, and he walked up to me in the dark and shined the flashlight right in my eyes. When I started to turn away, he said, "Look straight into this light, Madeline Beck." And I looked into the light, and I was blinded, and he said, "We're the Coast Guard. You did not see us here. You saw nothing."

Then I heard a man call out from the dunes. It sounded like he spoke a foreign language, but I couldn't tell for sure. Another voice told him to shut up.

Then the man with the flashlight told me to go straight home, and not tell anyone what I'd seen or I'd be arrested. He said they were engaged in a secret military operation.

"Your parents would be sad if you are arrested," he said. "Not one word about this, do you understand? Not one word."

I was so scared, I just said, "Yes, sir. I won't tell. I promise." I started walking away very quickly. Then I began running.

As I ran, I thought I heard some kind of engine offshore. I couldn't see a thing through the fog, though. I panicked and ran so fast, I kept slipping and falling. By the time I got home, I was caked with wet sand.

I can't tell anyone what I saw or heard, or I'll be arrested. I can't believe the Coast Guard would arrest a kid, but this is war. The military has to be cold-blooded in times of war.

Gee, Mom would die if she knew I'd been wandering the beach alone in the dark. Now that I think about it, I can't believe the Coast Guard didn't arrest me right there on the spot.

JUNE 13, 1942

Dear Diary,

I'm still in shock from what happened last night. I was so nervous all day, I never left home. I just sat on the front porch and prayed the Coast Guard wouldn't decide to come to the house and arrest me. After all, they know my name and address.

At one point I nearly jumped out of my skin because this black car slowed down in front of the house and a guy in a dark suit seemed to be staring straight at me. But then the car sped up and was gone, and I realized it probably had nothing to do with me or my being caught on the beach. Someone was probably just looking for a room and saw the NO VACANCY sign.

All day, though, I dreaded someone coming to the door, or the phone ringing. If Mom finds out what I did, her calm surface will crack for sure. Maybe she'll even get in trouble, too, for having a daughter who broke the law.

It's times like these I desperately wish Dad were here. He'd make everything all right.

JUNE 15, 1942

Dear Diary,

The last two days I've stayed close to home. I have the weirdest feeling that the Coast Guard really is keeping an eye on me. This afternoon I was loafing on the porch with Miss Burke, Theo, and Clara when a guy in a suit walked by the house. He paused and looked straight at me. He was wearing sunglasses and a fedora, so I couldn't see his face well.

Theo said, "Can I help you?"

Without a word, the guy turned and walked on.

"My, there's some odd characters in town these days," Miss Burke said.

Theo agreed with her. He went on to tell her about some of the strange people he'd seen down by the wharf.

Right now I'm about to jump out of my skin, thinking every sound I hear is the Coast Guard coming to arrest me. I don't know what to do. I feel like praying to Dad to help me.

JUNE 16, 1942

Dear Diary,

I felt a little calmer today. No sign of weird strangers. Still, I didn't sit on the porch, as I was afraid of being too exposed. I sat in my usual window seat, biting my nails and keeping watch for a telegram or letter. I know my nerves are shattered because of Dad. If we would just hear about him, I wouldn't be so afraid. My imagination wouldn't keep running away with me.

After dinner, from my window perch, I heard Theo and Clara talking on the porch swing. Miss Burke, Mrs. Rosenthal, and Mrs. Hawkins sat in rocking chairs, knitting. Mrs. Hawkins has been encouraging Mrs.

Rosenthal to leave her room more often. She even buys yarn for her.

Theo was telling them about the swordfish running off Montauk Point. He said the price would go down to thirty-five cents a pound now. He told her that great schools of mackerel and tuna have been seen offshore, too.

All their talk was such simple, normal talk, but it was music to my ears. My terror about Dad and my terror about what happened on the beach have made plain, ordinary life seem precious now.

JUNE 17, 1942

Dear Diary,

A horrible thing happened today.

I was sitting alone on the porch after dinner when a man strolled by, walking a dog. He was tall and thin, and had very white skin. He let his dog sniff the bushes near our walkway. Then he glanced casually at me and said, "Nice night, no?" He had a foreign accent.

I nodded and said, "Yes, sir."

"It's nice to be sitting outside in the fresh air, to be free," he said. "Is it not?"

"Yes, sir."

He stared at me a moment, then slowly smiled. "A person wouldn't want to be in prison on a night like this, would they?" he said.

"I beg your pardon?" I said.

"Nobody would like to be arrested for treason when they could sit in the open air like this," he said. "Would they?"

The deepest chill went through me, like someone had dunked me in an ice-cold pond. I could only nod and whisper, "No, sir."

He smiled again. Then he pulled his dog along, and they kept walking, as if nothing were wrong, as if he hadn't just warned me that I might be sent to prison.

At that moment, Theo, Clara, and Miss Burke wandered out to the porch and began chatting about the weather. I couldn't join in because I felt like I was about to have a heart attack. I excused myself and headed up to my room. My knees felt like jelly as I climbed the stairs.

I got into bed, and though the room was hot, I pulled

up the covers and just lay there, trying not to melt with fear. Treason! Who was that guy? Was he connected to the Coast Guard?

Somehow Clara picked up on my feelings. She tapped on my door and asked if she could visit.

"Please," I begged, my teeth chattering.

She asked how I was feeling. I was dying to tell her everything, but I didn't dare.

I just told her I get scared sometimes. I told her I was scared for my dad and I was scared of people, too. I was scared of some strangers, I said.

She said she knew just how I felt. And I know she really did. More than anyone else in the world, Clara would understand the terror of strangers.

As I lay there, agonizing, she began singing a song in German. Her voice was as clear as a bell. It's a miracle she can sing at all when her life has been so horrible. My nightmare is nothing compared with Clara's. Yet, *she* comforts *me*.

JUNE 19, 1942

Dear Diary,

I'm positively lucky to be alive.

I was riding my bike home from the Free Library today, and I was near the shore when a black car roared down the road. It swerved near me, making me lose control of my bike and crash into the curb. Then the darn driver of the car kept going, not even bothering to find out if I was okay!

I could hardly stand, my right leg was so painfully scraped up. My bicycle wheel was bent, so I was forced to leave my bike by the road and hobble toward home. Miraculously, Theo came by in his truck. I told him I'd carelessly run into the curb, and we went back for my bike. I didn't tell him about the car nearly hitting me, because I didn't want Mom to find out. It was just a little accident, but she'd have a fit.

Clara dressed my wounds, and Theo straightened out my bike wheel. Later, eating dinner with everyone, I felt especially lonesome. I was dying to come clean about what happened on the beach Friday night, and tell everyone about the man with the dog, and the black car on the road. I feel like my whole life is becoming a secret.

The fact is, I'm terrified. And I don't know what it's from, exactly. I mean, I won't get executed or anything. What I did wasn't *that* bad. Still, I'm terrified.

JUNE 20, 1942

Dear Diary,
I woke up with one clear thought in my head: I want to share my secrets with Johnny.

EVENING

Dear Diary,
All day I was as jumpy as a rabbit. I kept thinking, I've got to talk to Johnny before I explode.

But now I'm sweating over how to do it. I can't just walk up to his door and ask to talk to him. The Coast Guard might be following me. I might get his whole family in trouble if I'm seen visiting them.

This is nuts. I can go to Johnny's, doggone it. It's not against the law to walk up to a person's house and knock on their door. Golly, the United States is not a police state! It's not Hitler's Germany, for Pete's sake! I'm free to knock on a friend's door! My dad got wounded fighting for this freedom! Doggone it! Now I'm mad.

JUNE 21, 1942

Dear Diary,

Johnny wasn't home. He has a summer job as a pin boy at Palma's Bowling Lanes. His grandmother, though, seemed really happy to see me, and Bill hopped around, insisting I come look at the new flags on their map.

I took a quick peek, then asked Johnny's grandmother to give him a message when he came home. I gave her a piece of paper folded over. Inside it simply said: "Check the stump."

That was my first note. I put my second in the stump after I looked over my shoulder about a million times and didn't see any cars or people. The second note said: Eqog ugg Vjgq chvgt fkppgt. (Come see Theo after dinner.)

If the Coast Guard finds this note, they won't

understand its meaning. I'll stay on the lookout and waylay Johnny before he asks for Theo.

Right now I'm in my usual seat, peering out the window, watching for Johnny or for the man with the dog.

Theo and Clara are sitting in the porch swing. He's telling her that she should give singing lessons. She can use the piano in the parlor.

Right now Theo and Clara seem so innocent. They have no idea that I'm in the middle of a nightmare concerning top secret military activity.

My goodness! Johnny's riding up on his bike!

LATER

Dear Diary,

Johnny just left. On the way up to my room, I told him I was sorry for the way I'd been acting. I said there was no excuse for my mean behavior. He said yes, there was; I'd been upset about my dad. I could have hugged him for being so kind.

As soon as we got to my room, I didn't waste any more time. "Listen, I'm in serious danger," I said. "The Coast Guard's threatening me."

Johnny glanced around my room, as if expecting to see a nurse from an insane asylum.

I told him to sit down, so I could start from the beginning. Using my diary as a reference, I recalled every detail about the night I'd run into the secret Coast Guard operation. I told him all the strange things that have happened since.

When I finished, Johnny whistled, then said this sounded super serious.

I agreed. He wondered if the foreign speech I had heard could have been German. I said it was possible; then we both wondered if maybe the Coast Guard had caught a German saboteur. Johnny suggested that tomorrow we go back to the beach in broad daylight, when it's not off-limits. Then I could show him where I had stumbled onto the military operation.

I took a deep breath, worried I might be caught returning to the scene. But then that feeling of anger came over me. This is a *free* country, after all. "Why not?" I said.

"Good going, Colonel," he said, and he smiled that swell smile of his. I laughed, and for a quick moment, I did feel like my old self again.

It's time to hit the hay now. BIG day tomorrow.

JUNE 22, 1942

Dear Diary,

A scary discovery today!

Johnny came by on his bike while Mom and I were eating lunch. I told her we were going for a ride, and she looked really happy. I know she's been worried about my cutting myself off since we heard about Dad.

When I said good-bye to her, I felt guilty that Mom thought Johnny and I were heading out on a harmless bike ride when actually we were on a dangerous mission. But I have no choice. I have to keep facing the darkness. If I stand tall and face the thing I fear, I have a chance to conquer it. If I just keep dodging and hiding, it will conquer me.

We parked our bikes near the steps, then headed down the beach. We passed some kids playing in the sand, and grown-ups strolling in their swimsuits, but no men with bald heads or fedoras, and no Coast Guard.

Near the abandoned pier I showed Johnny the spot. He walked in circles, staring at the bright, silver-flecked sand as if he were Sherlock Holmes searching for footprints or a clue of some kind. I thought he was being silly, until he picked up something and called to me. When I ran over, he showed me a pack of cigarettes.

It was a pack of *German* cigarettes.

We both started talking excitedly. We figured maybe the Coast Guard *did* catch a German on the beach ten days ago. Jeepers, maybe the guy was a saboteur. Maybe he came off a U-boat.

The two of us stood in the white, glaring light of the sun, going over all these maybes.

Finally Johnny stuck the cigarette pack in his pocket. He had to hurry to his job at Palma's Bowling Lanes. But first he rode his bike with me all the way to the boardinghouse to make sure I got there safely.

Before we parted, we made a plan to meet tomorrow. I told him to be real careful on his way to Palma's. I even offered to go with him to make sure he was okay. He said then he'd have to ride back with me to make sure *I* was okay, and we'd end up going back and forth forever.

All through dinner, I debated whether or not I should at least tell Theo about our discovery of the German cigarettes. But I decided to keep my mouth shut. I'm still afraid that if I tell anyone in the house, I'll be putting myself in danger of treason. Plus, I positively don't want Mom to find out that I got into trouble with the Coast Guard. She's trying so hard not to fall apart because of Dad. One more terrible thing could give her a breakdown.

JUNE 23, 1942

Dear Diary,

I can't believe what I'm about to write. But this is what we discovered today, exactly what we discovered. (First, if anything happens to me — Mom, I love you so much, and Dad, I love you so much. And Clara, and everybody in this house — I love you all. Thank you for acting like my family. Oh, and I love the Roosevelts and our country so much, too.)

Okay, here's what happened:

Johnny came over after lunch, and we headed back to the scene of the military operation.

Again, no odd strangers or Coast Guard seemed to be on the scene. We ran barefoot over the hot sand, acting like two normal kids goofing around. When we got close to the pier, I suggested we explore the dunes.

We stopped to put on our shoes because the sand

around the dunes was really hot. As I was pulling on a sandal, I noticed a bunch of seaweed piled up nearby. I wondered aloud how it had gotten so high up on the beach.

Johnny wondered the same thing. He got a stick and began brushing away the sunbaked weeds. Soon he uncovered a shallow ditch in the sand. A wooden case bound with a rope was in the ditch. We used Johnny's pocketknife to cut the cord around the case, and when we opened it, we found a large tin inside. Inside the tin were a bunch of glass tubes and a sack of white powder.

We weren't sure what the powder and tubes were for. But we started poking around in the sand near the case, and the next thing we knew, we had uncovered two coats, and a pair of overalls, a pair of overshoes, and *three caps with Nazi swastikas.*

Johnny saw someone walking down the beach, coming our way. We quickly covered the stuff back up with seaweed and hid behind the dune. After a while, we peeked out, and the coast was clear.

We decided we'd better get the heck out of there. So we took off like lightning bolts and ran all the way back to the steps, jumped on our bikes, and hurried for home.

When we got to the crossroads, I turned and saw a black car following us. I screamed at Johnny to get off the road. We both leaped the curb and rode our bikes bumpily over the grass toward the baseball field. The black car drove on by. I couldn't tell if it was the same one that had almost hit me a few days ago or not. I might have just imagined it was after us. But I can't be sure.

When we got back to my place, Johnny and I zipped up to my room and sat on the floor and tried to get our bearings. He spoke first — and said exactly what I was thinking.

The facts are: We no longer think I ran into the Coast Guard at all. We think I ran into a band of Nazi saboteurs who had come ashore from a German U-boat. They buried their stuff in the sand, then disappeared. The Nazis are probably somewhere in the area right now, somewhere right here on Long Island. The powder in the case could be an explosive. They might be planning to come back for it and blow something up. Johnny and I think we are probably the only two Americans on earth who know this.

Furthermore, we think it was Nazi sympathizers who've been spying on me, who nearly hit me with the black car, and who warned me to be quiet!

Our plan now is for me to talk to Theo, not tell him what we know, but just ask him what *he* would do if he ever came across evidence that saboteurs were in the area. I'll tell him I need to know so I can tell K3F club members what to do in case such an unlikely event ever happens.

Theo's been fishing all day. I'm waiting for him in my room now, biting my nails off. I'm scared, but I've got to help our country for Dad's sake. Do it for Dad, do it for Dad, I keep telling myself. He sacrificed himself for America. Now it's my turn.

I just realized something. I'm actually in the middle of a "rendezvous with destiny," President Roosevelt's famous words. Mrs. Roosevelt's words taped on my wall fit my situation, too.

"You are going to have a great opportunity. There will be high moments in which your strength and ability will be tested. I have faith in you."

This *is* a great opportunity and a high moment, even though it doesn't feel that keen. It feels a little sickening. Actually, I feel nauseated. Victory does not come without a price.

LATER

Dear Diary,

Theo was great. I presented my "theoretical" situation to him and asked for advice.

He said there's only one thing he would do.

"What?" I breathed.

"Call the FBI," he said.

Golly, I couldn't imagine a better answer. I asked how a person called the FBI. He said it was listed in the phone book under Federal Bureau of Investigation.

"In our little phone book?" I asked.

He told me to wait, and he got his *Civil Defense Handbook* and found the FBI's number for me. He told me to give this to the kids in the club in case they ever needed it. That's what is so swell about Theo. He never acts like kids are too young for serious stuff like calling the FBI.

JUNE 24, 1942

Dear Diary,

Today I rode my bike to the hollow stump to leave a message for Johnny. I could swear someone was lurking down the road, but I left the note anyway. It said: Jcxg cpuygt!!

(Have answer!!)

Now I'm waiting for him to come over. My head's swimming with the facts. We've got to tell the FBI. But that seems impossible. Can two kids really get through to the FBI?

JUNE 25, 1942

Dear Diary,

Well, we did the impossible. We made our call from a pay phone near the bowling lanes. We had a bunch of coins, and we used up half of them before we even got an agent on the line.

I did all the talking. I tried to sound as adult as I could, lowering my voice and speaking calmly. I gave the basic facts, just the cold, hard facts of what I saw and what we found: the encounter on the beach, the cigarette pack, and the wooden case and clothes in the sand.

I didn't mention my life had been threatened. I was afraid the agent might think I was some crackpot who imagined danger all around her and was making up some story to explain it.

Finally I refused to give my name. I said, "I'm sorry, but I wish to remain anonymous."

The agent sounded only half-interested, though he asked for very detailed information about the location of everything. He didn't show one trace of excitement. In fact, he seemed bored! When I hung up, I was unsure of my success. But Johnny said that FBI agents are trained to sound bored.

Maybe so, but I feel a little let down. I mean, this was really big news as far as I was concerned. But I guess it was better for the guy to act calm; it was more professional.

Professional or not, I'm afraid the FBI agent's lack of excitement has thrown cold water on my own excitement. I'm wondering now if maybe I exaggerated the whole thing. Maybe the guy in the black car was just a reckless driver. Maybe the guy with the dog heard about me from some Coast Guard guy and was just making a joke. Maybe the stuff buried in the sand was . . . well, actually, it's hard to explain away that stuff on the beach, especially the three hats with swastikas.

What next?

I asked Johnny that before he headed off to Palma's.

"We wait and see," he said.

I'm not a person who likes to wait and see. I prefer action, but I have no idea now what action to take.

Also, I'm afraid that while I wait I'll go back to worrying about Dad all the time. I'll start to lose my mind again.

JUNE 26, 1942

Dear Diary,

An odd thing has happened. Since Johnny and I called the FBI, I've stopped being afraid. I don't feel I'm being watched anymore. Either the saboteurs and their Nazi sympathizers have all left town — *or*, they never even existed. Telling my story to the FBI has somehow lifted a big burden off me.

Maybe I'm being foolish, but I feel safe now.

JUNE 27, 1942

Dear Diary,

It came today. It came when I wasn't looking. (Isn't that always the way? Like if you watch a pot of water that's about to boil, it *never* boils. Why is that?) Anyway, I was up in my room, reading a movie magazine, when it came. Mom was home for a change. I heard her loudly calling my name.

I hurried out to the landing, not guessing at all what had happened.

"Maddie! Maddie!" she kept shouting, and when I looked over the banister, I saw her waving a piece of paper. "A letter — a letter about Dad —" she screamed. Then she burst into sobs, happy sobs. You can always tell a happy sob from a sad one.

"He's okay —" she said, gasping. "Dad's okay —!"

I burst into happy sobs, too, and by the time I got my shaky, sobbing self down the stairs, the whole household was gathered around us, and *everyone* was crying. Even Theo had a tear on his cheek. Mrs. Hawkins and Miss Burke and Mrs. Rosenthal were crying. And Clara was crying! Miracles! Clara, who'd forgotten how to cry. We were all crying and at the same time, laughing at ourselves for crying.

It was the single most wonderful moment of my life.

JUNE 28, 1942

Dear Diary,

Mom and I have read the letter so many times, we know it by heart. A nurse wrote it from the navy hospital at Pearl Harbor, Hawaii. She said she was writing at Dad's request. She said he was recuperating from his injuries. She said he wanted us to know that his wounds were healing, and he did not want us to worry.

The nurse gave us the address where we should write him. Some of the letter was censored — big black marks through whole sentences. But now we know what we most needed to know. Dad's alive. He's recuperating.

We don't know why he didn't write the letter himself. Mom says we're not going to worry about that. She says it doesn't matter what his wounds are. The only thing that matters is that he's alive and we're going to be completely grateful for that. If there's anything to worry about, Mom says, we'll worry about it later.

JUNE 29, 1942

Dear Diary,

This morning I rode to the bowling lanes to tell Johnny the good news. He was setting up pins when I shouted at him, "My dad is safe!"

He grinned and dropped the pins and came running. The bowlers all hollered at him, but he came to me, anyway, and gave me a giant hug before running back to do his job.

JULY 1, 1942

Dear Diary,

In three days I've written five letters to Dad. I've told him everything (except about the saboteurs, of course, and my call to the FBI. I don't want to give him a heart attack).

I described the weather in detail and all the swell things people have said and done since hearing the good news about him. (Mrs. Hawkins made a blueberry pie for us all, and Miss Burke had an announcement put in the local paper!) I told him how much I loved him about twenty times and how sad Mom and I had been and how grateful we are now. I told him that I pray all the time we will see him very, very soon. I told him that I was sorry I had not written to him enough, and now he'll get more letters than he ever wanted.

JULY 2, 1942

Dear Diary,

It's a riot. Everyone's writing to Dad. Theo and Clara sent him a get-well card. Mrs. Hawkins and Miss Burke wrote him cheerful notes. I saw Maxine and the Star Points and Bert Lyman at the movies, and they said they all wanted to write him! Oh, this is the best — Johnny and Bill are sending him a package from their whole family with books and socks in it! Plus some Italian pastries made by Johnny's grandmother! Isn't that swell?

It's not like people don't know other soldiers in the battlefield. (Maxine has two uncles on their way to Europe, Johnny's cousins are in training now, and Theo knows at least three fishermen who've gone into the navy). But Dad was the first one anyone knows to be injured. So even though he's never set foot in this town, he's like a special "hometown boy." I'd better write him and explain who everyone is so he won't be completely baffled by all his mail.

I'll tell him that Mom's eyes shine like stars these days. I know she's counting every minute until we see him again.

JULY 3, 1942

Dear Diary,

I'm writing Dad twice a day. Mom and I are waiting anxiously to hear again from his nurse. It's been a week since her letter. If she only knew how much another letter would mean to us, surely she would take the time to write more often. (I said those exact words in my last letter to Dad, hoping when the nurse reads them to him, she'll get the message.)

JULY 4, 1942

Dear Diary,

I'm getting ready to go with Johnny, Bill, Theo, Clara, Mom, Miss Burke, Mrs. Hawkins, and even

Mrs. Rosenthal to the fireworks at the ball field. Never has a Fourth of July meant more. Freedom. Family. Friends.

JULY 6, 1942

Dear Diary,

Johnny and I made an amazing discovery today. It's been a little over two weeks since we found the Nazi stuff buried in the sand, and for the first time we went back to the beach to take another look. Guess what. We couldn't find anything. *Not one thing!* We looked and looked everywhere. There was no indication of a shallow ditch, a case, any clothes, or the three Nazi caps. It was all gone, the sand swept clean.

I left there, half-feeling we'd dreamed the whole thing. But Johnny swore we hadn't. He thinks the Nazis might have cleaned up the area. Or maybe the FBI did.

It's strange, but for some odd reason, neither of us seems that interested in the subject anymore. Our fear and suspicions seem to have all blown away with the evidence. I'm only dreaming of the day Dad comes home, and Johnny seems to be thinking mostly about his swell job at Palma's and the bike scavenger hunt on Saturday for the USO Fund.

On our ride home, we had a contest to see who could ride the longest without using their hands.

We sat on the porch with Theo and Clara. Johnny and Theo talked about shark fishing, while Clara and I talked about the marionette show at Guild Hall. Miss Burke has roped the two of us into being usherettes there tomorrow night. What will we wear is our big question.

JULY 8, 1942

Dear Diary,

I'm still in shock. Johnny came by today. He asked if I had seen the paper. I said I hadn't. He said we should go somewhere private.

I led him to a bench in the backyard, and he pulled out today's local paper and pointed at the headlines:

NAZI SABOTEURS LAND DYNAMITE ON BEACH FROM U-BOAT

My eyes nearly popped out of my head. I pressed my hands against my heart and said, "Oh, my gosh!"

It seems that on the night of June 12, four Nazi agents came ashore from a submarine off our coast. The FBI and the Coast Guard found explosives, detonators, and other equipment in the sand. The men had plans for a two-year program of destruction of industrial plants, railroads, waterworks, and bridges stretching from New York to the Ohio Valley.

All four saboteurs had worked in the United States at one time or another. They all spoke English and had been trained at a school for saboteurs in Berlin. They're all expected to be executed once they are convicted in court.

Then Johnny came to the last sentence in the article. It simply said: "Officials revealed that a call from an anonymous tipster helped lead them to the scene of the Nazi landing."

When Johnny finished reading that sentence, I fainted. It's true. I've never fainted before in my life, but I just keeled over, my head landing on Johnny's shoulder.

He slapped my cheeks just like they do in the movies, and I came to. He told me to bend over and put my head near my ankles, and I did.

When I sat up again, I had a roaring headache. I felt like throwing up, too. It was all too much. I told Johnny I had to go lie down, and he helped me to the back porch and called for my mom.

Clara came instead and ushered me inside, and I told Johnny I'd see him tomorrow. Clara helped me upstairs, and I fell on my bed, feeling like I was in a fever. I went to sleep and slept for the rest of the day and night.

I guess I'm not much of a colonel if I can't handle the consequences of my actions.

Did Johnny Vecchio and I change the course of history?

JULY 9, 1942

Dear Diary,

I feel like my life has been changed forever. But life at Mrs. Hawkins's Mansion-by-the-Sea goes on as usual. Everyone in the house sat on the porch today and discussed the Nazi landing on the beach. Theo said he wasn't surprised. Mom, Miss Burke, and Clara thought it sounded more like a movie than real life. Mrs. Rosenthal just knitted and smiled. (I was relieved she didn't seem terribly upset, as Theo once predicted she would. I think she feels safer in America now.)

Everyone tried to remember what they were doing that night. Nobody asked me what I was doing. As the daylight faded, I just listened silently as they all talked about it. I felt like a ghost who'd come back to Earth and was listening to the innocent, naive voices of people she loved.

Johnny must be feeling the same strangeness. Without even saying it, we seem to have both agreed that it's no use to try to convince people of our role in the capture of the criminals.

Isn't that what you learn in church — Do good works for their own sake and not for the reward? That's a tall order. I'm not sure I could follow that order if fate had decreed a choice. The fact is: Johnny and I positively have no choice. Even if we wanted to be famous for changing the course of history, no one would believe our story. If we told our friends or families that *we* were the "anonymous tipster," they'd think we were lying for sure.

JULY 13, 1942

Dear Diary,

Johnny's working nearly every day at Palma's. The K3F club is taking a break since school's out. But in our free time, Johnny, Bill, and I plan to do some stuff for the war effort, like collect more scrap and newspapers. In fact, Johnny and Bill are coming by tomorrow afternoon, so we can all go together to the bike scavenger hunt for the USO Fund.

On the hunt, we'll ride our bikes and try to collect all the things listed on a piece of paper. We're supposed to find things the USO club needs, like ashtrays, hand soap, and drinking cups. The person who finds the most things wins.

JULY 14, 1942

Dear Diary,

Bill Vecchio won the scavenger hunt! Out of the forty-five kids who participated, he brought in the most complete list. (I think because he's so young and enthusiastic, a lot of townspeople gave him a helping hand.)

It's no surprise what he said when they gave him his little trophy: "Holy smokes!"

During the hunt, fifteen servicemen were brought to the USO Hall because the list called for "a man in uniform." They were all great sports. At the end of the day, the women's auxiliary sponsored a little party with a band and punch and cookies.

Theo, Clara, and Miss Burke came by. When the Four Hearts played a dance tune, Theo and Clara danced, and even with Theo's limp, they made a lovely couple, both dressed in white. Theo asked Miss Burke to dance the jitterbug. She laughed and said no, but I thought it was nice of Theo to ask.

Johnny was shy at first. But after about the third tune, he asked me to dance to "Taking a Chance on Love." He held me close as we clumsily stepped together around the room. We passed some grown-ups talking about the Nazi saboteurs and we didn't even poke or nudge each other. I think for some reason the truth scares us both to death.

JULY 17, 1942

Dear Diary,

Finally another letter from one of Dad's nurses! This one told us more about his condition. His hands were burned, so they are in bandages and that's why he can't write to us himself. His head injury is not completely healed, so he can't think as clearly as he'd like to. But he can understand all our letters, she wrote, and when she and others read them to him, he lights up like a candle.

Mom broke down when she read these touching words — "He lights up like a candle." And she sobbed over Dad's injuries. When I tried to comfort her, she kept sobbing. She said Dad must be suffering so much. "Burns are so painful!" she cried.

Even though I was crying, too, I told her we'd be with him soon. I told her we'd help heal his burns and his wounds. I said we'd touch him and talk to him and dance for him to help him get better. I kept talking and talking, saying anything to try to stop Mom's grief. I didn't worry a bit about prying.

One thing I know very deeply now: War is not about fun and games. It's about terrible sadness, pain, and fear.

JULY 21, 1942

Dear Diary,

My words to Mom have come true. A doctor from Dad's hospital wrote us today. He said we could be with Dad soon. He said they expect Dad to fully recover and resume his military duties someday. But it may take some time, and for that reason, they are sending him back to the states, to a hospital at the naval base in San Francisco.

At the hospital, they plan to have a bedside ceremony for Dad, to give him an Air Medal. If Mom and I move to San Francisco, we can attend the award ceremony and visit Dad every day.

I imagine he'll be a bit of a stranger to us at first. He'll be changed from his war experiences and from his wounds. But for that matter, Mom and I won't be the same people he knew before, either. We've both grieved our hearts out and fought our secret wars.

JULY 22, 1942

Dear Diary,

Mom quit her job at the defense factory today, so we can leave by Friday. Friday's just two days away.

We have to leave that soon, Mom says, so we can get to San Francisco and find a rooming house by the time Dad arrives. We'll get a train from New York City to Chicago, then another from Chicago to San Francisco. The trains are so full of servicemen these days, we might have long waits at the stations.

Mom explained these plans to everyone at dinner, and I saw tears in people's eyes. Mom herself wept a little and said, "Now, now, we'll write. We'll be back. And someday, you must all come to visit us — wherever we are."

But I know the truth. When you live a military life, you don't see people again. And you stop writing them after a short time. You just move along and make new friends. Then you move along again.

This time it feels especially sad, though. Maybe it's because of the war. Our "family unit" has become like a real family. Talking on the porch at night or gathered around the dinner table, we take a lot of comfort in each other. Why, right now I feel as close to Theo and Clara as if they were my big brother and sister. How can I say good-bye to them?

And Johnny . . . How the heck can I say good-bye to Johnny?

JULY 23, 1942

Dear Diary,

I rode my bike to Johnny's house this morning to tell him the news. I asked if I could speak to him alone. In case I cried, I didn't want his grandmother or Bill to see me.

We sat on his back steps and I told him Dad was getting an Air Medal.

"He deserves it," Johnny said softly.

Then I told him Mom and I would be leaving tomorrow to go live in San Francisco.

Johnny sucked in his breath and looked away from me. He didn't say anything for a long moment.

"So I guess this is good-bye," I said.

Still, without looking at me, he reached out and

grabbed my hand. He held it real tight. He squeezed it and didn't look at me. That's when a tear started down my cheek.

"I'll miss you, Mad," he whispered.

"Me, you," I whispered back.

Then he sighed and looked at me. He had a tear or two on his cheeks. He leaned over and kissed me.

But I had to blow my nose, so I couldn't linger long in that position. I sniffed and asked for a tissue.

Johnny jumped up and went inside. When he came back a minute later with the Kleenex box, his grandmother and brother were with him.

They both hugged me and said they'd miss me. His grandmother told me to write, and I told her I would.

As I started to leave, Johnny said he'd come by tonight after work to see me one last time.

LATER

Right now Mom's at the church saying good-bye to her friends. I just finished packing. It's not quite dark. I'm about to go downstairs and sit with everyone on the porch. Theo will report on the number of bluefish he caught today. Miss Burke will gossip about something, and we'll all talk about what my life in San Francisco will be like.

When it grows dark, Johnny will show up on his bike and join us. I have the feeling that he and I will hold hands. Right now the radio is playing "I'll Be Seeing You in All the Old, Familiar Places." Will Johnny think of me when he hears that song in the future?

The bond between me and Johnny is more special than most bonds. We're the only two people in the world who know the truth about how the saboteurs were caught. If one of us dies one day, the other will have to bear the secret alone. Except maybe I'll tell my children. Children always believe their parents, at least the small ones do.

Maybe Johnny will tell Bill. I suspect Bill will believe our secret, too. He has the heart of a hero, and believes the best about everybody. "Holy smokes," he'll say.

I've known another person this year who has the heart of a hero: Clara Rosenthal. Clara had her first singing student today, and I think it went very well. One thing haunts me: The day we got the great news about Dad, Clara cried for the first time in years. *Her* father will never come home to her, yet she cried with joy be-cause *my* dad was coming home to me.

Theo said Clara had faced the darkness and won the war. I know now what he meant. Though the war seems far from over, Clara has already defeated the Nazis. With all their storm troopers and bombs and U-boats, they could not kill this one seemingly small thing: Clara Rosenthal's goodness.

It gives me hope for myself. It gives me hope for the whole world.

EPILOGUE

Maddie Beck took the long train ride to San Francisco with her mother and was happily reunited with her father. Captain Beck's wounds prevented him from flying again during the war, but he did recover well enough to remain in the navy. Over the next few years, Maddie attended school at a number of naval bases. She graduated from high school while stationed near Virginia Beach, Virginia.

Contrary to her prediction, Maddie and her mother *did* remain in close touch with the household of Mrs. Hawkins's Mansion-by-the-Sea. In fact, Theo and Clara got married and named their first child Maddie in honor of their friend.

Maddie went back to meet her namesake the summer after her senior year in high school. She and Johnny Vecchio began dating that summer. And to no one's surprise, they became engaged two years later.

After graduating from college (Maddie from Mary Washington College in Fredericksburg, Virginia, and Johnny from Georgetown University in Washington, D.C.), Johnny and Maddie were married in the summer of 1949. They settled in Washington, D.C., where Johnny worked for many years for *National Geographic* magazine, and Maddie worked as an organizer for the American Red Cross.

LIFE IN AMERICA
IN 1941–1942

HISTORICAL NOTE

World War II began two years before the United States joined the fight. From 1939 until 1941, while Americans watched helplessly, Adolf Hitler's German troops invaded country after country in Europe. One of the most horrendous aspects of Hitler's brutality was his campaign against Jews and other minorities. After the war, it was learned that over 8 million European Jews had been murdered by the Nazis. The annihilation of the Jews came to be called the Holocaust.

During the time of Hitler's aggression, the nation of Japan was also seeking to expand its empire. It had moved into Indochina and was planning to conquer other parts of the Pacific. When the Japanese attacked the U.S. military base at Pearl Harbor, Hawaii, on December 7, 1941, the United States was finally brought into World War II. The United States declared war against Japan and, quickly thereafter, against Germany.

Once the United States got involved in World War II, the nation threw itself wholeheartedly into the struggle. Inspired by President Franklin Delano Roosevelt and First Lady Eleanor Roosevelt, millions of Americans "fought the war" on the home front. Thousands of women went to work in defense factories and shipyards to help make weapons and ammunition, ships and planes. Children ran scrap metal drives, fat drives, and book drives. Civilians trained to be auxiliary firemen, policemen, nurses' aides, and air-raid wardens. They served as plane-spotters and had Victory Gardens. Women stopped wearing silk and nylon stockings so that silk and nylon could be used to make parachutes and medical supplies. Families sacrificed gasoline, sugar, meat, rubber, tinfoil, and many other things to help in the war effort.

While Americans sacrificed on the home front, great numbers of military men and women were sacrificing abroad. In the Pacific alone, more than one hundred thousand American sailors and marines were wounded and more than five hundred naval ships were sunk.

America was the only major power whose land was not physically shattered by the war. There were times, however, when the enemy was close to American soil.

Japanese submarines sometimes operated off the Pacific coast of the United States; and in the early months of the war, German submarines, known as U-boats, patrolled the Atlantic Coast of the United States. The U-boats sank a number of Allied ships during the winter and early spring of 1942.

Eventually, the U.S. Navy and Coast Guard developed ways to detect and sink the German submarines, and the U-boat threat declined. On June 12, 1942, however, two German U-boats delivered eight Nazi saboteurs onto American soil. One group of four landed in north Florida, and the other landed near the tip of Long Island, New York. The four Nazis who landed on Long Island buried boxes of explosives in the sand, planning to destroy American industrial companies and transportation facilities. Eventually the saboteurs were turned in by two of their own group, and all but the two informers were executed.

In 1945, World War II ended in victory for the United States and its Allies. In May of that year, Germany surrendered; in August, Japan surrendered. Altogether, more than 57 million people had been killed in the war.

The December 8, 1941, edition of The New York Times *announces the December 7 bombing of the United States military base in Pearl Harbor, Hawaii. This attack led the U.S. to declare war against Japan, and soon after, against Germany.*

During the attack on Pearl Harbor, the U.S.S. Shaw's magazine was hit, detonating ammunition and explosives held there.

The U.S.S. Lexington, *a navy aircraft carrier, was badly damaged during the Battle of the Coral Sea on May 7–8, 1942. This battle was an indication of a new kind of warfare, in which dive bombers and torpedo planes would cause most of the damage; enemy ships never came in sight of one another.*

President Franklin Roosevelt declared that there was "one front and one battle where everyone in the United States — every man, woman, and child — is in action. That front is right here at home." Here, President Roosevelt with Eleanor Roosevelt, whose public service endeavors led to changes improving the welfare of American soldiers, and increased assistance for women who went to work to support the war effort and their families.

In response to President Roosevelt's message, American civilians eagerly accepted their role in World War II. In spite of wartime hardships, the collective efforts of rationing, recycling, and carpooling made many people feel more united with their fellow Americans than at any other time in history. Here, a group of Manhattan children called the Tin Can Club of America salvages cans for the war effort.

Rubber was necessary for the production of airplanes and tanks, but Japan controlled the Southeast Asian plantations that were the world's largest source of natural rubber. In June of 1942, President Roosevelt called on American citizens to turn in "old tires, old raincoats, old garden hose, rubber shoes, bathing caps, gloves." Across the country, groups emerged with the sole purpose of collecting rubber. Top, organized by the North and South Lawndale Citizens Defense Youth Organization, this enthusiastic group of Chicago children went collecting from house to house with bicycles and wagons. Bottom, one hundred and six trucks carrying more than eighty tons of rubber are led by members of a Boy Scout troop in Stevens Point, Wisconsin.

This ad encouraged people to plant a Victory Garden to supplement their wartime rations. Each household was issued ration books that held coupons for weekly and monthly allotments of items like meat, butter, cooking fat, shoes, and gasoline.

Along with food, rubber, and tin, the war effort also needed money. War bonds, which could be purchased for $18.75 and turned in after ten years for $25, covered one-sixth of the nation's $304 billion war expenses.

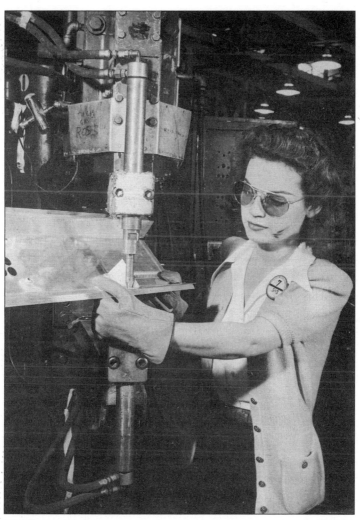

The United States government drew women to defense-industry jobs with ads reading, "If you've sewed on buttons, or made buttonholes on a machine, you can learn to do spot welding on airplane parts." Because defense jobs gave them a sense of responsibility for the war effort, women responded enthusiastically. Here, a woman works in the spot welding department for Lockheed, an aircraft manufacturer.

During World War II, millions of Americans joined the Red Cross effort as volunteers in the Nurse's Aide Corps, the Gray Lady Service, the Junior Red Cross, the Hospital and Recreation Corps, and in other services benefiting the armed services and the war effort.

Americans volunteered to serve as plane spotters and ground observers. This young girl works at the observation post of the Bangor, Maine Filter Center, where she reports on multi-motored aircraft, aircraft formations, aircraft that can be heard but not seen, and "unusual occurrences and unusual objects," such as "blimps, helicopters, balloons, accidents, strange objects."

Top, *the June 12, 1942, edition of the* Journal American *announces the landing of two German U-boats,* bottom, *on American soil; one in Florida and one on Long Island, New York. Four Nazis buried boxes of explosives on a Long Island beach, intending to return, and with them, destroy industrial companies and transportation facilities.*

REMEMBER PEARL HARBOR

History, in every century,
records an act that lives
forevermore.
We'll recall, as into line we fall,
the thing that happened on
Hawaii's shore.

Let's remember Pearl Harbor
as we go to meet the foe.
Let's remember Pearl Harbor
as we did the Alamo.

We will always remember
how they died for liberty.
Let's remember Pearl Harbor
and go on to victory.

"Remember Pearl Harbor" was based on a popular World War II saying and became an instant hit with the public. It was played by every radio station and was sung at social, family, and religious gatherings across the country.

WAR CAKE

★ ★ ★

1 c. brown sugar

1 c. water

1 c. raisins

2 T. margarine

1 t. cinnamon

½ t. ground cloves

1½ c. flour

½ t. salt

½ t. baking powder

½ t. baking soda

½ c. chopped walnuts

Preheat the oven to 350° F. Grease and flour an 8" x 4" baking pan. Place the brown sugar, water, raisins, margarine, cinnamon, and cloves in a heavy-bottomed saucepan and bring to a boil. Turn down heat and cook gently for 5 minutes. Remove from heat and let cool until the mixture is lukewarm. Sift together the flour, salt, baking powder, and baking soda. Add flour mixture to the cooled sugar mixture, beating until the batter is smooth. Stir in the walnuts. Spread evenly in the baking pan and bake for 25 to 30 minutes or until a toothpick inserted in the center of the cake comes out clean. Let cool in the pan 10 minutes, then turn onto a rack to cool completely.

Because sugarcane could be converted into gunpowder, sugar was among the staples that were rationed. Creative cooks baked War Cake, which required less sugar than a standard cake recipe, and no eggs or milk.

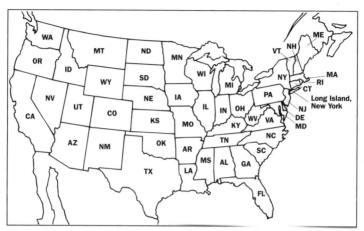

This modern map of the United States shows the location of Long Island, New York.

ABOUT THE AUTHOR

MARY POPE OSBORNE's father, like Madeline Beck's, was a career military officer. "Growing up in the fifties and sixties, my brothers and I often heard stories from our dad about his WWII experiences in New Guinea and stories from our mom about waiting for him on the home front," she says.

"I first heard about Nazi U-boats patrolling in American waters while we were living on an army base on the coast of Virginia. As my brothers and I played on the abandoned coastal artillery emplacements once used to defend the shore, we imagined what it would have been like to confront the enemy on the beach. Many years later, I read that Nazi saboteurs had actually come ashore on Long Island in 1942. That story captured my imagination and I seized upon it as the centerpiece of Maddie's story."

Mary Pope Osborne has written many books, in

almost every genre, for children and young adults. Her impressive backlist includes the Magic Tree House series, and, most recently, her novel *Adaline Falling Star* (Scholastic Press, 2000). For the Dear America Series, she is the author of *Standing in the Light: The Captive Diary of Catharine Carey Logan,* and for the My America series, *My Brother's Keeper: Virginia's Diary.* She lives in New York City with her husband, Will.

To the memory of my father,
Colonel William P. Pope,
who served in the Pacific during WWII

ACKNOWLEDGMENTS

I am deeply grateful to Robert Schnare, Jr., director of the Naval War College Library, for his tremendous research assistance; and to Tracy Mack, my editor, for her invaluable editing and inspiration.

Grateful acknowledgment is made for permission to reprint the following:

Cover portrait: Super Stock.
Cover background: FPG International.

Page 166: *The New York Times*, Culver Pictures.
Page 167: U.S.S. *Shaw*, Ewing Galloway.
Page 168 (top): U.S.S. *Lexington*, AP/Wide World Photos.
Page 168 (bottom): Franklin and Eleanor Roosevelt, Corbis/UPI.
Page 169: The Tin Can Club of America, AP/Wide World Photos.
Page 170 (top): Chicago children, AP/Wide World Photos.
Page 170 (bottom): Trucks carrying rubber, AP/Wide World Photos.
Page 171: Victory Garden, Stock Montage.
Page 172: War bonds, Stock Montage.
Page 173: Woman welder, Ewing Galloway.
Page 174: American Red Cross Ambulance, Ewing Galloway.
Page 175: Ground observers, U.S. Civil Defense.

OTHER BOOKS IN THE DEAR AMERICA SERIES

A Journey to the New World
The Diary of Remember Patience Whipple
by Kathyrn Lasky

The Winter of Red Snow
The Revolutionary War Diary of Abigail Jane Stewart
by Kristiana Gregory

When Will This Cruel War Be Over?
The Civil War Diary of Emma Simpson
by Barry Denenberg

A Picture of Freedom
The Diary of Clotee, a Slave Girl
by Patricia McKissack

Across the Wide and Lonesome Prairie
The Oregon Trail Diary of Hattie Campbell
by Kristiana Gregory

So Far from Home
The Diary of Mary Driscoll, an Irish Mill Girl
by Barry Denenberg

I Thought My Soul Would Rise and Fly
The Diary of Patsy, a Freed Girl
by Joyce Hansen

A Light in the Storm
The Civil War Diary of Amelia Martin
by Karen Hesse

A Coal Miner's Bride
The Diary of Anetka Kaminska
by Susan Campbell Bartoletti

Color Me Dark
The Diary of Nellie Lee Love
by Patricia McKissack

One Eye Laughing, the Other Weeping
The Diary of Julie Weiss
by Barry Denenberg

While the events described and some of the characters
in this book may be based on actual historical events
and real people, Madeline Beck is a fictional character,
created by the author, and her diary and its epilogue
are works of fiction.

All rights reserved. Published by Scholastic Inc.
557 Broadway, New York, New York 10012.
DEAR AMERICA®, SCHOLASTIC, and associated logos
are trademarks and/or registered trademarks of Scholastic Inc.

Library of Congress Cataloging-in-Publication Data available.

ISBN 0-590-68715-8;
ISBN 0-439-44574-4 (pbk.)

10 9 8 7 6 5 4 3 2 1   02 03 04 05 06

The display type was set in Bernhard Gothic.
The text type was set in Janson Text.
Book design by Elizabeth B. Parisi

Printed in the U.S.A. 23
First paperback printing, October 2002

Early Sunday Morning

★★★

The Pearl Harbor Diary of Amber Billows

BY BARRY DENENBERG

Scholastic Inc. New York

Washington, D.C.
1941

Monday, October 20, 1941
Washington, D.C.

When Daddy tapped his fork on his water glass last night and announced (in his usual, upbeat fashion) that he had "exciting news for the entire Billows family" (he always refers to us as "the Billows family," as if we were one of his favorite radio shows), everyone knew what was coming next. We might as well start packing.

We were moving — yet again — and the only question was where and when.

Equally certain was that the next sentence would be (which it was): "Who can guess where we're headed?" — which Dad says in a way that makes you think he had four, first-class train tickets to heaven tucked safe and sound in his back pocket. (Dad's kind of a positive thinker. Someone else's problems are his golden opportunities. Fortunately, Mom's not-so-sunny disposition provides the necessary balance. She's not nearly as upbeat as Dad. For her, disaster is lurking around every corner.)

I could see that this time even Mom didn't know where we were going.

Dad insists everyone be *really, really* serious about their guesses. If you blurt out the first thing that comes to your mind, just to get it over with, he'll get that disappointed look on his face that only prolongs the process, so everyone concentrates real hard.

Mom guessed (hopefully) back to Boston because, for one thing, that's where she was born, and for another, it's where Grandma and Grandpa live.

Dad didn't say anything, so I knew it wasn't Boston. If it was, he would have told her right away, before me and Andy, because it would have made her *so* happy. I had the feeling wherever we were going wasn't going to make her that happy.

Andy guessed St. Louis, but that's just because they have a National League team there — a team that would play his beloved Brooklyn Dodgers. (He's still recovering from the Dodgers winning their first pennant in twenty years and then losing the World Series to the Yankees because the catcher dropped the ball, or something like that.)

After Andy, Dad gave me his I-will-not-reveal-our-true-destination-until-everyone-has-guessed look, so the pressure was really on.

Like Mom, I, too, wished we were going back to Boston, but since Mom had already guessed that (Dad hates it when you guess the same city) and I knew it wasn't Boston I decided to pick a long shot: San Francisco. That really perked up the crowd, who got even more perked when Dad, obviously delighted with my effort, said, "Close, very close," and he paused, basking in the spot-light of our startled stares.

"Hawaii," he said. "We're going to Hawaii."

Now I think if you would have given each of us a million guesses, Hawaii would have been number one million and one on each of our lists.

First of all, the last time I looked, Hawaii wasn't even in the United States. I didn't know where it was and I could tell by the looks on their faces that neither did Mom or Andy.

Fortunately, Mom had the good sense to ask the question that was on everyone's mind: When?

"Next week," Dad said, as if it were the greatest news in the world.

That's when I had the fit.

It all came out.

I told Dad I didn't ever remember starting school in September like everyone else. I told him how horrible it was: being escorted to my homeroom by the principal; standing there and being introduced to an entire room of strange faces, knowing mine must have been turning as red as the stripes on the flag hanging over my head; pretending that everyone in the class wasn't really staring at me and that my glasses couldn't have been fogging up that badly; praying that at least one girl didn't think I was the biggest fool she ever saw in her life.

Now that the dam had burst, it was too late to hold back.

I told him how it takes me a year just to figure out the bus trip, where the classrooms are, which kids to avoid, and which teachers (if any) I could trust.

And how by the time I get ever-so-slightly settled in, it's time to move to the next city.

All I asked was that we move in the summer, like everyone else. There were families whose dads got transferred places but they did it over the summer, in an orderly fashion. Not next week.

Sometimes, I said, certain that this would be news to him, they even went to see the city first. They looked for a nice place to live. They saw what the schools were like. Sometimes just the moms went, and sometimes just the dads. And sometimes the entire family.

But they always, always did the actual, physical moving over the summer because it made everything so much easier for everyone. The packing, the moving, the going, the arriving, and most important (and here I had the feeling someone was actually screaming), SO THAT THE CHILDREN COULD START SCHOOL ON THE SAME DAY AS EVERYONE ELSE.

Then I ran to my room (which is in the basement), ran into my closet, slammed the door, sat on the floor, and chewed my bottom lip because I had sworn I was going to stop chewing my nails down to the quick every time we moved.

I was so angry, I forgot to cry.

When Mom knocked on the closet door and whispered that she wanted to talk, I knew I was a goner. (Whispering might be fine for other people, but coming from Mom it was a bad sign. It meant she was at her most, most serious.)

For some reason, which I can't quite figure out, I don't like to fight with Mom. It just isn't any fun. She never yells, never loses her temper, and never says anything she has to be sorry for later. It's really awful.

She's always very serious about it. Mom doesn't like it when anyone in the family disagrees with anyone else in the family, and when it happens she won't let up until the offending family member SEES THE ERROR OF THEIR WAYS. You don't even have to apologize, you just have to SEE THE ERROR OF YOUR WAYS. I *hate* seeing the error of my ways.

Fortunately, Mom gets to the point a whole lot quicker than Dad. She said that no one hated how much we had to move more than Dad. And that he hated it even more that we had to move at the drop of a hat (Mom and Dad are about equal on the corny expression meter).

But, she said, looking at me with the serious stare she has, that's one of the sacrifices your father has to make if he wants to be a good reporter. I'd had enough, but Mom wasn't finished. She explained that, besides his family, being a good newspaper reporter was the most important thing in Dad's life and that we were lucky to have a father who loved what he did and would I want him to do something he didn't like just so we didn't have to move, till I wanted to shout, "STOP, STOP, STOP," which I did, although I didn't shout it, I just said it.

We shook hands, which is one of the things Mom insists we do after a disagreement.

I was still mad, though, and decided to stay in my room, even though I knew that would make Dad sad.

I couldn't help it.

I decided I wasn't mad at Daddy anymore because I was so mad at Andy. I'm the only one who *ever* says anything about moving. The one thing Andy does complain about is that we never live in a city that has a National League team. Dad told him that cities like Philadelphia, Milwaukee, and Cincinnati don't have much going on, so his paper doesn't want him to live there. Andy said that Hawaii was a new low for us because they don't have any baseball teams at all. At least it was something. But as long as there's a ball, a bat, and a glove somewhere, Andy doesn't care where we live. (He doesn't have trouble making friends, like I do.)

He's afraid to say anything to Daddy. Daddy's his hero. Andy wants to be a reporter just like him. (Although he likes to say "journalist." He told me it sounds more distinguished. He hasn't figured out yet that "Andy" is about the most undistinguished first name you can have.)

Andy thinks being fifteen is a big achievement and because I'm three years younger than him I should worship the ground he walks on.

He's right about one thing, though. There is a silver lining to this dark cloud: At least we won't have to live in Washington anymore. *Everyone* hates Washington: Andy, because the Dodgers don't play here; me, because of the long, hot summers and the long, cold winters.

Even Dad hates it, although he won't admit it. Mom hates it more than any of us. She says that everyone in Washington spends every waking minute thinking up what to lie about next. (Dad says Mom "doesn't suffer fools gladly." I'm not sure what that means, but if it means she doesn't stand for anyone's nonsense, he's right.)

When Daddy announces that we're moving, I begin a brand-new diary. (It makes me feel better.) So far I have three. There's my Washington diary, my Boston diary, and my back-to-Washington diary. By the time I'm done I suppose I'll have about a million.

We've lived in Washington, Boston, Baltimore, and New York City. New York is where I was born, but I don't remember much about that because we moved when I was two.

Andy says New York was the best because he liked living in an apartment more than a house. There were lots of kids in the building, and Mom didn't have to do all the things with the house that drive her nuts.

My favorite place was Boston. We lived right near the Boston Public Garden, which is the best place on earth. I wish we had never had to leave.

Andy says Dad took him to a Dodgers game when we lived in New York, but he doesn't remember it too well.

The only time I was ever in New York, besides when I was born, was two years ago, when we all went to the World's Fair.

I had such a good time. I can still picture the parachute jump. The parachutes were red and white, with yellow, red, and green Life Savers on the top. They were like collapsed umbrellas on the way up and opened ones on the way down.

Mom and I went up in one chute, and Daddy and Andy in another. We were hundreds of feet up in the air — so high, you could see the whole fair and all the teeny-tiny people scurrying around down below.

It felt like it took forever to get up to the top. (Dad told us later it only takes forty-two seconds, and that when you go down it's like falling off a twenty-story building.) The ten seconds it took to come down made me lose my breath. (Mom said it almost made her lose her lunch.)

We went on all sorts of other rides, took a bus around the whole fair, and saw the General Motors Futurama exhibit, where they showed what the future would be like in the year 1960 (so far away, who could even imagine it?). They had a car with a transparent plastic body so you could see how it worked, and this strange new thing called "television," which was like radio with a picture.

At the end we got a button that said: I HAVE SEEN THE FUTURE.

The only problem was that you had to stand in line for pretty much everything, and it was really, really hot. My feet were aching, so I took off my shoes and dangled my feet in this big pool with a nice fountain, and Dad said not to do that but then he and Mom looked at each other, started to laugh, took off their shoes, and dangled them in, too.

Wednesday, October 22, 1941
Washington, D.C.

As soon as I told Allison we were moving, she got mad, which was not at all the response I was expecting. I told her it wasn't my fault we were moving, and she said it was. She said I told her when we first became best friends (in the middle of last year) that I didn't think we would be moving for a while because (thanks to the war) there was all sorts of good stuff for my dad to report on right here in Washington. I only said that because that's what Mom told me.

I tried to explain that the war might be spreading. That it might not just be in Europe anymore but all over because of Japan. (Although I'm not 100 percent sure what Japan has to do with all of it.)

I was hoping this would make her less angry, but I could see that it wasn't, because the tears were just streaming down her face and she walked away even before I could finish, which wasn't very nice.

Thursday, October 23, 1941
Washington, D.C.

I spent all yesterday afternoon in the library reading about Hawaii.

It's a territory of the United States, I discovered. I didn't know the United States had territories. I didn't know we had anything besides the forty-eight states.

And it's not one thing, it's lots and lots of things — islands, almost a hundred of them.

It's even farther away than I'd thought: 2,390 miles from the coast of California.

It sounds like it's in the middle of nowhere.

They used to be called the Sandwich Islands, in honor of the same guy they named the sandwich after. He must have been a big deal to have a whole place named after him and a meal.

The name Hawaii means "paradise," and from the pictures, the islands do look pretty.

They have exotic fish and exotic-sounding

tropical plants whose names I can't even pronounce: bougainvillea, hibiscus, jacaranda, al-
garoba.

It's hot and dry in summer (what a relief that
will be) and about 70 degrees morning, noon, and
night, 365 days of the year, so they don't wear a
lot of clothes because it's spring all year-round.

We're going to live near Honolulu, which is on
one of the larger islands. There's a really nice
beach there called Waikiki, and the beach boys
surf the waves. It's near Pearl Harbor, which is
where the U.S. Navy parks its boats, at least according to Mr. Military (my brother).

He assures me, as if I really cared, that there
are battleships, destroyers, and aircraft carriers
there. He's excited because Dad said he knew an
admiral or two who can take us for a ride.

Hawaii doesn't sound like it's very American,
though. Once it was ruled by a queen whose name
was Lili something. And I read that if you were found
standing in a position that was higher than the

king's, you would be put to death. When the king was inspecting a ship and decided to go below, everyone had to dive overboard so that they would be below him and therefore avoid execution.

That's not the only bad news.

There are volcanoes that are active (which means, I think, that they work) and earthquakes. There are so many volcanoes that they have to have their own personal goddess, Pele.

I thought volcanoes and earthquakes were extinct, like dinosaurs. Or, if they weren't extinct, at least they were far, far away, so you didn't have to worry about them. Of course, Hawaii is far, far away.

From the pictures and what I read I don't think the people there look like me. They look very, very tan and have long, black hair. They're Polynesian (whatever that is), Japanese, Chinese, and from places I've never even heard of: Korea, Vietnam, and Cambodia.

They don't even speak English there. They do,

but they speak other things, too (like Hawaiian). It'll be just great if I have to learn another language and, instead of taking math in English, which is plenty hard enough, I'll have to take it in Hawaiian.

Andy's right. It's like we're moving to another planet.

Friday, October 24, 1941
Washington, D.C.

I talked to Mom about Hawaii while she was preparing The Last Dinner Party.

She says we will be able to cook some really exotic food, like stone-cooked pig.

Mom loves to cook more than almost anything in the world, and she's really, really good at it. She read about the stone-cooked pig in one of the books I brought home from the library. Unfortunately, it explained precisely what you do.

You kill the pig the night before, dip it in some really, really hot water, take out the insides, rub the outside with salt, and hang it up overnight. (Mom read all this to me like it was "sauté until golden brown and turn over.")

Then in the morning you dig this really gigantic pit, make this really gigantic fire, put rocks on top of the wood, and then hot rocks inside the poor pig. Then you cover everything with dirt and ashes from the fire, cook for two hours, and serve with sweet potatoes and yams.

Yummy.

Mom's really looking forward to going to Hawaii. She thinks it will be nice and quiet and that it will be nice for all of us to take it easy for a while. I think she means that it's going to be good for Dad to get away from all the hubbub in Washington.

And, course, there's the new baby.

The baby's due in May. Mom says she doesn't

care if it's a boy or a girl, but I think she wants a girl. It better be a girl.

Saturday, October 25, 1941
Washington, D.C.

I can't believe Mom and Dad are having a dinner party tomorrow night when we're leaving in just four days. Luckily, for the first time, we don't have to pack everything ourselves. Dad's paper is having a moving company come in and do it for us. Mom says that's because Dad's a pretty big deal now, which is only right, given how hard he works and how much he cares.

I hope he has a nicer office than the one he has here, which is so small that he has to pile everything all over the place.

Of course Dad insists on packing his books himself. Dad takes great pride in his library, and I think a lot of the books are old and fragile and he's afraid to let the moving men do it.

I don't know why they are called dinner "parties" rather than just plain "dinner." There really isn't a party, just lots of smoking, drinking, eating, and talking. Talking is the whole reason we have so many dinner parties. (Besides the fact that Mom loves to show off her cooking skills. No matter what city we're living in, everyone's always pleased to get an invitation to one of Mom's dinner parties. I think she has some kind of reputation or something.)

That's how Dad gets a lot of his information. "Background," he calls it. He's real serious about things like politics and world affairs, especially lately.

Dad's a real master at getting his guests to do all the talking. To me it's kind of obvious, but maybe that's just because I know how he operates.

First there're the cocktails.

Dad mixes the drinks and makes sure the martinis are very dry and the bourbon is very old-fashioned. I don't understand the very "dry" part, but I think the "old-fashioned" part means that there are lots of cherries and pieces of orange in it.

Mom shows the ladies around the house and conducts what she calls "girl talk": cooking, clothes, the neighborhood, school, and stuff like that, none of which (other than cooking) actually interests Mom. That way, Dad can concentrate on the guys and the small-talk segment.

During the small-talk segment, Dad will do plenty of talking as long as it's about nothing much like sports, cars, sports cars, and the weather.

He talks so much, you begin to think he's a pretty forthright guy, willing to talk about anything under the sun. It kind of gets you in the mood, helped by what Dad calls "the universal lubricant," alcohol. Of course no one ever notices that all Dad ever drinks is seltzer. He doesn't like alcohol; he says it clouds the mind. Dad likes to keep his mind very uncloudy.

When we were younger, Mom would give me and Andy dinner first. Then, when the guests arrived and they saw how tall we were (although Andy's pretty much a shrimp), we would go up to our rooms for the rest of the evening. Now that we're older they let us eat with them, which can be pretty boring. But I think it would hurt Dad's feelings if I said I would like to eat first and spend the night reading in my room.

By the time everyone's sat down to dinner, having had a drink or two, Dad delivers a line like: "I don't know, the whole thing just confuses the hell out of me, Senator (or General), and I'd really like to hear your views on the matter," and that's pretty much all they need. They're off and running, blabbing away, pausing only briefly to praise Mom's Coq au Vin or Veal Cordon Bleu, and then it's back to Roosevelt, Hitler, Churchill, and Mussolini.

After dessert, coffee, cigars, and brandy, Mom and Dad, like two little tugboats, ferry their bloated guests toward the front door, where Dad invariably has to say, "Here's your coat and hat, what's your hurry."

We're having an isolationist to dinner tomorrow night. The reason I know is Mom's making meat loaf, mashed potatoes, and apple pie. Mom says that isolationists are so American that that's all they eat for every single meal, which I find hard to believe. (Sometimes you don't know whether or not to believe some of the things Mom says. Dad says she has a very dry sense of humor, like a martini, I guess.) Even if you're an isolationist you must get bored eating meat loaf, mashed potatoes, and apple pie for every single meal.

Mom says isolationists live in a dream world and they may be kidding themselves but they're not kidding her. She especially hates Charles Lindbergh, even though the rest of the world loves him. Mom says he's the King of the Isolationists and just because he knows how to fly an airplane, everyone listens to what he has to say. Mom says if he didn't have that deceptively boyish grin, no one would care so much about what he had to say.

She doesn't call him the Lone Eagle; she calls him the Lone Ostrich, because that's what Walter Winchell, her favorite radio commentator, calls him. (Mom hardly ever misses his program. I love the way it begins: "Good evening, Mr. and Mrs. North America and all the ships at sea.") Lindbergh is trying to convince everyone that the war in Europe is not something we should get involved in, that it need only concern England, France, Germany, and Russia. It's their war, not ours, Lindbergh says. We don't have to worry, because we have the gigantic Atlantic Ocean protecting us like a moat that surrounds a castle. That's why Mom calls him the King of the Isolationists, because he acts like he's the king and the United States is his castle. Mom thinks he wants to be president someday.

She thinks that what Lindbergh is saying is utter nonsense.

I'm not sure what Dad thinks, although he knows enough not to say anything good about Lindbergh in front of Mom. He seems more concerned lately and talks about "the dire state of the world"; "darkening clouds on the horizon"; and "leaving us no choice" more and more frequently.

We'll see if Mom pulls her "scalding soup attack" trick tomorrow night. If Mom doesn't like someone, she makes sure their bowl of soup is about a billion degrees Fahrenheit. Then, when they take the first spoonful, she waits to see them wince in pain and says (in her most sincere manner), "I hope the soup's hot enough for everyone," carefully avoiding looking at her victim.

Sunday, October 26, 1941
Washington, D.C.

Mom and Dad got into an argument after dinner, which is a rare occurrence. They don't usually argue — I'm not saying they *never* argue, but it's rare and when they do, it's BEHIND CLOSED DOORS. They don't even raise their voices, so it's impossible to hear what they're saying even if you put a glass to the wall. (Frankly, I think that's a big waste of time. All it does is make your ears red.)

The argument began while Dad and I were helping clear the dessert dishes, coffee cups, and ashtrays from the dining room table. (Andy, who is unbelievably lazy and gets away with it because he's a boy, was already up in his room.)

Dad always helps Mom with the dishes, even drying them and putting them away. (He doesn't like to wash, because that makes his fingers wrinkle and he has trouble typing his articles. When he says this, Mom calls him Mr. Hunt and Peck.)

I'm a great eavesdropper. I do it at school with the teachers all the time. It's all in where and how you stand. You can't be face-to-face or even back-to-back (too obvious). You just have to stand sort of sideways *and* off to the side. Just far enough away so they don't notice you're near them but close enough to hear what's being said. You don't need to be so close you can hear every single word. Don't be greedy — that's the key.

The funny thing about the argument was that there's a swinging door connecting the dining room and the kitchen, so Dad would be taking some plates into the kitchen and I would hear him up to when he went through the door and then as he came back out I would hear him and Mom until the door swung closed and then I could just hear him and not Mom, so I couldn't really make out everything but I caught most of it.

One of the guests at dinner was Senator Mucky Muck. (That's not his real name — I can never remember his real name — that's just what Dad says. Dad says he's a "real big mucky muck." I call his wife Mrs. Mouse because she's so teeny tiny and never says a word. Boy, does she wear a lot of perfume. The only time she ever utters a sound is when she wants her martini "freshened," as she puts it. Mom said that she recently recovered from a complete nervous breakdown. I'd like to have seen her before she recovered.)

Mom was mad because Dad didn't say anything in response to Senator Mucky Muck's views. Senator Mucky Muck is an isolationist. (I noticed that he gobbled up all his meat loaf and mashed potatoes and asked for seconds on both. Maybe Mom is right.)

Dad gets even more patient than usual when Mom gets like this, which is a good idea, I can tell you from experience.

He explained to her that the entire purpose of the dinner party was to find out what important people in government were thinking, so he could

SERVE HIS READERSHIP PROPERLY. (This is a very serious phrase for Dad and one of the few things you can't joke about.)

Mom, who, of course, knows all this, said she was willing to listen to most anything but this "isolationist garbage." She said that she didn't have any readership to serve (I thought Mom was getting awful close to crossing the line here) and she wasn't sitting still for it anymore. The next time, she was going to speak her mind.

She told Dad he was "duly warned." Dad looked "duly warned."

Monday, October 27, 1941
Washington, D.C.

I wasn't going to talk to Allison even if she talked to me, but she didn't. I had to be with her every day in every class for all of last week, pretending every single minute that she didn't exist.

Mom was right. I should have more than

one friend. Mom thinks it would be better if I had two or three friends or even a group of friends, but I don't like that. I like to have just one best friend I can depend on. As soon as I move to a city I find someone to have as a best friend and that's it.

It's too complicated having more than one friend. But Mom says that sometimes having more friends can be less complicated.

I wish I had listened to her, because now I dread going to school because I don't have anyone else besides Sylvia Prescott to be friends with. Sylvia's nice and pretty much worships me, which is kind of the problem because she's a little boring.

I don't see why I have to go to school, anyway. We're leaving soon for Hawaii, so what does it matter? I'll just be missing a couple of days more.

Mom just laughed when I said that. She's even more serious than Dad about school.

There seems to be an endless list of things to

do, and everyone's running around, bumping into one another like balls on a pool table.

I have to figure out what I'm going to be taking, because Mom says we're going to stay in a hotel until our stuff comes. I have absolutely no idea what all the kids in Hawaii will be wearing. I am definitely taking my shaggy sweaters, even though I know it's really warm there. I took my pleated skirts, including my two houndstooth ones, the black and white and the brownish one, and all my kneesocks. I wonder if they wear kneesocks in Hawaii.

I've been so busy, I haven't had time to properly concentrate on how terrified I am of going on my first airplane flight.

Andy said it's nothing and then started telling me everything I never wanted to know about air travel. Of course I don't know how he would really know since he's never been in a plane, either.

I don't know why my first flight has to be a thousand hours long.

Mom said I should make sure I bring enough books to read on the airplane. I don't know how much is enough, but I'm bringing two Nancy Drews — *The Secret of the Old Clock* and *The Bungalow Mystery* — *The Little House in the Big Woods* and *The Yearling*. That should last me for a while.

After dinner I was in my room looking at this picture book of Hawaii that I took out of the library. There was a knock on the door. Our family has a strict door-knocking policy. Dad's a big believer in privacy — his and everyone else's (which is odd for someone whose job is basically to snoop on other people, but I've never said that to him).

If you're in your room with the door closed, no one can enter under any circumstances (unless it's a real emergency) until the person inside says it's okay. We do a lot of knocking, and you come to recognize everyone's knock.

Andy's is boomboomboom, three knocks right in a row with no space at all in between, like he's going to crash down the door if you don't answer right away. Dad's knock is also three, but it's more a tap, tap, tap. Very polite and patient, like Dad. Mom and I are both two knocks. Mine's knock, k-n-o-c-k, one short and one long, and Mom's knock, knock, simple and to the point.

So when I heard knock, knock I was sure it was Mom and said, come in.

I was shocked when I looked up from my book and Allison was standing at the foot of my bed.

She looked so stricken that I forgot to act like I was mad, which I kind of was but I kind of wasn't. I thought maybe something had happened to her father, who has been in and out of the hospital, although Allison doesn't know why. No one in her family will tell her. Allison's family doesn't like to talk about *anything*. They give me the creeps, although I never say anything to Allison, because I think they give her the creeps, too, and if I said anything it would just make her feel even worse.

That's why she loves to spend so much time with my family and which is why Mom let her come right up to my room. At least I think that's why.

Before I could even ask her what was the matter, she said she would like to start the conversation about my moving to Hawaii over again, from the beginning, which I thought was a good idea. But when I said that we were moving to Hawaii, she just started crying again and said she would miss me so much, she could hardly bear to think about it and that she would never find a better best friend, ever.

I really hate it when people cry and I really hate it when they say something nice to you. I don't think it's one of my better characteristics. (As a matter of fact it might be my worst.) It makes me feel really, really embarrassed, and when it happens I act really strangely.

So I started to laugh.

I was just trying to cheer Allison up. I told her I would write once a week no matter what and that I was the most reliable pen pal, which isn't at all true, as Allison knows (when she went to Maine for the summer, I didn't answer a single one of her letters), but which was such an outrageous lie that it actually made her start laughing and I knew that was my chance and I asked her if she wanted to go downstairs and have ice cream with my mom and dad. Having ice cream with my mom and dad is one of Allison's favorite things to do. Mom and Dad are always counting calories (Dad's a little on the plump side of things, and Mom's been extra careful ever since the baby), but after-dinner-before-bed-ice-cream is a family ritual.

Fortunately we were distracted over ice cream because Andy's still upset that Daddy has to sell the Chevrolet. The one with the nifty gadget that squirts clean water onto the windshield when you press a button. Dad told Andy he could help him pick out the new car when we get to Hawaii, but I don't know if that helped.

Andy wants to learn to speak Hawaiian (not that he's doing that well with English), and so he's practicing. *Aloha* means "welcome," "love," or "farewell"; *mahalo* means "thanks." We will be *mahinis,* which is "newcomers," and I'm a *wahine,* which is "girl."

So I guess it's so long, Washington, D.C., and *aloha,* Oahu, Hawaii.

Oahu, Hawaii

Friday, November 7, 1941
Oahu, Hawaii

The flight from Washington to San Francisco took forever, and the flight from San Francisco to Hawaii took forever and a day (over eighteen hours). I must say it was pretty exciting and not as scary as I thought it would be.

At San Francisco we boarded the *China Clipper,* which is a flying boat — it's like a really, really big motorboat with a giant wing on top of it. We took off from a floating pier and landed on the water. The four huge propellers are way high up so they don't get dunked in the water. When we landed we putt-putted up to the pier.

We left at 3:00 P.M. and arrived in Honolulu 9:00 A.M. the next day. I slept a lot of the time (the San Francisco to Hawaii part is half overnight).

I'm a pretty good sleeper, especially when we travel anywhere. When we're in the car I lay my head on Andy's lap and I'm sound asleep in five minutes.

I read almost all of the books I brought and did crossword puzzles. We played Information Please, Monopoly (for three hours — Mom won), and then tried to see if all of us together could name the capitals of all forty-eight states. We couldn't. No one knew the capital of Michigan (Lansing) or Kentucky (Frankfort).

Dinner was quite elegant (Mom was *really* impressed). It was served in the dining lounge and the tables were beautifully set with white linen tablecloths, sparkling silverware, and very pretty china plates.

Now I know where the sun was all the time we lived in Washington, right here in Hawaii. Andy's right, this is another planet. A planet where they only have nice weather. It was 78 degrees the day we arrived (and it's been that way every day since) — 78 degrees in November! The air even *smells* different: clean and sweet. Mom says that's because of the ocean.

She thinks the climate will be good for Andy's asthma. Sometimes his attacks are so bad, he has to get under a kind of tent and inhale mentholated steam so he can breathe.

We went to the beach at Waikiki. There are *actually* beach boys there who surf the waves. They have really good tans and lots of muscles. There were supposed to be boys who dive off the piers and swim out for the coins the tourists throw in the water, but I didn't see them.

Dad says that if you give the surfers some money, they will take you for a ride. I don't think I'm quite ready for that yet, thanks to my brother.

Andy said there used to be twice as many surfers (as if he would know — Andy has to pretend he knows *everything*), but the rest were eaten by sharks. Sharks eat so many surfers because turtles are their favorite food and when they look up and see someone paddling on a surfboard, they think it's a turtle and accidentally eat them.

Unfortunately he succeeded in getting me completely nuts about the sharks (not that it took that much), and I've crossed surfing off my Top Ten list of things to do while in Hawaii.

I wish we could have stayed at the hotel longer. The Royal Hawaiian Hotel is the prettiest hotel I've ever seen. It's coral pink, and there are panoramic views of the towering mountains poking their peaks up through the clouds. The whole island seems to be bright green except for the turquoise sea and the blue sky.

We had breakfast brought up to the room, and one day I had waffles and the next sliced papaya, Portuguese sausage, and eggs (none of which, except for the eggs, I had ever had before).

I really, really like my new bedroom. It's sunny and airy and much bigger than any bedroom I ever had before. Of course, the whole house is about twice as big as any house we ever lived in.

There are three bedrooms and three bathrooms, so that we can each have our own. (In Washington and Boston I had to share a bathroom with Andy, which is one of the worst experiences imaginable.)

Mom's spent the past forty-eight hours organizing the kitchen. (She's trying to get ready for Thanksgiving.) We both think the kitchen is the prettiest room in the house because it has this big bay window that lets in the morning sunlight.

Dad said I can paint my room lavender (which is my favorite color). As much as I liked living in the hotel, it's nice to be sleeping in my own bed again.

Sunday, November 9, 1941
Oahu, Hawaii

Now I know the real reason Dad was transferred to Hawaii. It was so he could play more golf. Of course, according to him it's *strictly* business. He claims it's even better than dinner parties for getting the "inside story."

Dad likes to do a lot of what he calls "socializing" and Mom calls "schmoozing." (I think there's a big difference.) Besides her dinner parties (which, frankly, she does mostly for Dad's sake), Mom's pretty much a loner. The only social activity Mom really likes is playing hearts. Mom likes to play hearts (even more than she likes to listen to Benny Goodman).

She tried to teach me to play, but I'm not real good at card games (or any kind of games, now that I think of it). You need at least three to play, and, fortunately, Dad and Andy know how, so that takes some of the pressure off me. Mom doesn't like to play with me, anyway. She says I just get rid of all my bad cards at the very first opportunity without any sense of what's happening in the game (which she's pretty much right about). I thought getting rid of the bad cards (hearts and the queen of spades) as soon as you could was the whole point. Basically I hate card games.

Dad's playing at the Oahu Country Club with one of the navy men who is related to Senator Mucky Muck. He got up real early because they have to "tee off" by 7:00 A.M.

Dad doesn't dress like golfers are supposed to dress. I watched out the window when Senator Mucky Muck's nephew (I think) came to pick Dad up.

He looked like he had spent hours in front of the mirror trying to decide how to assemble clothes that had the most amount of checks and plaids (he succeeded). But Dad just had on his old Harvard sweat suit (that's where he went to school) and a towel around his neck.

He already has a golf date for the next three Sunday mornings. We'll never get to see him anymore on Sundays.

Tomorrow, school.

This time, I'm going to take Mom's advice. I'm not going to have one best friend, even if someone begs me. I'm going to have two or three friends, maybe even more.

Mom's going to drive me in the new car. It's a brand-new four-door Hudson, and it has a foot-controlled radio-station selector that is really, really fun (although I have to scrunch down a little in the driver's seat so I can reach it).

Monday, November 10, 1941
Oahu, Hawaii

School wasn't as bad as I thought it would be. Of course I did have to go through the being-escorted-by-the-principal-and-being-introduced-to-the-entire-class routine.

Most of the kids look like me, but there are also Hawaiian, Japanese, Chinese, and lots of kids who look like they're all of these combined.

Everyone's pretty friendly. One girl stopped me in the hall and said that if I needed help going over any of the stuff I missed to just let her know. She's in most of my classes and has really, really white teeth and the nicest smile I've ever seen. Her name is Kame Arata.

I was surprised she spoke English so well. I never knew anyone Japanese (at least I think she's Japanese), and it's funny seeing someone like her who sounds pretty much just like me.

Wednesday, November 12, 1941
Oahu, Hawaii

It was Andy's birthday yesterday (he's sixteen, so he'll be even more obnoxious). Mom and Dad gave him binoculars, and Grandpa and Grandma sent him a silver dollar, which they always give us on our birthday.

Dad said he would take Andy up to Aiea

Heights with his binoculars so he could see all the way down to Pearl Harbor, which is where the boats are.

Andy wants to join the Boy Scouts. Mom asked if I wanted to become a Girl Scout, but I don't. Rules and regulations aren't my favorite things in the world. Most rules don't really make any sense — like looking both ways but what if it's a one-way street? Plus, I don't think I look so nice in a uniform.

Thursday, November 13, 1941
Oahu, Hawaii

Mom and Dad went out to a big-deal dinner on the Waikiki Terrace, which is up on the roof of the Royal Hawaiian Hotel. The reason I know it was a big deal is because Dad wore his white tuxedo jacket and Mom wore a gown.

Mom said the Royal Hawaiian Orchestra was going to play (from the way she said it, I think they're famous), and there was going to be lots of champagne, which Mom really likes.

Friday, November 14, 1941
Oahu, Hawaii

Dad's writing his first article since we got here. One of the Ten Commandments of the Billows family is THOU SHALT NOT INTERRUPT DAD WHEN HE'S WRITING AN ARTICLE. This is in effect no matter how urgent you think it is that you've lost your tooth. (I used to interrupt him quite a bit when I was younger).

I hardly ever interrupt him now, though. It's not that he yells or anything like that. Frankly, that would be better. He just looks up slowly from his precious Smith-Corona (another commandment: DON'T TOUCH THE SMITH-CORONA — "it's not a toy") and asks what you came to see him about. He's not really too glad to see you, but he thinks that being polite and getting to the point of your unannounced and unwanted visit is simply the fastest way to get rid of you.

I'd rather he just yelled, "GET OUT." Dad's the type who can kill you with kindness.

His articles always look nice and clean when he starts out. But by day two, he's scribbled all over the margins; by day three, he's crossed out some things, circled others, and drawn arrows showing where he now thinks some things should go. When it's impossible for anyone but him to decipher what he's written, it's ready to be read to Mom (he always changes anything that Mom says doesn't sound right). Then it's ready for its final retyping (Dad's a ferocious two-finger typist), which means he will be awash in a sea of crumpled-up white typing paper for the next twenty-four hours (at least) and won't eat or drink anything except coffee.

Monday, November 17, 1941
Oahu, Hawaii

This is the first time in my entire life that I have needed *anyone's* help with my schoolwork. Each time we move, though, it gets harder because I miss so much, and now that I'm in the sixth grade the work is *really* getting hard. (Last year was the first year I didn't get straight A's because of that stupid A– in science — thanks to Mr. Gould, better known as Mr. Ghoul.)

Science is where I'm having trouble. History, math, English, and social studies are fine. But what they're doing in science is *so* different that I really need some help.

Kame said that after school Wednesday we could walk home to her house together and then my mom could pick me up after dinner.

Mom said that means she's inviting me to stay for dinner and it would be rude to say no.

One of the class mothers called Mom and asked if she would like to join the PTA. Mom said we were still getting settled and just as soon as we were "unpacked" she would "check back." Mom says the same thing in every city we move to.

Tuesday, November 18, 1941
Oahu, Hawaii

Mom picked us up after school, as usual, but the surprise was that Dad and I were going to the Hawaiian Book Exchange (Mom was taking Andy to his first Boy Scout meeting).

Dad's finished with his article and he was celebrating. Dad celebrates almost everything by buying some more books. He's not comfortable when we move to a new city until he's found a "decent" secondhand bookstore. That's where he met Mom. Dad was working part-time in a secondhand bookstore while he was going to college. Mom came in wearing her nurse's uniform — that's what Mom was before Andy was born — and was standing on her tiptoes — she's pretty petite — trying to get a cookbook off a really, really high shelf. That's when Dad swooped in for the kill. He snatched the book down off the shelf, blew off some imaginary dust, and said, "Al Billows, at your service." (That's why I was named Amber, and Andy, Andy. Mom's first name is Anne, and since Dad's Al, everyone's initials had to be A. B.) Then he handed her the book with a flourish, and as they say, the rest is history.

Mr. Poole's Hawaiian Book Exchange is pretty dusty and dark, which is precisely what Dad means by "decent." It has to have at least a million books, and the more disorderly the better. It must have at least a million books just up in the balcony. I didn't go up there, though, because it looked to me like the whole thing was about to collapse.

Dad really hit it off with the man who owns the store. He had wild, gray hair that went all over the place and looked like it had *never, ever* been combed; wore glasses that hung by a string around his neck but which he never put on his face; and smoked a cigar that he never lit. But he sounded the opposite of the way he looked. He seemed so intelligent and had a soothing, soft voice that was as gentle as a whisper.

Just listening to him talk made you feel everything was going to be all right.

Usually Dad likes to have everyone else do all the talking, but this time Dad was. The bookstore man wanted to know what people "back on the mainland" thought about the war, especially the people back in Washington.

Mr. Poole asked me if I liked to read, and when I said very much, he seemed delighted. He said in that case he had a delightful surprise for me, and disappeared down one of the long, dimly lit aisles that separated the endless rows of floor-to-ceiling bookcases. When he returned, he handed me a copy of *The Secret Garden* and said he hoped I enjoyed it half as much as he did.

When Dad paid for his books, Mr. Poole wouldn't let him pay for mine, pointing to the sign over his head: CHILDREN READ FOR FREE.

Dad liked Mr. Poole so much, he asked me if it was all right if he joined us for dinner. It was fine with me — I didn't even know we were going to have dinner out.

When we left, the man just turned the OPEN/CLOSED sign the other way, and off we went. He suggested we take a streetcar to his favorite restaurant, which was a lot of fun. I had two orders of the best spareribs.

We were all having such a good time (when Dad genuinely likes someone, which is actually quite rare, he *really* likes them), Mr. Poole came with us to the movies.

Dad *loves* the movies, and so do I. (Mom would rather read, and Andy would rather play baseball.) And Dad *loves* Charlie Chaplin, so we went to see *The Great Dictator* at the Princess Theater.

Dad and I prefer to go to the movies in the afternoon, and so, it turns out, does Mr. Poole. Mr. Poole said that going to the movies in the afternoon is the best because there aren't enough people there to ruin it for you by talking. And, besides, he said, it's more fun going in the afternoon because "it's so wicked" — he winked at me when he said that.

Charlie Chaplin was really, really funny, especially when he was imitating Hitler. I don't understand, however, how everyone can laugh at someone who's supposed to be so awful.

Wednesday, November 19, 1941
Oahu, Hawaii

Kame's house is very pretty. There were two peacocks roaming around the gardens.

There are photographs and things all over the walls. In the living room there was a picture of someone who looked like he must be the king of

Japan, and two swords, one long and one short. Kame said that they were samurai swords, and that her ancestors had been samurai warriors back in Japan.

When we sat down to dinner I was surprised that there were no forks, only chopsticks. I didn't have the vaguest idea what to do with them. Everyone, including her two younger brothers, was looking at me like they were expecting me to do something miraculous, like actually eat with them.

Kame realized what my dilemma was and brought a fork and spoon from the drawer. Now that I had utensils I could use, it seemed to be a kind of signal that everyone could begin passing the food around.

There were steaming bowls of noodles, platters of rice cakes, little bowls of dried squid, tempura, and tofu, which I had never even heard of. The tofu was nicer than I thought, smooth and velvety, like custard but not nearly as tasty.

Kame explained that tofu was made from ground soya beans, hoping, I think, that that would mean something to me.

Mr. Arata asked me how I liked living in Hawaii, and I said that, although I had only been here a short time, it seemed quite nice. (I hate it when people say something is "quite nice.") He said that Hawaii was *tenjiku*, which means it is a "heavenly place." Mr. Arata owns a tea importing company.

After dinner he played the samisen, which is a three-stringed Japanese guitar, and everyone (except me, of course) sang Japanese songs. Even though I couldn't join in, I liked being there, because her family is very sweet.

When we were in Kame's room waiting for Mom to pick me up, she said that her mother didn't speak at dinner because, in a traditional Japanese family, the woman must always defer to the man.

She said the Japanese have a saying: "There is

no prosperity in a family where the hen crows." Which means that women are silent, and men rule the roost.

She sounded like she thought she owed me an explanation.

She asked me if my family was traditional or modern. I had never thought about that. The only thing I knew was that Dad sure didn't rule our roost, but I didn't know if that made us traditional or modern. The only thing I knew about our family is that we were real different from most families.

She said her family favored her brothers because Japanese parents only want boys for children.

She sounded very sad.

She told me her name means "turtle" in Japanese, and I couldn't help but laugh. It took me quite a while to stop while Kame was saying, "What? What? What's so funny?" I finally calmed down enough to tell her about Andy and the sharks and the surfers, and she started laughing again and said now she was never going in the ocean again, thanks to me.

Sunday, November 23, 1941
Oahu, Hawaii

Dad's already off to golf, so I stayed in bed later than usual and reread Allison's letter, which arrived yesterday.

She said that she already misses me just as much as she thought she would. She's sure by now I've already found a new best friend. She said she saw Sylvia Prescott once or twice, which was fine, but every time she would wear something Sylvia liked, Sylvia would go out the very next day and buy it (her father is rich) and then wear it to school.

She wants to know everything about Hawaii, especially what all the kids in school are like.

She said she misses me and misses being with my family, especially having ice cream after dinner. Allison loved to talk to Mom. She would tell Mom things she wouldn't even tell me (that's how I knew about her father being in the hospital). Mom's a great listener — something that most people (including me) aren't too good at. Mom said that's because people just like to hear the sound of their own voice.

Mom said that if I don't write Allison back this week, she's going to strangle me. She said she had no intention of raising an inconsiderate daughter, which I thought was unnecessary.

Monday, November 24, 1941
Oahu, Hawaii

Andy is having a heart attack because he discovered that one of his new friends (he already has about a thousand) has an even better baseball-card collection than he does. Andy basically judges people on the size and quality of their baseball-card collections (which partially explains why Andy doesn't know any girls — but only partially).

According to Andy, this one boy has a 1937 Joe DiMaggio, and the big news is that he's willing to trade it, but Andy says he wants too much in return. Andy's a pretty shrewd bargainer, especially when it comes to his baseball cards.

Mom and I went shopping for all the stuff we need for Thanksgiving dinner. It's going to be really strange having Thanksgiving dinner without, one, Grandma and Grandpa; and, two, snow. It's not even cold!

On the way there, Mom said she was hoping we could find a nice, fat pig so she could make stone-cooked pig for everyone. (Dad's invited Mr. Poole and Lieutenant Something, his golfing friend.)

Tuesday, November 25, 1941
Oahu, Hawaii

Kame's trying to convince me to join the Shakespeare Club. Now I'm sorry I told her how much I like acting and about all the stuff Allison and I did last year. They're going to do *Much Ado About Nothing,* which is one of my favorites, so it's tempting.

I still feel too new here and not comfortable enough to be in a play yet. To be in a play you have to really, really feel comfortable with the other people, and I don't even know anyone besides Kame.

She said they will be holding auditions over the next two weeks, so I don't have to decide right now, which let me off the hook. I can tell, though, that Kame is going to be disappointed if I don't do it.

At least she's happy I promised I would go to the big dance with her on Sunday, December 7. It's in the big hall at school, and Mom said she would drive us, pick us up, and take Kame home.

Sunday night we went skating at the Waikiki Skating Arena, which was a lot of fun. We skated with some boys Kame knows. Kame is really, really pretty, so she know lots of boys.

Kame likes to do all sorts of stuff, which is good. She's never boring, which is my greatest fear in life. If someone asked me what would be my least favorite way to die, I would say being bored to death.

I'm trying really hard not to have a best friend. But it seems to be happening without my doing anything. It's not my fault because Kame is just like me, and she's popular and pretty so it's not like she was lonely until I came around. It's just that she likes to be with me the most, and I feel the same.

She's staying with her aunt, Miss Kozuke, for two nights. Kame loves her aunt, who is much younger than her mother and more modern. Kame says her aunt believes you take what is best from the land of your ancestors and the land of your birth. One is not necessarily better than the other.

Her aunt is the reason Kame speaks English as well as she does. Her aunt believes it is very important to speak English properly. When Kame stays at her house, they don't speak any Japanese and they read the newspaper aloud so that Kame can keep practicing. Kame said that if her mother found out, she would be very angry.

I asked Kame if she was worried that America and Japan might soon be at war with each other. (This is what Daddy wrote about in his article. He titled it "Collision Course.")

She said she would be very sad because if that happened, she knows it would trouble her mother and father terribly because they were born in Japan. But she was born right here in Honolulu, and she's American, not Japanese.

She just hopes it doesn't happen.

Thursday, November 27, 1941
Oahu, Hawaii

You could tell that Thanksgiving this year was not going to be like previous years from the moment the guests arrived. Lieutenant Lockhart came in a chauffeur-driven car with flags flying from the fenders, and Mr. Poole by bike wearing tennis shoes and his yellow rain slicker, although there wasn't a cloud in the sky.

I think it would have been better if there were wives, but Mr. Poole isn't married, and Lieutenant Lockhart's wife is back home in Pasadena, California.

I'm not sure if Dad thought Mr. Poole and Lieutenant Lockhart would get along or if he thought about it at all and it was just that neither of them had anyplace special to be on Thanksgiving. You can never tell with Dad: It's very hard to read his mind.

Whatever he was thinking, it was not one of

his better ideas. As Mom likes to say, "The tension was so thick, you could cut it with a knife."

The only thing they agreed on was how good Mom's turkey was. (Of course, I'm the only one who knew how close they came to having a nice, fat, juicy pig instead of a turkey for Thanksgiving dinner.)

Early on, Dad tried to loosen things up by telling a lame joke. Dad thinks he's a great joke teller, but he isn't — neither in his choice or delivery. He said that, as everyone knew, some of the Hawaiian street names were very hard to pronounce. One day a new policeman, who had just come from the mainland, found a dead horse on Halekauwila Street, and rather than call it in he found someone to help him move the horse to King Street and then he called it in.

Ha. Ha.

Usually dinner party conversation starts out nice and relaxed, like everyone's just passing the time, with nothing particular on their minds, even though everyone knows that isn't the case. This time it didn't start off like that at all.

Once Lieutenant Lockhart got started, there was no stopping him. The only time he paused was when he asked to have his drink "freshened," which was something I thought only Mrs. Mouse said.

Mr. Poole was pretty quiet, and Dad hardly said a word, which was a sure sign he was delighted with the conversation and had already started mentally writing his next article. Even Mom, who usually joins in quite readily, was on the quiet side. But you could tell she was listening intently to every word.

Right before dessert, Mr. Poole got this funny look in his eye, like he'd just had an inspiration. He asked Lieutenant Lockhart if he was aware that war with Japan was "just around the corner," and it was just a question of where and when.

Lieutenant Lockhart laughed, like he had heard

the best joke ever. He started to lecture Mr. Poole as if he were talking to someone whose intelligence he considered way below his.

Japan, he explained, was a second-rate country with a third-rate military. Their aviators had such poor vision, they couldn't even fly their airplanes properly — their air force had the highest accident rate in the world.

Lieutenant Lockhart's voice was getting louder with each sentence, as if the size of his audience were growing and he wanted to make sure he was being heard, even in the back rows. He sounded like someone who was used to having the final word on any subject.

Japan wouldn't dare face the United States in battle, he went on. It was inconceivable that the Japanese government was unaware of these facts and the risks involved and would refrain, he was sure, from doing anything foolhardy.

The only sign that Mr. Poole was thinking anything at all was a slight downturn at the corners of his mouth, and a lowering of his eyelids, like he was growing tired of the conversation.

Sometimes Mr. Poole talks in riddles, and it's not quite clear precisely what he's saying, although you usually have an idea of what he's getting at. Dad says Mr. Poole's a poet and a "true scholar."

He picked up his unlit cigar and looked at it for a moment and then said to Lieutenant Lockhart: "Experience is a costly school, Lieutenant. But a fool will learn in no other."

He said it in his usual, friendly, off-the-cuff way, like he was simply notifying you that it might rain tomorrow and perhaps you should take an umbrella.

By now, Lieutenant Lockhart was visibly agitated and didn't even respond when Mom asked him if he would like another piece of pecan pie. Instead, he downed his drink and signaled to Dad that he was ready for another.

When he spoke, he was angry and his pupils had become tiny black pellets.

The Japanese in Japan didn't worry him one bit, he said. It was the Japanese living right here in Hawaii who worried him. Only he didn't say "Japanese." He said "Buddha-heads." He said, "Almost half the population of Hawaii is 'Buddha-heads,'" and he wouldn't be surprised if they begin sabotage operations any day now.

He bragged that the entire Pearl Harbor military base was on full alert, twenty-four hours a day, to guard against any sabotage attempts that "these Buddha-heads think they can make."

He suggested that Mr. Poole stick his nose back in his books and not where it doesn't belong. He said he should leave military strategy to military strategists like himself.

That's when Mr. Poole got up.

He shuffled over to where Lieutenant Lockhart was sitting and stood behind him so that Lieutenant Lockhart would have to turn around in his chair if he wanted to face him.

Mr. Poole asked him, still in his soft, gentle

voice, how long he had lived in Hawaii. Two months, Lieutenant Lockhart replied, quickly, without moving.

Mr. Poole said he had lived in Hawaii fifty-four years, all his life. He said that he was fortunate to have gotten to know many, many Japanese during that time. He said he could assure the lieutenant that, although Japan was their homeland, America was their chosen land, and we had nothing to fear from them.

He leaned over, as if what he had to say was private, between Lieutenant Lockhart and himself. He was almost whispering. "The Japanese have an ancient proverb, Lieutenant Lockhart," he said. "Roughly translated it is as follows: Behold the frog, who when he opens his mouth, displays his whole inside."

Then he thanked Mom for "a glorious repast," told Dad he hoped to see him at the bookstore soon, winked at me and Andy, and said he would see himself to the door.

Sunday, November 30, 1941
Oahu, Hawaii

After Thanksgiving dinner I wasn't at all sure we were going on the tour of Pearl Harbor that Lieutenant Lockhart had offered to take us on. I'm not sure what Dad would have done if it were up to him, but he knew that Andy would be really disappointed if we didn't go. So the three of us went. Not Mom, though. She wouldn't budge. She told Dad that she had seen and heard enough of Lieutenant Lockhart to last her a lifetime. This must be what Dad means when he says Mom doesn't suffer fools gladly.

I hadn't seen Andy this excited since the Dodgers won the pennant. He asked Lieutenant Lockhart so many questions, he could hardly catch his breath. He was talking so fast, I was afraid he was going to have an asthma attack right then and there.

We all went over to Hickham Field, where the American bombers are, and to Wheeler, where the fighters are based. The fighter planes were lined up neatly on the ground, wing to wing and close together so they could more readily be protected from sabotage, Lieutenant Lockhart explained.

I had to hand it to Andy: He knew what each plane was, how fast it could go, everything. Lieutenant Lockhart said he was quite impressed, and you could see that he was.

We saw battleship row, and got to see the cruisers, destroyers, and the battleships. We were lucky, because all the battleships were there for the first time in months.

But Andy was disappointed because the aircraft carriers (his favorites) were out on maneuvers and weren't there.

The last thing we did was take a tour of Lieutenant Lockhart's own ship, the U.S.S. *Arizona*. We watched a boxing match that was held onboard. The ship was most impressive. It was so clean, it gleamed in the sun, and the crew wore their white dress uniforms and saluted us as we passed.

Monday, December 1, 1941
Oahu, Hawaii

I got another letter from Allison. Amazingly enough, they're doing *Much Ado About Nothing* also. I think I'll join the Shakespeare Club with Kame and be in the play. Then Allison and I can be doing the same play at the same time. Maybe even the same role!

Mom said this was my last warning: If I don't write back to Allison by the end of the week, it's "curtains."

Mom said as far as she's concerned, life is easier here. Just not wearing so many clothes all the time is a relief.

Mom asked me how I liked school and if I was

making lots of friends. I think she was hinting at our best-friend discussion, but I know she likes Kame so she didn't say anything else about it.

Kame and I have to decide by Thursday what we're going to wear to the dance Sunday night.

Tuesday, December 2, 1941
Oahu, Hawaii

While I was helping Mom prepare everything for dinner, I asked her if she liked living in Hawaii and if she missed the United States.

She said she was glad we were living here, because she thinks Dad is taking things a little easier. (Frankly, I hadn't noticed this. He seems to be working just as hard here as he did in Washington or Boston. Although there aren't nearly as many dinner parties, and maybe that's what Mom means. In Washington, there was one practically every weekend.)

Friday, December 5, 1941
Oahu, Hawaii

Dad's playing golf with another reporter. He's a friend of Mr. Poole and writes for the *Honolulu Advertiser.* Lieutenant Lockhart can't play this Sunday because he's on duty.

Saturday, December 6, 1941
Oahu, Hawaii

Mom and I went shopping. She needed new shoes, and so did I. After shopping we saw *Dark Victory.* Mom doesn't like to go to the movies as much as Dad and I do, but she does if it's a Bette Davis movie. It was a pretty gloomy story, if you ask me, but Mom likes gloomy stories.

Sunday, December 7, 1941
Oahu, Hawaii

This is the third time I have attempted to write, but my hands have been shaking so badly that my writing is illegible. It seems steady enough now, and I will try to record all the horrible events that have taken place in the past twelve hours.

At first I thought I was still dreaming. I heard an incessant droning, like the sound the *China Clipper*'s propellers made, only much louder, more high-pitched.

Oddly, my mother was in the dream. She was saying, "Amber, Amber, wake up, wake up," her voice barely audible above the whining sound that was getting louder and closer. I could tell by the force of her voice that she was speaking as loudly as she could.

The dream was disturbing, but I didn't want to wake up because I was too sleepy. But now Mom was shaking me. I would have to get up.

The dream was over, and the nightmare was about to begin.

"Go wake your brother right now," she said.

I have never heard fear or panic in my mother's voice before, but I heard it then. There was no mistaking it.

I hadn't noticed that the droning in the dream was still there.

Without questioning what was so urgent or why I should get Andy up, I barged right into his room and told him Mom wanted him to get up right away.

I think some of the fear in Mom's voice must have been transmitted to mine, because Andy didn't question me any more than I questioned Mom.

We both ran downstairs, out the kitchen door, and onto the back patio, where Mom was, looking up at the sky.

She told Andy to go back and get his binoculars.

There were hundreds of planes in the sky. That's where the droning was coming from.

In the past few weeks I had gotten used to the sound of planes flying over my head while the army was on maneuvers. But this sound was different — it was louder, deeper, and there were more planes than I'd ever seen before. And, besides, the army never had maneuvers at eight o'clock on a Sunday morning.

They were coming in unbelievably low, barely clearing the treetops, circling in the sky and then peeling off, forming smaller groups of four and five.

Andy scanned the skies with his binoculars. He knew all the planes by heart: torpedo planes, high-level fliers, dive-bombers, horizontal bombers. Something was wrong, he said. They weren't the same color as our planes, and the red-ball insignias on the wings weren't American.

I was astonished when I looked through the binoculars. The planes were flying low enough that you could see them plainly even without the binoculars. But with them I could see right into the glass-paneled canopy that covered the cockpit where the pilot sat. I was going to wave like I had done so many times before, but I stopped.

The pilot had a white cloth tied around his forehead, and he looked just like Mr. Arata. He was Japanese! These were Japanese planes, not American planes on maneuvers. The pilot was smiling at me, looking close enough that I could reach out and touch him. Then he banked into a turn and was gone.

"It's Pearl Harbor! It's Pearl Harbor!" Andy was screaming. He was pointing to the column of black smoke that was rising up in the skies above Pearl Harbor. The smoke was mixing with the rays of the early morning sun, creating an eerie, bloodred sky.

There was machine-gun fire in the distance that sounded like Fourth of July firecrackers, and dull, booming explosions that were so loud, you could feel the ground shaking beneath your feet and hear the dishes rattling in the kitchen cabinets.

Mom had the radio on as loud as it would go. For a while there was no news, only a church service and some music.

I was praying Dad would call. I so wanted to hear his voice and know that he was all right.

Finally the announcer interrupted the program. "This is the real McCoy," he said. "We are under attack. The Japs are here." He kept repeating it and repeating it, like he was trying to convince himself it just wasn't another drill.

Andy was right. They were attacking Pearl Harbor.

But that was all we knew. We didn't know if anyone had been killed or hurt or even if there was anyone left at Pearl Harbor.

Outside, there were more explosions, different from the ones earlier. Andy said they were anti-aircraft guns.

Directly over our heads we saw the first American plane. He was going after a Japanese fighter. They were desperately trying to outmaneuver each other. We watched the struggle transfixed and horrified.

Finally the American plane's stream of bullets found their target.

The Japanese plane exploded with such violence that in a moment it ceased to be a plane. It was a flaming, orange inferno hurtling toward the earth.

There were more announcements and more instructions on the radio: Don't drive, stay off the streets, don't use telephones, prepare buckets of sand, and fill tubs with water in case of fire.

The announcer sounded frantic, his voice faltering.

He said all doctors and nurses who were in the area should come immediately to the army's Tripler General Hospital.

When Mom said she had to go, I looked at her

in utter disbelief. It was another incredible shock on top of the ones I was still trying to absorb. I couldn't understand how she could even consider leaving us here. We hadn't heard from Dad — we didn't know where he was, or even if he was all right.

My whole world was disintegrating right before my eyes, like that Japanese plane that had been shot down only minutes ago.

Mom looked at me like she was depending on me for something. *I have to do this, please help me,* her look said.

I said nothing, and that was sufficient.

She told us not to leave the house, no matter what. That we should stay away from windows and doors and wait until Dad got home and tell him where she went and not to worry. If anything happened, we should lock ourselves in the basement. This was an insight into the state of Mom's mind. We don't have a basement.

Then she hugged us, got in the car, and drove off.

I decided I would be safer if I was hiding under something. Andy helped me turn over the couch and the two big chairs, push them together in the middle of the living room, and drape our blankets and sheets over them.

It took a lot of time and it was hard to move everything around, but it was worth it. I decided I needed one last thing. I went to the kitchen and got Mom's big cleaver. Once I was back inside the couch-fort I felt safer, although I could only stay for fifteen minutes at a time because I could hardly breathe.

A little after we built the couch-fort, Dad called.

He was all right and wanted to know if we were all right. Andy told him we were, and then I spoke to him. I told him Mom had gone to help out at the hospital, and he didn't say anything for the longest time. Then he said he would go there first, get Mom, and come home.

Like Mom, he wanted me to tell him that it was okay, so I did, although I wish Mom hadn't gone to the hospital, or Dad to play golf, and that he would just come home and that we had never left Washington in the first place.

I was too terrified to do anything besides listen to reports on the radio. They kept repeating the same instructions as before and urging everyone to be calm.

Andy, despite instructions, stayed outside till it was dark, looking up at the skies with his binoculars, tears streaming down his face. I don't know what he was looking at. There was nothing to see. There had been no planes, no explosions since Mom had left.

I remained inside under the couch until Mom and Dad came home.

Monday, December 8, 1941
Oahu, Hawaii

Andy and I slept in our sleeping bags on the floor in Mom and Dad's room (although I don't think any of us got much sleep).

I don't know what I would have done if they hadn't come home or if anything had happened to them. I feel much better now that we're all together.

Mom made breakfast like there was nothing unusual happening. Andy and I just sat there at the kitchen table, waiting for Dad to say something.

He said when they had seen where the planes were headed, they'd driven to Pearl Harbor. The skies overhead were already turning gray from the black smoke spewing up from the badly damaged ships along battleship row.

It looked like the entire fleet had been destroyed. All of Pearl Harbor was in flames, and the harbor itself was a lake of fire. The beach was littered with the limp bodies of the men who had been washed ashore.

Everyone was running all over the place. It was the first time many of the men had seen any real action. When Dad said this, he put his head in his hands for a few seconds. I looked quickly at Mom and could see she was trying not to cry.

Some of the men became unglued, others panicked, and still others were frozen with fear. Some of the men were badly burned from swimming in the scalding water trying to save themselves and their buddies. Others, heroically, refused to abandon their antiaircraft guns, ignoring the flames that were about to engulf them. Many risked their lives going belowdecks to help their trapped crewmates.

Hundreds had been killed, maybe more.

Worst hit were the *Oklahoma* and the *Arizona*, Lieutenant Lockhart's ship.

The *Oklahoma* took five torpedoes, and most of the men were trapped and drowned when the ship capsized. Some are still alive in a compartment at the bottom of the ship that is now the top of the ship.

They can hear them tapping, but it's nearly impossible to tell precisely where the tapping is coming from because the sound echoes throughout the vessel. The rescue workers had been using acetylene torches to cut through the ship's hull, but the flame used up all the oxygen and suffocated some of the men to death. They switched to safer cutting equipment, but that is taking longer and they know that every second, the water inside is rising.

The men from the Navy Yard plan to work all night long.

The *Arizona* was hit the worst. At least eight bombs landed, and one went straight down one of the ship's funnels. It landed in the part of the ship where all the ammunition was stored, and there was a horrendous chain reaction that ignited cans of black powder, thousands of rounds of machine-gun bullets, and all the torpedoes. The whole front part of the *Arizona* exploded, and fire raged all over the ship.

Dad said he didn't see how anyone could have survived.

Nearly all the planes at Hickham and Wheeler have been destroyed also. Some Japanese pilots who had been shot down aimed their mortally wounded planes at hangars and rows of parked planes in one last suicide attack.

We all remained silent while Dad spoke. When he was done, we looked at Mom. But Mom obviously didn't want to talk about last night at the hospital. When she came home she looked dazed, and her pretty yellow dress was splattered with dried blood. All she said was that she wanted to lie down for a while.

"I have to go back," she said, staring down into her coffee cup.

But this time I was ready for her.

I told her I was going with her.

I had thought about it all last night. I wasn't going to spend another day hiding under the couch, wondering where everyone was, if they would ever come back, and hoping that the Japanese planes didn't drop a bomb on my head.

I was going, and there was nothing she or Dad could do to stop me.

I knew my face had to show how determined I was. Any signs of second thoughts, doubts, or any weakness whatsoever and Mom was sure to make me stay behind.

I showed none.

She looked at Dad wordlessly.

Dad said Andy could go with him, to Honolulu.

As we drove to the hospital we could see that the destruction had not been confined to Pearl Harbor.

There were houses wrecked by bombs, stores that were smoldering ruins, and bomb craters so deep, a man could stand in them.

There were roadblocks everywhere. The MPs,

carrying rifles with long bayonets, stopped our car, looked inside, and asked Mom what her destination was. When Mom told one she was a nurse and she was going to Tripler, he immediately waved us through.

It still took three times longer than it usually did. There were traffic jams wherever we turned. Accidents littered the road and the roadsides, making for slow going.

As soon as we arrived, there were a thousand things to do.

There were hundreds of men lined up in the halls, still lying on the stretchers that they had been brought in on by the litter bearers and the ambulance teams. Emergency ambulances continued to drive up depositing more badly wounded men, including some of the men who had finally been freed from the *Oklahoma*.

Patients who had been hospitalized before the Japanese attack willingly gave up their beds. Still, some of the stretchers had to remain outside on the grass until there was space available in the constantly overcrowded halls.

The stench was overpowering. Some of the men were burned so badly, their flesh had turned black. It's a smell I don't think I will ever forget.

A medical officer walked up and down the halls deciding who was fortunate enough to be treated next. Doctors and nurses worked furiously at the operating tables while orderlies, frantic that they were running out of sterilized instruments, sutures, and bandages, searched for the necessary equipment while seeing to the patients waiting their turn.

It is a miracle they were able to concentrate on the grim tasks before them.

Everything and everyone was moving so fast, it was a blur, with barely enough time to react and realize how truly horrible it all was.

Mom told me I should help organize the people who were lined up to donate blood. She told me to work fast because some men were going into shock since they were losing so much blood. There were so many people in line that they had run out of proper containers, and we had to use sterilized Coke bottles.

Many of the people in line were Japanese, which surprised me. I know it shouldn't have, but it did. It was the first time since early Sunday morning that I had thought about Kame, if she was all right, if her family was safe, and how awful this must be for her.

One man was so nervous about giving blood, I told him that maybe he shouldn't. He insisted, saying he wanted to do his part. But when I asked him to roll up his sleeve, he fainted.

After that, I cleaned all the dirty bottles and tubes I could find, gathered containers that were scattered all over, washed them, and filled them with water so Mom could sterilize the instruments.

When I started to take off the soiled sheets from one recently vacated bed, thinking I would put on fresh, clean ones, Mom stopped me. We had no time for that. The next patient would just have to be put in the bed as it was.

These poor boys bore their excruciating pain in stony silence, most moaning quietly to themselves, as if they didn't want to cause any trouble or disturb anyone.

One patient was in shock from loss of blood. Mom said I should just do my best to comfort him. I put my hand under his head, lifted it up, and gave him a drink of water. He smiled, as if to say thanks.

He was trying so hard to talk, desperately wanting to tell me something that seemed terribly important to him. But no matter how hard he tried, he couldn't utter a sound. I summoned all my acting ability so he would think that I understood, and, in a way, I think I did.

When I returned a few minutes later to check on him, he didn't look too good. I found Mom. She felt for a pulse and put her ear to his mouth to see if he was breathing. There was nothing. With no emotion showing on her face, Mom pulled the sheet over his head and, in a matter-of-fact voice, said that I should see to the other patients.

There was one man who had been screaming the same thing over and over for hours.

"Where are they? Where are they?" he kept shouting. It seemed that no one dared approach him, and I felt bad for him. I wanted to do something, although, God knows, I didn't know what.

I held his hand, which was cold as ice and soaked with sweat. He stopped screaming, at least for the moment. I brought a basin of cool water with me and I dipped a ragged piece of cloth into the water, then gently laid it on his brow, which seemed to be burning up with fever.

He was lying there with his eyes wide open, wild with fear and distorted with pain.

He looked familiar, but I couldn't remember where I knew him from. Then, I realized who he was.

It was Lieutenant Lockhart.

He started screaming again, as if my recognition had caused him to cry out. I hurried to find Mom.

I think at first she didn't believe me. It had already been a hideously long and awful day. I think she thought I was delirious. I didn't blame her for thinking that, but I wasn't.

When she looked down at Lieutenant Lockhart, her expression was difficult to decipher. It was disdainful and sympathetic at the same time.

She told me not to leave his side and returned within seconds with a syringe, which she immediately poked into his arm. In moments he was sleeping soundly.

On the way home, Mom told me she discovered that Lieutenant Lockhart had been thrown clear of the *Arizona* when the explosions first began. Although both his legs were severely injured, he was able to swim to shore where he collapsed. He was rescued and taken to the hospital, where they had to amputate both his legs in order to save his life.

Saturday, December 13, 1941
Oahu, Hawaii

This is the first night I've been able to write. For the past three nights I've just been too tired. As soon as Mom and I get home from the hospital, I stick something in my mouth, crawl into my sleeping bag, and I'm out like a light.

I feel a little rested now, and tomorrow we're not going to the hospital, which is quite a relief.

We're now under martial law, which means that the military has taken over the government. Mom said that she doesn't see why anyone would want the military taking over after the fine job they did of preventing the attack in the first place. I don't think Mom and Dad quite see eye to eye on this point, so the less I say, the better.

There are all sorts of stories going around about the attack. The Japanese on the island cut arrows in the cane fields pointing toward Pearl Harbor to guide the pilots; some of the pilots who were shot down have turned out to be graduates of high schools right here on Oahu! One of them was even wearing a McKinley High School class ring!

Andy and Dad went to look at one of the Japanese planes that was shot down. Andy said they had all the pilot's clothes laid out. He had American money, and he didn't wear a uniform. He wore American slacks and a typical, colorful sport shirt. All this so no one could tell where he came from if he survived the crash.

Andy has been going out with some of his friends and looking for souvenirs. So far they have found a half-burned Japanese flag, some bullets, and a wing section with the Rising Sun insignia on it. They're going to make key chains out of the bullets and sell them.

Andy and his friends want to go see the Japanese prisoner they captured from the midget submarine. According to my brother, these midget subs were launched on the backs of the regular-sized, mother subs and had only one or two men in them. One was rammed and sunk, and the man who was driving was captured.

And there are rumors that it's not over: The Japanese are coming back to destroy any ships and planes that survived the first attack; they're going to launch a ground invasion and take over all Hawaii; they've poisoned our reservoirs, and it isn't safe to drink the water; the Japanese on the island are going to rise up and kill all the *haoles* ("white people") on the island. And there's even a rumor that the United States has surrendered.

Dad says this is preposterous. The United States has declared war on Japan. He read President Roosevelt's speech to us. The president called December 7 "a date which will live in infamy," and said the attack was "unprovoked and dastardly."

People are trigger-happy, shooting at anything that moves. Last night a poor cow that got loose and was roaming around got shot.

People are rushing to the markets and grabbing anything they can off the shelves and putting it in their baskets without even looking at what it is.

Mom and I went shopping on the way home from the hospital, and it was awful. We had to wait an hour before we could even get into the Kaimuki Supermarket. They were told not to sell to people who were hoarding, just to sell the regular amount. But it was nearly impossible to control everyone. People were cradling ten-pound bags of rice, carrying cartons of canned milk and toilet paper out to their cars.

They finally had to close the doors and let in only a few people at a time.

Mom was a little worried because she wants to eat right because of the baby. She's getting a little big now, and you can feel the baby kick.

Mom's due in May. Maybe the baby will be born on my birthday, May 9!

Sunday, December 14, 1941
Oahu, Hawaii

Dad and Andy are almost finished making sure the kitchen and the bedroom are completely blackout proof.

For the past week (I can't believe it's only been a week — it seems like ten lifetimes) we have had sheets covering the windows, but that isn't working well enough.

Thursday night the air-raid warden came to our door and told us light was escaping from the kitchen window. (There can't be any light visible from sundown to sunup, and civilians are not allowed on the streets during that time.) The blackout is so no one accidentally or on purpose can give signals to the Japanese, should they return.

Mom thinks the blackout is pretty silly because Pearl Harbor is lit up all night long while the vessels are repaired. Dad said the military claims they can turn the lights off immediately if they need to. Mom wasn't exactly buying that.

Andy went around and stuffed cracks with newspapers. Now he and Dad are painting all the windows in both rooms black so that absolutely no light can escape.

Sometimes it gets too stuffy at night with the windows closed, so we open one. (We all sleep in Mom and Dad's room — Andy dragged in his mattress, but I still use my sleeping bag.) I can't go to sleep without reading at least a little while. So, to be on the safe side, I get into my sleeping bag before I turn on my flashlight.

We spend most of our time now either in the kitchen or the bedroom because they're the only two rooms that are blacked out.

Tuesday, December 16, 1941
Oahu, Hawaii

Mom asked if I wanted to go see Kame. I did and I didn't. Of course Mom sensed immediately what was going through my mind. In her let's-get-to-the-point tone of voice she said, "It's not Kame's fault."

We've decided to go see her tomorrow.

There hasn't been any school since December 7. The military has taken over our school buildings and turned them into administration offices and a processing center.

The military needs not only the buildings but our teachers, too. They are going door-to-door helping get all residents over the age of six fingerprinted so they can be issued I.D. cards.

We'll have to carry the I.D. cards at all times. Andy said that one of the reasons is so our dead bodies can be easily identified in case of an attack. That took a big load off my mind.

School might not resume until February,

which is fine with me. I love spending time with the whole family, especially helping Mom with all the things we have to do.

Wednesday, December 17, 1941
Oahu, Hawaii

I was nervous all the way over to the Aratas', but as soon as I saw Kame's pretty face I knew in my heart how much I had missed her. I gave her a big hug, and I could feel how scared she was and could see it in her face.

Kame made tea, and we sat in the kitchen while she told us what had happened.

The Sunday night of the attack some MPs and a man from the FBI came to talk to her father.

They asked if he had a radio, and when he showed it to them they took it out to the car saying that they wanted to look it over at the lab.

One of the MPs took down the photograph and the samurai swords on the living–room wall and carted those out to the car also. Kame had told her father that morning to bury them, but he wouldn't listen to her.

After that her father, accompanied by the FBI man, went up to the bedroom. When he came down he was carrying a small suitcase. Mr. Arata said he was going downtown with the men to answer some of their questions and he would be back soon.

As her father was going out the door he turned to Kame and motioned for her to come close to him. He hugged her and told her, "You are the strong one. Take care of your mother and your brothers."

Then the man from the FBI put handcuffs on her father, put him in the car, and they drove away.

They haven't seen or heard from him since.

Kame tearfully told us that she and her mother are arguing over everything. Her mother yells at her for leaving a window open a crack, because she's deathly afraid one of the air-raid wardens will see some light and take her away, too. She said she has tried to obey her father's wishes but that she and her mother barely speak. (The whole time we were there, Mrs. Arata was upstairs with the two boys.)

One night her mother was on the telephone talking to Kame's aunt, and the operator came on the line and said something that her mother didn't understand. Kame's aunt explained, in Japanese, that the operator didn't want them to speak Japanese and that if they didn't start speaking English, they would have to get off the line.

Her mother hung up and started crying because she doesn't speak English well enough to do that.

All she ever says is *shikata ga nai,* which means "it can't be helped."

Kame is ashamed. Ashamed that she is Japanese. Ashamed that she has the face of the enemy. She is worried about her father. There are rumors that some of the men who have been rounded up by the authorities have been shot trying to escape. And she is worried about what will happen to her. She said she is afraid to go anywhere.

Mom said that she should remember that she is an American just like us, not the enemy. She told Kame she would have to give it time. Mom's a great believer in giving things time. Time is a healer, Mom likes to say.

Mom told Kame she would talk to Dad and see what he could find out about her father.

Then we invited Kame and her family (including her aunt) to Christmas dinner. Mom is determined to have Christmas dinner no matter how hard it is getting food.

You could see how pleased Kame was with the invitation — she even smiled a little. She said her aunt was an excellent cook and would prepare some delicious Japanese delicacies.

When we got home, we talked to Dad. He said the situation is grave because there is a great deal of hatred directed at the Japanese on the island. He said there is no telling what has happened to Mr. Arata, but he will do his best to find out where they have taken him.

Dad said he and Andy spent the whole day at his office trying to place calls to the mainland. He was able to speak to his paper's headquarters in New York City; to Grandma and Grandpa (who were relieved to hear his voice); and to the principal of our school in Washington. Dad wanted to let everyone know that we are all okay. That's the kind of thing Dad does all the time that makes him so sweet.

They got a late start coming home from Dad's office and had to drive the last two miles in the dark. Dad said it was really hard driving at night because the roads are so dark (there are no streetlights), and the headlights don't emit much light at all.

Last Thursday, Dad and Andy took the car down to the police station to have the headlights painted blue. Andy was pretty annoyed because they got blue paint all over the front of the car and, as with everything these days, they had to wait in line for over two hours.

Fortunately the car has running boards, so Andy stood on them and told Dad when he was getting too close to the side of the road.

Thursday, December 18, 1941
Oahu, Hawaii

Andy and Dad have been working nonstop for the past two days building our bomb shelter. It's supposed to be at least ten feet long and five feet wide, but ours doesn't look that big.

Dad got some corrugated iron that he's using for the roof. All they have to do is pile the dirt on the top and finish filling the sandbags for the back wall.

Mom said that from what she can see, it would be best if we were hit by a very, very small bomb.

Friday, December 19, 1941
Oahu, Hawaii

We had to stand in line for two hours today at the library waiting to get our gas masks. The man showed us how to put them on.

You have to place your chin in the mask first, then strap it over your head. There's this big, tubular part that comes down from your nose and mouth, so you look like an elephant with a mutated trunk.

I think there's as good a chance of suffocating to death from putting the gas mask on wrong as there is dying from a Japanese poison-gas attack.

You have to make sure it's on real, real tight so that no gas can get in. I feel like there's a squid attacking my face.

You're supposed to carry it in this ugly, green canvas bag with a shoulder strap. You have to take it with you *everywhere* — even to the bathroom. If the soldiers see you don't have it, they will make you go home and get it. And if you lose it, you have to pay $3.75 to get a new one.

The regular masks are too big for really little children and babies. They get "bunny bags," which their whole bodies go into, and there's a clear plastic area where their faces are. The bag has bunny ears, so they look like bunnies from outer space. It's pretty funny.

We went into a room to test and see if they actually worked. We put on our masks, and then they put tear gas in the room. My eyes got red and teary and felt real sore, so I raised my hand (which is what they told us to do if you were experiencing some gas), and they took me out immediately.

The man said my mask didn't fit right, which I had pretty much figured out by then.

Dad said the reason my mask doesn't fit is that my head is too small and that perhaps we should consider having it enlarged. Dad doesn't have the best sense of humor in the world. He said I

shouldn't worry, because it's unlikely that anything is going to happen.

If it's unlikely that anything is going to happen,
why do I have to wear it? (I didn't ask him that,
because he has enough on his mind.)

Saturday, December 20, 1941
Oahu, Hawaii

I thought things couldn't get any worse, but I was
wrong.

Mr. Poole is dead.

Dad and Andy went to see him at the bookstore.
There was no bookstore. One of the American
antiaircraft shells accidentally struck the building when it missed its target and set it on fire.
It burned to the ground.

Mr. Poole lived in an apartment in the same
building as his store, and he died in the fire.

The whole block is still roped off.

Mom told me all this. Dad is still in the

bedroom. He hasn't come out since late this morning, when he and Andy got back. Andy said he's never seen Dad this upset about anything.

Sunday, December 21, 1941
Oahu, Hawaii

Dad's found out where Mr. Arata is. Since he was active in the Japanese Businessman's Association, he is suspected of somehow being involved in the December 7 attack. He's being held on Sand Island for questioning. That's all Dad knows.

Kame is relieved to know that her father is alive.

Monday, December 22, 1941
Oahu, Hawaii

Every time there's an air raid we rush out and cram ourselves into the bomb shelter. (Everyone except for Mom, that is. She said she would "rather be blown to smithereens than spend time in that crazy cave.")

Dad said people are building bigger and more elaborate ones. All we have in ours is a kerosene lantern, some canned food, but no can opener, and some bottled water.

It has two benches on either side when you walk in (or, more accurately, crawl in), a crude wooden floor, and a pipe going up through the roof so you can breathe, sort of.

There's always water seeping up from the ground, and there are mosquitoes, spiderwebs, snakes (I'm sure), and all sorts of horrible creatures with at least a thousand legs creeping and crawling around.

I wanted to ask Dad when he was going to put in the shower and bath, but I didn't dare. Dad hasn't been exactly ecstatic about his new building career. He works on his articles late at night in the kitchen because he spends so much time during the day on stuff like the bomb shelter.

Mom made a sign and put it over the entrance. It says: BILLOWS FAMILY — PLEASE KNOCK.

In the beginning I was always the first one down there because I was so scared. But now I don't rush down so fast, which is what I think Dad and Andy are doing, because no matter how slow I am, I'm still the first.

Tuesday, December 23, 1941
Oahu, Hawaii

This is going to be, without doubt, the worst Christmas of my life.

For one thing, there's downtown. They've painted all the buildings so that they're camouflaged. That way, they can't be seen from the air. From down here it doesn't look to me like it would fool anyone. They just look like badly painted buildings. Maybe from up in the air you would think it was a mountain or something. There are sandbags placed all around them, and the windows are taped to prevent flying glass. You couldn't see in the windows if there was anything to see, which there isn't. They hardly have anything in them because there have been so few shipments from the mainland.

They've taken down all the Christmas lights and holiday decorations so it doesn't even look like Christmas, and it certainly doesn't feel like it.

This year we have soldiers instead of Santas.

The only thing that reminds you that it's Christmas when you're downtown is the Salvation Army people with their kettles and tinkling bells.

We're not even going to have a tree. The trees come from the mainland, and, of course, there are none. Although Mom and I have decorated the house, it doesn't really look like much without a tree.

Mom's really happy about the butcher, though. The butcher really, really loves Mom, so he saves her some of her favorite cuts of meat. He knows how much care and pride Mom puts into preparing a meal. For Christmas he is saving her a nice big leg of lamb. And Mom's going to make twice-baked potatoes, Dad's favorite.

The other thing that makes Mom happy is that she can still get Walter Winchell on the radio. The local radio stations have been off the air since the attack. This is so that the Japanese planes can't follow the radio beams, which seems pretty silly to me. The Japanese were capable of finding Pearl Harbor the first time and, since they've already been here once, I would imagine they know the way without radio beams.

Andy tunes in the police radio and listens to the dispatcher telling the police cars all the suspicious things that have to be investigated. It's really spooky listening to that.

I was going to write Allison today, but I'm afraid of the censors. Dad says they take out anything they think is unacceptable. You have to be especially careful not to say anything about the weather, because they consider that essential information. They cut out any offending words and then reseal the envelope with censor's tape.

I told Mom I didn't think this was a good time to write, because I didn't want to get into any trouble. She said she "wouldn't even dignify that with a response."

At least we can still go to the movies. We decided to see *How Green Was My Valley*, although Andy voted for *Dumbo* (which is about, of all things, a flying elephant. The world is coming apart at the seams, and people are making movies about flying elephants).

I cried from beginning to end. I don't usually cry at movies. I don't know what came over me. Lately I feel real sensitive, and the movie made me think about how much I care about my family. Even Andy was choked up, you could tell.

After the movie we had to turn in our American money and get the new Hawaiian money. The authorities are afraid that if the Japanese invade, they'll take all our money. The new money has HAWAII printed big on both sides. That way the Japanese won't be able to use it. Andy thinks we should all just use Monopoly money.

Naturally we had to stand in line at the bank for forty-five minutes (the line was around the block). We spend half our lives standing in line now. We line up to be immunized for smallpox, and we line up for gasoline rationing coupons. We're only allowed ten gallons of gasoline a month. Dad takes the bus now when he goes into Honolulu, but even taking the bus is a problem. There aren't enough drivers, so sometimes Dad waits so long, he just comes home.

I didn't take my gas mask with me to the movies or to the bank, and Mom and Dad didn't say anything. The masks are such a pain. They weigh about a million pounds and look ridiculous.

Wednesday, December 24, 1941
Oahu, Hawaii

Mom went to a meeting about school. They still don't know when we're going to resume class, but it's not going to be where it was. The military still needs the facilities. When we do go back, we'll be divided up into smaller groups, classes will be held in private homes, and the teachers will go from house to house to save on gas.

Christmas Day, 1941
Oahu, Hawaii

I heard Mom and Kame's aunt talking in the kitchen while they were preparing dinner. Miss Kozuke said that they all had to be very careful because they were Japanese. Their telephone conversations are being monitored, and the older Japanese, like Kame's mother, are not wearing traditional kimonos or sandals because they are afraid.

When Kame and I came in, they stopped talking about it. Kame's living with her aunt now. Mrs. Arata and the two boys did not come to dinner.

Miss Kozuke brought fresh vegetables from the victory garden she and Kame planted. It's very difficult to get fresh vegetables, so it was a real treat for everyone except Dad. Dad doesn't eat any vegetables except potatoes. He says they're rabbit food.

Kame's aunt was going to prepare sushi, but she was unable to get the ingredients she needed.

She also brought beans that had been soaked in water and cooked the night before. She and Mom ground the beans, pressed them through the cheesecloth, and poured them into wooden bowls. Kame's aunt said that tofu has lots and lots of protein.

Mom showed Miss Kozuke how to make twice-baked potatoes and said they have lots and lots of starch, which made all of us laugh. It was an odd sound, laughter.

At the dinner table Dad stood up to make a toast. I was really taken by surprise. Dad's never done anything like that. But I could see that something was on his mind. Plus, it was the first time I had ever seen Dad take a drink. Even Mom had never had sake before, and Dad tried it and thought it was "wonderful." He had quite a few of those little cups Miss Kozuke brought to serve the sake in.

He held up one of the little cups and said he wanted to make a toast to those who were unable to join us tonight but who he hoped would be able to very soon: Mr. and Mrs. Arata and the two boys.

Then he said he would like to make a toast to someone who will not be able to join us in the future, Mr. Poole.

He had something more he wanted to say, something about Mr. Poole, but he couldn't do it.

After dinner I told Dad that you could see how much his toast meant to Kame and her aunt. And what a nice way it was to begin Christmas dinner. I told him that he always thinks of everything. "If I thought of everything," he said, "we wouldn't be here."

I told him not to be so hard on himself and gave him a big, big, hug. I love to hug Dad; he smells like an ice-cream soda.

Kame and her aunt left pretty early. They wanted to get home before it got dark. Dad, Andy, and I helped Mom in the kitchen.

Dad tapped his fork on the little sake cup and said he had an announcement. I couldn't believe what I was hearing.

I looked at Mom and could see that this time, she knew.

"They want to evacuate as many people from the island as they can," Dad said. Evacuation will help ease the housing and food shortage. Top priority is being given to women and children, especially pregnant women (which Mom more than qualifies for).

"So we're moving," Dad said, just like he always does, only this time it was so different. How long, was all I could think, praying it would be soon.

"The day after tomorrow," Dad said, answering my question without my even having to ask.

"Amber turned out to be right after all," he said. "We just had a little detour. We're moving to San Francisco."

I didn't know what to say. I was so relieved. It was like a bad dream was finally ending.

Isn't it ironic?

The shortest diary I ever kept, and the saddest.

Epilogue

★★★

Lieutenant Lockhart and his wife were divorced in 1943. A year later, by then addicted to painkillers and alcohol, he committed suicide.

Mr. Arata was released from Sand Island in 1942. The family, including Miss Kozuke, was sent to the Jerome Relocation Center in Arkansas. It was impossible to trace anyone besides Kame after that.

In 1949, Kame married and gave birth to Grace a year later. When Grace was fourteen months old, Kame and her husband were killed in a freak automobile accident.

Amber Billows lost track of Kame immediately after December 1941. She spent years trying to find her, finally succeeding (with the help of her father) only in time to learn of Kame's tragic fate.

Amber then located Grace in an orphanage and adopted her. She and her husband (a documentary filmmaker friend of her brother's) brought her back to their Boston home, where Grace grew up. She was the couple's only and much loved child.

Life in America
in 1941

Historical Note

★★★

"A date which will live in infamy." That was how President Roosevelt described December 7, 1941. It was a day no one expected to be different from any other. Instead, the events of that day changed world history.

By 1941, much of the world was already at war. While the Nazis occupied and terrorized most of Europe, Japan was busy with its own imperialist mission in the Far East. In 1937, conflict between Japan and China escalated when Japan captured the city of Nanking and went on to massacre 300,000 Chinese civilians. Although anger at Japan was evident in the world and in the United States, Americans wanted no part of anyone else's war. This country's usual reaction would have been to protect vulnerable China from an aggressively advancing Japan. But during this period of isolationism and fear, the idea of participating in another war was met with apprehension from the American people. From 1935 to 1937, Congress passed three Neutrality Acts designed to keep us out of conflicts by forbidding arms sales and other supports.

Roosevelt was in a bind. Without the backing of the people, all he could do was ask Congress to amend the Neutrality Acts in some way to allow our government to send supplies to our European allies. By 1941, Roosevelt had the Lend-Lease program to give aid to Great Britain. The program allowed America to provide allied nations with defense supplies without engaging their enemies. Roosevelt was inclined to do more. He would have liked to give more to Great Britain in its fight against Germany. He would have liked to contribute American resources and manpower toward this fight and toward China's fight in the East.

Yet in America, there was an air of quiet denial. Only moderately concerned about the problems in Europe, Americans were even less interested in Japan's actions. Detached geographically from these wars, the American people were reluctant to become involved in them physically or financially. Indeed, they were adamant about staying out of it.

So it wasn't until the summer of 1940 that Roosevelt decided to take some steps toward war. When Japan took Indochina from France, it put the Japanese very close strategically to the Philippines, a group of islands in the Pacific ruled by the United States. America began to strategize. While Congress saw to a renewal of America's naval fleet, Roosevelt banned the sale of certain goods to Japan. As far as Japan was concerned, these were acts of aggression, and they would be answered.

Answered they were. Japan, led by Emperor

Hirohito, allied itself with Adolf Hitler's Nazi Germany and Benito Mussolini's Fascist Italy in a pact under which each leader vowed to support the other if any one of them were attacked by the United States. This was the Tripartite Pact. In light of this alliance, Roosevelt tightened America's purse strings and exports even more. His plan was to cut off Japan's war plans at the source. He placed an embargo on all oil, steel, and iron exports to Japan. Great Britain followed suit. What would Japan run on now? What would they build with? How could they continue this war they had started?

In order to seize the resources that they would need to recover momentum in the war, Japan's navy would have to take the Dutch East Indies, along with British Malaysia and the American Philippines — areas extremely rich in raw materials. This would be impossible unless they defeated America's Pacific fleet first. Hideki Tojo, a

Japanese army general who had just become Prime Minister, decided not to hesitate. A surprise attack in the Pacific was in order. The preparations began.

America had long ago made the islands of Hawaii a territory. By 1941, half of the U.S. Naval Fleet was docked in Oahu's Pearl Harbor. It was a strategic move that enabled America to have a military presence in the Pacific. But even as it accomplished this, it opened the door to a risky proximity to Japan and its dreams of total command of the Far East. Pearl Harbor became a target.

Because Japan's attack on America could only be pulled off successfully if it came as a complete surprise, the bombing of Pearl Harbor was perhaps the riskiest military mission in history. Even as Admiral Isoroku Yamamoto laid his plans, diplomats from both Japan and the United States sought a peaceful resolution. And even while all this was happening, American military intelligence had finally broken the codes that revealed the alarming news that Japan was planning surprise attacks somewhere in the Pacific. But when? Where? Would it be the Philippines? Would they dare attack even closer to American soil?

The Japanese sent out warnings. One was sent to American officials in the Pacific after the first part of Japan's mission, sending war ships in the direction of Hawaii, was put into action on November 26. And another was intercepted on its way to Japanese diplomats in Washington, in town to break off any further negotiations with America. It was a long message. By the time it was decoded, it was early Sunday morning in Hawaii — December 7, 1941. It was too late. What had been a dreamy night in the Pacific harbor turned into a nightmarish dawn.

At 7:55 A.M., bombs crashed down, exploding ships on contact. Anyone who could tried to help the others. But it was no use. The surprise attack had worked. By 9:30 A.M., it was over. Eighteen American ships were lost. Over 300 American military planes destroyed. Over 2,400 American lives were lost and 1,178 people were wounded. The next day, President Roosevelt made the report to the rest of the country. And America went to war.

Many popular Sunday afternoon entertainment programs were interrupted when news of the "sneak attack" was broadcast to the American public via radio bulletins. The news sent a shock wave across the nation, uniting it behind the president and effectively ending isolationist sentiments in the country. The United States was gripped by war hysteria. This was especially strong along the Pacific coast of the United States, where residents feared more Japanese attacks.

People who once lived peacefully side by side became paranoid. Communities demanded that the residents of Japanese ancestry be removed from their homes along the coast and relocated in isolated inland areas. Later, President Roosevelt would sign into effect an order for forcible internment of Japanese people in America. It was a dark time in America's history. While we were fighting wars abroad against fascism and imperialism, America was depriving its own citizens of their civil rights.

All around the country, people were driven by fear. The bombing of Pearl Harbor had brought war too close to home. Posters hung everywhere: "Remember Pearl Harbor!" This was the call to arms that kept Americans enthusiastic. Rationing began and victory gardens sprung up as people were encouraged to grow their own food to avoid shortages. The war raged on for nearly four more years. On August 6, America dropped the first atomic bomb on Hiroshima, Japan. On August 9, another was dropped on Nagasaki. On August 14, 1945, Japan surrendered to the Allies. No country has tried to invade America's shores since.

Luxury yachts dropped anchor in the Ala Wai harbor in Honolulu, Hawaii. The palm tree-lined, mountainous island of Oahu was the base for almost half of the American military fleet in 1941.

The streets of Honolulu in December 1940 were decorated with Christmas lights. But in 1941, after the December 7 attack on Pearl Harbor, public festivities for the Christmas holiday were cancelled, and lights and decorations removed because of strict blackout regulations imposed by the American military.

142

In 1941, in retaliation for an American-led embargo on the export of oil, steel, and iron to Japan, Japanese Prime Minister Hideki Tojo, a former army general, sent an armada of four aircraft carriers transporting 350 bombers, Zero fighters, and torpedo planes to attack the American naval and army bases in the U.S. territory of Hawaii. On Sunday, December 7, 1941, the Japanese aircrafts reached their destination at 7:53 A.M.

The commander of one of the four Japanese aircraft carriers, Shokaku, *watches the jets take off to attack Pearl Harbor early in the morning on December 7, 1941. The Kanji inscription on the wall behind the officer is an appeal to the pilots to do their duty.*

143

This photograph was taken by a Japanese pilot during the raid on the island of Oahu, Hawaii. The American battleships moored in Pearl Harbor, called the Bay of Pu'uola in Hawaiian, were attacked by torpedoes and bombs. In this picture, the USS West Virginia was torpedoed, and the Japanese torpedo planes are visible in the right center of the photo. Eight U.S. battleships were destroyed by the Japanese, leaving the American naval presence in the Pacific crippled.

144

In the above photograph, the USS Arizona lists and sinks after being hit by at least eight Japanese bombs. Over one thousand U.S. servicemen were killed aboard this battleship. American destroyers USS Cassin and USS Downes were also hit while in drydock. Anti-aircraft shells fired from American crafts explode above the destroyed ships. Below, a photograph snapped from an automobile that was traveling alongside Pearl Harbor shows many of the other American ships that were damaged during the raid.

Wheeler Army Airfield, in central Oahu, was the U.S. Army's main fighter base and was heavily attacked during the raid on Pearl Harbor. Of some 140 planes on the ground there—mainly P-40 (as shown in the photo below) and P-36 pursuit planes—nearly two-thirds were destroyed or put out of action. The Japanese pilots set planes afire with machine gun and cannon fire and sent bombers in to wreck them with explosives.

Hickam Army Airfield, which was adjacent to the Pearl Harbor Navy Yard, was also attacked by the Japanese. Many men were killed at Hickam when the Japanese bombed their barracks, and approximately two-thirds of the jets housed in this airstrip were so badly wrecked, they had to be grounded. However, the American planes, such as the B-17E bomber pictured above, that managed to escape damage flew on defensive missions, shooting down Japanese planes.

Hawaiian civilian volunteers formed the Women's Ambulance Service Patrol (WASP's) in 1942, after the sinking of the American ship USS Wasp. *They provided emergency ambulance service throughout the duration of the war.*

8 PAGES—HONOLULU, TERRITORY OF HAWAII, U. S. A., SUNDAY, DECEMBER 7, 1941—8 PAGES ★ PRICE FIVE CENTS

WAR!

(Associated Press by Transpacific Telephone)

SAN FRANCISCO, Dec. 7.—President Roosevelt announced this morning that Japanese planes had attacked Manila and Pearl Harbor.

OAHU BOMBED BY JAPANESE PLANES

SIX KNOWN DEAD, 21 INJURED, AT EMERGENCY HOSPITAL

Attack Made On Island's Defense Areas

By UNITED PRESS

WASHINGTON, Dec. 7.—Text of a White House announcement detailing the attack on the Hawaiian Islands is:

"The Japanese attacked Pearl Harbor from the air and all naval and military activities on the island of Oahu, principal American base in the Hawaiian Islands."

Oahu was attacked at 7:55 this morning by Japanese planes.

The Rising Sun, emblem of Japan, was seen on plane wing tips.

Wave after wave of bombers streamed through the clouded morning sky from the southwest and flung their missiles on a city resting in peaceful Sabbath calm.

According to an unconfirmed report received at the governor's office, the Japanese force that attacked Oahu reached Island waters aboard two small airplane carriers.

It was also reported that at the governor's office either an attempt had been made to bomb the USS Lexington, or that it had been bombed.

CITY IN UPROAR

Within 10 minutes the city was in an uproar. As bombs fell in many parts of the city, and in defense areas the defenders of the Islands went into quick action.

Army intelligence officers at Ft. Shafter commenced officially shortly after 9 a. m. that the fact of the bombardment by an enemy had long previous army and navy had taken immediate measures in defense.

"Oahu is under a sporadic air raid," the announcement said.

"Civilians are urged to stay off the streets until further notice."

CIVILIANS ORDERED OFF STREETS

The army has ordered that all civilians stay off the streets and highways and not use telephones.

Evidence that the Japanese attack has registered some hits was shown by three billowing pillars of smoke in the Pearl Harbor and Hickam field area.

All navy personnel and civilian workers, with the exception of woman, have been ordered to duty at Pearl Harbor.

The Pearl Harbor highway was immediately a mass of racing cars.

A trickling stream of injured people began pouring into the city emergency hospital a few minutes after the bombardment started.

Thousands of telephone calls almost swamped the Mutual Telephone Co., which put extra operators on duty.

At The Star-Bulletin office the phone calls deluged the single operator and it was impossible for this newspaper, for sometime, to handle the flood of calls. Here also an emergency operator was called.

HOUR OF ATTACK—7:55 A. M.

An official army report from department headquarters, made public shortly before 11, is that the first attack was at 7:55 a. m.

Witnesses said they saw at least 50 airplanes over Pearl Harbor.

The attack centered in the Pearl Harbor, Army authorities said.

"The rising sun was seen on the wing tips of the airplanes."

Although martial law has not been declared officially, the city of Honolulu was operating under M-Day conditions.

It is entirely reported that enemy objectives under attack were Wheeler field, Hickam field, Kaneohe bay and naval air station and Pearl Harbor.

Some enemy planes were reported shot down.

The body of the pilot was seen in a plane burning at Wahiawa.

Oahu appeared to be taking calmly after the first spread of panic.

ANTIAIRCRAFT GUNS IN ACTION

First indication of the raid came shortly before 8 this morning when antiaircraft guns around Pearl Harbor began sending up a thunderous barrage.

At the same time a vast cloud of black smoke arose from the naval base and also from Hickam field where flames could be seen.

BOMB NEAR GOVERNOR'S MANSION

Shortly before 9:30 a bomb fell near Washington Place, the residence of the governor. Governor Poindexter and Secretary Charles M. Hite were there.

It was reported that the bomb killed an unidentified Chinese man across the street in front of the Schuman Carriage Co. where windows were broken.

C. E. Daniels, a welder, found a fragment of shell or bomb at South and Queen Sts. which he brought into the City Hall. This fragment weighed about a pound.

At 10:05 a. m. today Governor Poindexter telephoned to The Star-Bulletin announcing he has declared a state of emergency for the entire territory.

He announced that Edward L. Doty, city secretary of the major disaster council, has been appointed director under the M-Day law's provisions.

Governor Poindexter urged all residents of Honolulu to remain off the street, and the people of the territory to remain calm.

Mr. Doty reported that all major disaster council wardens and medical units were on duty within a half hour of the time the alarm was given.

Workers employed at Pearl Harbor were ordered at 10:10 a. m. not to report at Pearl Harbor.

The mayor's major disaster council was to meet at the city hall at about 10:30 this morning.

At least two Japanese planes were reported at Honolulu department headquarters to have been shot down.

One of the planes was shot down at Ft. Kamehameha and the other back of the Wahiawa

Hundreds See City Bombed

Hundreds of Honolulu men hurried to the top of Punchbowl soon after bombs began to fall, sur spread out before them the whole panorama of surprise attack and defense.

Far off over Pearl Harbor the white sky was polka-dotted with antiaircraft smoke.

Sailing away from the navy base were billowing clouds of white black smoke. Just above the smoke could be seen the dark puncture of the antiaircraft fire.

Out from the silver surfaced waters of the harbor's bottle of billowing black smoke was pouring out.

Names of Dead and Injured

Far off over Pearl Harbor the white sky was polka-dotted with antiaircraft and it injured.

The complete list will be corrected here. Here is a partial list: Peter Lopes, 24, of 3801 Kaimuki Rd. St., was reported at 9:30 a. m. to be in serious condition from wounds in the upper abdomen.

Matao Onuma, 23, 2745 Kalihi St., was injured on the left arm.

Au injuring thru a reporter assumed at hospital.

Schools Closed

All schools at Oahu, both public and private, will remain closed today, Superintendent of Public Instruction Oren E. Long announced. Announcement of whether schools will remain closed for the duration of the emergency will be made from time to time, he said.

Editorial

HAWAII MEETS THE CRISIS

Honolulu and Hawaii will meet the emergency of war today as Honolulu and Hawaii have met emergencies in the past—coolly, calmly and with immediate and complete support of the officials, officers and troops who are in charge.

Governor Poindexter and the army and navy leaders have called upon the public to remain calm; for civilians who have no essential business on the streets to stay off; and for everyone and woman to do his duty.

That request, coupled with the measures promptly taken to meet the situation that has suddenly and terribly developed, will be needed.

Hawaii will do its part—as a loyal American territory. In this crisis, every difference of race, creed and color will be submerged in the one desire and determination to play the part that Americans always play in crisis.

BULLETIN

Additional Star-Bulletin extras today will cover the latest developments in this war move.

The headlines of the Honolulu Star-Bulletin *newspaper scream the news of the December 7 Japanese aerial attack on the American military base at Pearl Harbor, Hawaii.*

Fifteen officers who were killed during the Pearl Harbor raid were laid to rest the following day, December 8, 1941. A marine rifle squad fires volleys over the graves. More than two thousand Americans lost their lives during the attack.

The crew of the USS Ward were cited for firing the first retaliatory shots on the morning of the Pearl Harbor raid. The crew of this destroyer spotted a Japanese submarine lurking just outside the harbor, fired, and sank it.

149

United States President Franklin Delano Roosevelt delivered a speech to Congress on December 8, 1941, following the attack on Hawaii, in which he asked for a formal declaration of war against Japan. Roosevelt favored entering the war earlier, however America's isolationist tendencies prevented him from sending aid to the Allies in Europe. The raid on Pearl Harbor, which Roosevelt called "a date which will live in infamy," gave him ample reason to join the effort to defeat the Axis powers. Below, American servicemen aboard the USS Wichita listen to President Roosevelt's address to Congress on the radio.

Following the attack on Pearl Harbor, residents of Hawaii feared the prospect of a food shortage. With a closure imposed on civilian ships running from the mainland, women lined up at the markets and bakeries to buy food and other necessary provisions. Eventually Hawaii created a food stamp rationing system, and residents planted victory gardens.

All civilians and off-duty military personnel were encouraged to evacuate Hawaii during the Second World War, after the raid on Pearl Harbor. Residents of Hawaii had the choice of whether to stay or go, but the wives and children of military employees were forced to leave. Evacuation and air-raid drills were carried out frequently during war times, to ensure preparedness in the case of a second attack.

Two children are shown with their government-issued gas masks. Everyone in Hawaii was given a gas mask, which they had to carry at all times. The American government promised punishment of a fine if civilians were caught without their gas masks. Also, all residents were told to blackout their homes and to build bomb shelters in their yards in case of another attack by the Japanese.

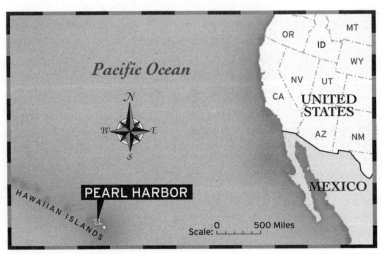

Map of western United States mainland and U.S. territory of Hawaii. Pearl Harbor is shown.

152

About the Author
★★★

Barry Denenberg is the author of several critically acclaimed books for young readers, including three books in the Dear America series, *When Will This Cruel War Be Over?: The Civil War Diary of Emma Simpson*, which was named an NCSS Notable Children's Trade Book in the Field of Social Studies and a YALSA Quick Pick; *So Far from Home: The Diary of Mary Driscoll, an Irish Mill Girl*; *One Eye Laughing, the Other Weeping: The Diary of Julie Weiss*; and two books in the My Name Is America series, *The Journal of William Thomas Emerson: A Revolutionary War Patriot* and *The Journal of Ben Uchida, Citizen 13559, Mirror Lake Internment Camp*. Praised for his meticulous research, Barry Denenberg has written books about diverse times in American history, from the Civil War to Vietnam.

Denenberg's nonfiction works include *An American Hero: The True Story of Charles A. Lindbergh*, which was named an ALA Best Book for Young Adults, and a New York Public Library Book for the Teen Age; *Voices from Vietnam*, an ALA Best Book for Young Adults, a *Booklist* Editor's Choice, and a New York Public Library Book for the Teen Age; and *All Shook Up: The Life and Death of Elvis Presley*. He lives with his wife and their daughter in Westchester County, New York.

Acknowledgments

The author would like to thank Kristen Eberle, Kerry McEneny, Daniel Martinez, Janelle Grey Kensmo, Kylie Kovita, Amy Griffin, Beth Levine, Lisa Sandell, Elizabeth Parisi, Chad Beckerman, Manuela Soares, Kate Lapin, Victoria Maher, and Jeanne Hutter.

Grateful acknowledgment is made for permission to reprint the following:

Cover Portrait: SuperStock

Cover Background: AP/Wide World

Page 142 (top): View of Pearl Harbor, Bishop Museum Archives.

Page 142 (bottom): Christmas in Honolulu, Bishop Museum Archives.

Page 143 (top): Japanese plane, Official U.S. Navy Photograph, now in the collections of the National Archives, Photo #80-G-182249.

Page 143 (bottom): Japanese officer, Official U.S. Navy Photograph, now in the collections of the National Archives, Photo #80-G-182248.

Page 144: Aerial view of attack on Pearl Harbor, U.S. Naval Historical Center Photograph, Photo #NH 50930.

Page 145 (top): U.S.S. *Arizona* under attack, Official U.S. Navy Photograph, now in the collections of the National Archives, Photo #80-G-40056.

Page 145 (bottom): View of Pearl Harbor raid from car window, Official U.S. Navy Photograph, now in the collections of the National Archives, Photo #80-G-33045.

Page 146 (top): Wheeler Field, U.S. Naval Historical Center Photograph, Photo #NH 50473.

Page 146 (bottom): Destroyed aircraft at Wheeler Field, Photograph from the Army Signal Corps Collection in the U.S. National Archives, Photo #SC 134872.

Page 147 (top): B-17E bomber at Hickam Field, Photograph from the Army Signal Corps Collection in the U.S. National Archives, Photo #SC 127002.

Page 147 (bottom): WASP volunteers and ambulance, *Star Bulletin,* November 20, 1943; War Depository Collection, University of Hawaii.

Page 148: Front Page of *Honolulu Star-Bulletin,* December 7, 1941–*Honolulu Advertiser*.

Page 149 (top): Officers' burial, Official U.S. Navy Photograph, now in the collections of the National Archives, Photo #80-G-32854.

Page 149 (bottom): U.S.S. *Ward* gun crew, Official U.S. Navy Photograph, from the collections of the Naval Historical Center, Photo #NH 97446.

Page 150 (top): President Roosevelt's address to Congress, UPI/Acme.

Page 150 (bottom): U.S. servicemen listening to President Roosevelt on the radio, Official U.S. Navy Photograph, now in the collections of the National Archives, Photo #80-G-464088.

Page 151 (top): Food line, *Star Bulletin,* December 8, 1941; War Depository Collection, University of Hawaii.

Page 151 (bottom): Evacuation of Pearl Harbor, *Star Bulletin,* November 5, 1943; War Depository Collection, University of Hawaii.

Page 152 (top): Children with gas masks, from the book *Pearl Harbor Child* by Dorinda Makanaonalani Nicholson, civilian survivor of the attack on Pearl Harbor.

Page 152 (bottom): Map by Jim McMahon.

Other Dear America books
by Barry Denenberg

When Will This Cruel War Be Over?
The Civil War Diary of Emma Simpson

So Far from Home
The Diary of Mary Driscoll, an Irish Mill Girl

One Eye Laughing, the Other Weeping
The Diary of Julie Weiss

My Name Is America books
by Barry Denenberg

The Journal of William Thomas Emerson
A Revolutionary War Patriot

The Journal of Ben Uchida
Citizen 13559, Mirror Lake Internment Camp

While the events described and some of the characters in this book may be based on actual historical events and real people, Amber Billows is a fictional character, created by the author, and her journal and its epilogue are works of fiction.

Library of Congress Cataloging-in-Publication Data available.

ISBN 0-493-32874-8;
ISBN 0-439-44575-2 (pbk.)

10 9 8 7 6 5 4 3 2 1   02 03 04 05 06

The display type was set in Minister Book.
The text type was set in New Aster.
Book design by Elizabeth B. Parisi
Photo research by Zoe Moffitt

Printed in the U.S.A. 23
First paperback printing, October 2002

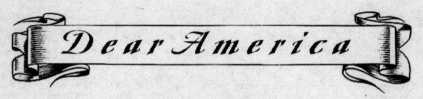

So Far from Home

The Diary of Mary Driscoll, an Irish Mill Girl

BY BARRY DENENBERG

SCHOLASTIC INC.

New York Toronto London Auckland Sydney
Mexico City New Delhi Hong Kong Buenos Aires

Skibbereen

County Cork, Ireland

1847

Thursday, April 1, 1847
Skibbereen, County Cork, Ireland

'Tis true.

I will be going to America.

I can remember when I first heard the name. AMERICA.

Visiting Aunt Nora, we were, just Ma and me. As far back as I could remember Kate and Da stayed behind. Ma would be baking morning and night, while Da smoked his pipe as if 'twas his last bowl. I could always smell a visit coming.

Before we left I'd work on my lessons. Aunt Nora was teaching me English. Ma was proud that Aunt Nora was a teacher and could read and write. Ma wished she could, too, I think.

To be sure, Aunt Nora was always glad to see us, she having no children of her own, only the children she taught.

I was eight the last time we visited. After that she left for America. 'Twas then I first heard the name.

Sitting on the beach, we were, watching the waves come in and breathing the fresh, salty ocean air. Aunt Nora loved the ocean.

"Come sit by me, Quiet One." She called me Quiet One because Kate, my older sister, was rarely still.

She motioned for me to come closer. I was thinking she was about to tell me a great secret. I scurried across the sand like a crab until I was as close as could be.

"Do you know where America is?" she whispered.

I didn't.

"Look out toward the horizon. What do you see?" she said.

"Only sea and sky," I answered. Try as I might 'tis all I saw.

"Can you see past the sea and the sky?" she asked.

I couldn't.

"There lies America," she said. "Past the Isle of the Blessed, where the mermaids bask on the rocks. Past the Land of the Lost, whose earthly forms cast no shadow."

I dared not move, charmed as I was by the sound of Aunt Nora's voice and the stories she told.

"Even past the Land of the Fallen Angels, where the seagull has no voice. There lies America. 'Tis a sacred place where everyone dresses in red, the color of magic, and the roads are paved with gold.

" 'Tis in America that you'll live someday, Quiet One."

Then Aunt Nora fell silent, worn out, it seemed, by the thought of this faraway land, this America.

I told Ma as soon as we returned to Aunt Nora's cottage, so excited was I by this news. Ma smiled and put her arms around me — she smelled of spice and honey. "Your aunt is as sweet as a whistle but there are times when her speech is more crooked than a ram's horn. Pay it no mind, Mary dear."

Now Aunt Nora's letters from America are the only bright spot in our lives. Ma and Da sit silently while I read them aloud. She writes of the opportunities in America and urges us all to join her. America, she says, is the land of hope.

She has sent a ticket for my passage along with this last letter. I can't help but think back to that day by the sea. I was thinking Ma was right, that 'twas just Aunt Nora's way of talking, and I paid it no mind. I never dreamt it might someday come true.

Friday, April 2, 1847
Skibbereen, County Cork, Ireland

I will be leaving in three weeks. Ma said it this morning, and I have been like a cat on scissors ever since.

Da was not pleased, though I am not sure why. Maybe 'tis because the family is being further scattered about. Maybe because Ma had not told him of her decision. He gave no sign.

His silence made me uneasy — as it always does. Relieved, I was, when Ma began speaking.

"All the girls are parting. Kate has been there

two years, and Nora six. 'Tis Mary's time now. My sister will look after her."

Da stood up, his pipe gripped tightly in his teeth, and walked to the door. "Fine, fly away then. At once, across the sea to America. 'Tis all anyone cares to talk about anymore. America. A place where people have lost their senses. I wish you Godspeed, daughter."

When Da was gone, Ma turned to me. I have never seen her look that way.

"Mary, you are no longer a child. Praise God you are young and strong. Go to America — 'tis our only hope."

Ma is right. I am strong. Although I am only fourteen — three years younger than my sister Kate — I do not mind. I have always depended on Ma and Da. Now 'tis my turn. I won't let them down.

Maureen is the only one I told. We've never had any secrets. She would like to go with me, but her family has no money for the passage. She said she will be lonely when I'm gone. 'Tis sad. I miss her already.

'Tis best I go. We are down to nothing. Once the potato provided us with all we needed. Now we are always hungry. 'Twas two years ago — I will never forget — when the fog came in and I heard the dogs. They could smell the foul odor. 'Twas warning us, they were, howling until the morning light.

At first Da was thinking soot had fallen on the potato crop. But the blackness spread to the dark green leaves and the purple blossoms. The leaves crumbled to ashes at his touch. When he dug down into the ground he discovered only a slimy mass of rotten potatoes. Fear in his eyes, there was.

Now there's not a loaf of bread in all Skibbereen. We line up for soup, but 'tis of poor quality and leaves us hungry just the same.

Our neighbors kill their animals to last another day. We have sold our furniture so we could have money for food.

Da talks of help coming from England, but Ma says that is foolishness. The English care nothing about the Irish. You can't get blood from a turnip, she says. I suspect she is right.

The roads are littered with lifeless souls wandering about. They look more like walking ghosts than flesh and blood. One funeral follows another. Fathers bury their daughters, wives their husbands — all without a tear being shed.

Now there is only an eerie silence. No cackling chickens disturb the morning silence. No dogs bark in the night — for they are either dead or too weak to cry out.

My hand is trembling as I write. I sleep little and wake often, soaked in a cold sweat.

The world is coming apart at the seams.

May God have mercy on our souls.

Wednesday, April 7, 1847
Skibbereen, County Cork, Ireland

Two more weeks. I thank Almighty God for Aunt Nora sending the money to bring me out. She is working hard in America, teaching her students, so I can come. I am fortunate to have such a generous aunt. She says the ticket is a gift from Kate as well, but I doubt if that's true. Kate is not one to share any of her wages with me. She has yet to send us money for food.

When I am settled in America, 'tis me who will be sending the money home so Ma and Da can join us.

Aunt Nora says there is a need for girls who wish to be maids-of-all-work in respectable homes — such as where Kate works. American girls do not care for that kind of work. 'Tis beneath them, she says.

Kate likes the work. She works for the wife of the mill agent, Mr. Abbott. Aunt Nora asks that I tell her if 'tis factory work I would be seeking. If 'tis she will talk to Kate. Aunt Nora is sure Mr. Abbott can help me find work in the mills.

Ma is relieved to know that Kate is getting on well, since we never hear from her.

Aunt Nora also asked that we write her what ship I will be on. She will be sure to meet me in Boston.

I would like to work in the mills. 'Tisn't for me

to be someone's servant, like Kate. A day's pay for a day's work, that's what I say.

Living in a rich lady's home is not for me. I don't like being at someone's beck and call. I'd rather know what my tasks are and then be left on my own. Even helping Ma with the chores I prefer it that way. When we still had the sheep I would do all the clipping. When Ma taught me to card and spin, I did it all on my own so Ma could tend to other things. The same with baking the bread and feeding the pigs. Lord knows, the work was never finished, but there was no one looking over my shoulder.

'Tis best I work in the mills. That will suit me. Aunt Nora writes that the pay is better in the mills, and the higher the wages, the faster we will all be together as a family.

Her letters make America sound filled with promise. 'Tis a place, she says, where a girl can work hard and be rewarded. 'Tis all I ask.

Monday, April 12, 1847
Skibbereen, County Cork, Ireland

All around us the landlords are evicting people. The Dalys had their cottage tumbled down three days ago. 'Twas brought to the ground in the wink of an eye. A frightful scene there was. Mrs. Daly was racing about clinging to her doorpost — the only thing remaining of her home.

Ma fears we will be next. If Mr. Hughes takes our cottage from us, we will have to turn to the poorhouse for relief. Ma says she will never allow that. She says that those who go in do not come out alive.

I can hear her sobbing at night, although I dare not stir.

We will be happy in America, God willing. I can hear it in Aunt Nora's letters.

Ma says it's counting our blessings we should be. Unlike those around us we are not ill. The Sweeneys are suffering from the black fever. Their youngest son has already died from the looseness and only nine, he was.

Monday a beggar woman came with her two young sons. She was covered only by a filthy sack and her mouth was stained green from eating grass. I was in the field looking for herbs. I was thinking that the two boys might be up to no good. They had the wild eyes, darting this way and that, trying to see if anyone was around. Ma was alone in the house. Da was off in hopes of catching a fish.

The beggar woman sat down on a pile of stones to rest. She looked tired, and her face, 'twas as white as a cloud. The boys threw themselves into the pigsty and began gobbling up what the pigs had left.

Ma came out to see what the noise was about. She hollered for the boys to leave, but they just stood there. Finally their mother rose up from the pile of stones and told them to stop.

The woman turned to Ma and asked, "Is there a bit of bread for the hunger?" She said her husband had been killed by a runaway horse, and she held up her arms to show the loose skin hanging from her bones.

Ma told her she had nothing to spare and sent her on her way.

I dared not look Ma in the eye. I know how hard 'twas for her to send the poor woman away. Ma has always been the first to help a neighbor in need. Now all that has changed. We must watch out for ourselves.

Thursday, April 15, 1847
Skibbereen, County Cork, Ireland

It has been two weeks since Da killed the pigs. That was the last meal that could be named such.

What I wouldn't do for just one spoonful of potatoes and buttermilk.

'Tis food that fills my dreams at night — a big bowl overflowing with a bubbling stew. Thick chunks of fish bobbing up in between large pieces of carrots, onions, and turnips. I barely have time to give thanks. But when I lift the first spoonful to my mouth, one of the chunks of fish turns into the head of a terrible snapping turtle and bites my lip. I awake terribly hungry.

When I get to America, I will eat and eat and never stop.

Thursday, April 22, 1847
Skibbereen, County Cork, Ireland

I have bundled what little I have. I fear 'tis not enough. The voyage can take a month or more.

I have said my good-byes and called on everyone we know in the village.

Maureen said she will miss me dearly. She is as shy as a flower, that one. A true friend like her I will never find. Mr. Connelly talked about what life in America would be like. I don't know how he knows about America since he's never been outside Skibbereen.

Mrs. Connelly made me some dried oatmeal cakes for the voyage. She said they will taste just fine dipped in hot tea. She gave me woolen stockings to keep my feet warm and a sleeping gown that closes in the front. Mrs. Connelly said that she was after speaking to any number of people, and she knows 'tis hard to lie in your sleeping berth and try to hook and eye from behind.

Not a word came from Da all night. He just sat there smoking his pipe. He's been like this since Kate left.

Father Mullaney provided the blessing.

By the time the Connellys and Father Mullaney were gone, Ma's eyes were brimming with tears. She searched my face with a look so fierce I could feel the heat. I am thinking she wanted to make sure to remember what I looked like for fear we would not see each other again.

I sat down on the bed next to her. She held my face in her hands and smiled. She told me she would miss me awfully and that she had prayed to Sweet Jesus every night that we would not have to say good-bye. "But," she said, "these are terrible times, and there are too many sad memories here already."

I told her I was not afraid, although I surely was. She said 'tis a strange and far-off land I am going to, but to be sure, the Holy Mother of God will watch over me. "Remember," she said. "The Blessed Lord would never close one gate without opening another."

All that night Ma's words sounded over and over. How much I will miss her.

'Tis Mr. Nevin taking me in the morning. He still has his horse and cart. That way we do not have to walk the thirty miles to Cork.

We leave at first light.

Atlantic Ocean

Friday, April 30, 1847
Cork, Ireland

There are more people on this boat than in all of Skibbereen. I swear to Almighty God there are. They are everywhere — running every which way, carrying their cases and dragging their frightened children behind them. 'Tis all I can do to make sure I am not trampled underfoot.

There was quite a scare when we boarded. I was huddling against the inside wall of the ship with my bundle to my chest, and humming the lullaby Ma always sang to me when I was a wee girl:

> *On the wings of the wind*
> *Over the dark rolling deep*
> *Angels are coming*
> *To watch over thy sleep*

While I was humming, one of the crewmen came by carrying a long pole with a sharp nail sticking out of one end. He poked the stick into the dark corners of the ship and called out. Looking for something, he was.

Soon he was joined by two others who used hammers and chisels to break open some barrels. They turned one of them upside down. A man was hiding inside. He cried for help, and they let him out. He begged them to let him stay on the ship. Fell to his knees and pleaded for mercy, he did. Said he didn't have money for his ticket.

They laughed and put him ashore just the same.

I gripped my ticket tighter, pulled my bundle closer, and set out to find a place to sleep. The berths were jammed top to bottom. I feared there was no place on the ship for me.

I am thanking the Lord a man and his wife saw my sorry state and asked me to join them. Mr. and Mrs. O'Donnell are from Killarney. Mrs. O'Donnell has shiny red cheeks and blue, blue eyes like Ma. They are going to America to be with their daughter Alice. Mrs. O'Donnell says that Alice is almost my age — she is thirteen — and looks just like me. Mr. O'Donnell laughed. He told Mrs.

O'Donnell that Alice is surely pretty but couldn't compare with a "beauty" like me. His speech made me blush.

They are traveling with others from Killarney.

My sleeping berth is crudely made of splintery wood planks. The ceiling is so low, only the children around me are able to stand without hitting their heads on the underside of the deck. There are crawling things in every corner.

When we left port people rushed on to the main deck to say farewell to Ireland. What's done is done, I thought, and stayed below.

Thursday, May 6, 1847
At Sea

We must all sleep one above the other and within arm's length. I dare not undress to change into my sleeping gown. My berth is so narrow and uncomfortable, I must sleep on my side. 'Tis difficult to write down here.

The O'Donnells have been kind enough to share their food with me. Today we had butter and bread. If it were not for them, I would be hungry most of the time. My hard-boiled eggs and the oatmeal cakes are already gone. I was unable to get any tea for the oatmeal cakes and had to eat them as brittle as they were. The ship's crew provides little to eat besides these awful biscuits.

Tonight the O'Donnells cooked a stew with the Corcorans. Everyone eats from the same kettle. The rolling of the boat caused the kettle to sway. The stew spilled over the sides and put out the fire. Thankfully I do not suffer from seasickness like so many around me.

The Corcorans have two pretty twin girls — Molly and Sophie — and Brendan, who is nine.

I asked Mrs. Corcoran how old the twins were, and they shouted out, "Guess!" I pretended to give the question great consideration. "Three," I said, and they shook their heads, delighted that they had fooled me on my first guess. Again I appeared lost in thought. "Two?" This caused even greater delight. 'Twas true I was going off track, leaving them no choice but to tell me. They looked at each other, deciding who would tell. "Seven," Molly said. "My, my," I said. "I have never met twins that old. Never in all my days."

"I'm the oldest," Molly said proudly.

The whole while Brendan kept his distance. He doesn't trust me, that one, but that's just because I'm a girl.

Mrs. Corcoran is fine company. She is lovely to talk to and spends most of her time watching the children. Mr. Corcoran reminds me of Da, smoking his pipe and keeping to himself. When the weather is fair he plays cards on deck.

I went up with the Corcorans this morning to have water pumped into our cans from the large barrels on deck. 'Tis barely enough to satisfy our thirst, and there is hardly any left for cooking. We save the cooking water and use it to wash.

One of the barrels leaked and another was undrinkable because it once held vinegar. 'Tis a shame because there is not enough to waste.

There are only two privies for all of us. Both are above deck at the front of the ship. 'Tis impossible to use them without becoming soaked from the wind and the spray.

Worse than the long wait and the drenching are the rats that are always lurking about. Mrs. O'Donnell tells me to make as much noise as possible in order to scare them off. I do, but they don't seem to be too afraid.

Many take care of this below decks. There is a constant foul odor down there. In good weather, the main decks are so crowded during the day that 'tis difficult to find a place to stand.

Mrs. O'Donnell has offered me the use of their chamber pot. She is so kind to watch over me. She showed me how to keep it clean. Once a day now I go up on deck, tie the chamber pot to a rope, and empty it over the side. Then I dip it into the ocean and pull it back up by the rope. Glad, I am, to be a help in some way.

The twins have taken a liking to me. I tell them a story every morning now. It helps pass the time. They are more easily entertained than Brendan. The wee girls, especially Molly, are bolder than their brother. He is timid as a fawn, that one. This morning we played hide-and-seek. The girls raced down the cluttered aisles and found many clever places to hide. When I found them, they shrieked with joy. But I never could find Brendan's hiding place. He only came out after I had given up. Mrs. Corcoran thanked me for playing with the children. She said that this sorrowful voyage is hardest on them. I think so, too. There is nothing to occupy their time and much that is bewildering.

A violent gale began two days ago. The ship has been rolling awfully ever since. The wind whips around, and the storm-tossed sea bursts upon the decks with terrible force. The waves are so fierce that they rush down into the lower decks. Everything is closed off below to keep the water out. I expect at any moment for the ship to cave in, sending us to the bottom of the salt-sea ocean. 'Tis like a dark, airless dungeon down here. Lord knows I am frightened, but I do my best to hide my fears so the children won't be any worse for it.

Last night I could hear Brendan crying out my name. The Corcorans' sleeping berth is not far from mine. I made my way to him as best I could. 'Twas so dark, I tripped over people who shouted angrily at me. I whispered, "Brendan," as loud as I dared. Finally I heard, "Mary, over here."

Poor boy. He says he wants to go home. I explained that he is going to a *new* home. A *better* home. But he was having none of it. "Why," he cried, "can't we go to my old home? What's the matter with my old home?" Then he buried his head in my lap and cried himself to sleep while I sang to him softly:

> *On the wings of the night*
> *May your fury be crossed*
> *May no one that's dear*
> *To our island be lost*
>
> *Blow the winds gently*
> *Calm be the foam*
> *Shine the light brightly*
> *To guide them back home*

Thursday, May 13, 1847
At Sea

Three days now have I been forced to stay below because of the storm. I was kept awake by Mr. O'Donnell, who is suffering from the ship fever. He moans day and night and cries out for water. I made my way slowly over to their berth and asked Mrs. O'Donnell if there was anything I could do. She shook her head and squeezed my hand. I stayed with her for a bit, both of us silent. After a while I could stay down there no longer and went above.

The wind had stopped, though 'twas still raining as fast as it could. I crawled under a sail that lay on deck, hoping 'twould protect me. After a time I felt another leg touching mine. 'Twas a boy. Older than me, to be sure. But there was barely enough light to see. I couldn't tell if his eyes were open or closed. Didn't I think that he was sleeping or just keeping still. I prayed he wasn't dead.

We stayed like that for the longest time. I dared not move or make a sound. I hardly took a breath.

Finally he spoke. "I'm Sean Riordan," said he, as if that were something to be proud of. I told him my name. Then silence. The rain had stopped. He said we should come out from under the sail — now that the storm had passed. He had a cheerful voice.

He showed me how to stretch the sail so we could catch the rainwater in a water can. Moved like a cat, he did. Cautiously.

"I'm going to find work in America," he said.

His uncle Patrick Quinn sent the money for his ticket. He has been living in Boston for five years now. He owns a tavern.

I told Sean about Aunt Nora and my plans to work in the mills.

"Do they hire Irish?" he asked.

I must have made a queer face.

"Some places don't hire Irish, you know," he said.

Sean said that someday he would like to be rich. What would I do if I were rich? he was asking.

"I would bring Ma and Da to America," I told him.

"And then?" he went on. "What would you do then?"

I told him I would live in a big house on a cliff overlooking the ocean. And I would spend my days watching the waves come in while the seals sunned themselves on the rocks.

"And you?" I asked.

He thought carefully and looked away before talking. He said he would bring everyone from Ireland to America. "That would leave the English with what they deserve, a country with no people."

Suddenly I felt cold. "I must be off," I said. I had been away too long. I had to go below and see how Mr. O'Donnell was faring.

Sean wanted to lend a hand, but I said no, I thought it best I go alone.

Monday, May 17, 1847
At Sea

Mr. O'Donnell is still feverish.

I sat with Mrs. O'Donnell while she wiped his damp brow with a cloth. He sleeps most of the day, thank the Lord.

Mrs. O'Donnell is knitting a sweater for her daughter whom they haven't seen in two years. She is living with a family in Boston. Mrs. O'Donnell says 'twas best for the child. 'Tis certain she misses Alice greatly. I think this is why she has been so kind to me.

She said it must have been hard for Ma to let me go to America. "'Tis hard for all the mothers," she said. The O'Donnells are eager to see their daughter again. "We will make it all up to her then," she said, though I am not sure of her meaning. She went on for some time. Mrs. O'Donnell says I am very patient for a wee girl. I suppose I am. I like listening to people, if that's what she means by patient. Besides, I told her, I'm not a wee girl. I'm fourteen.

Wednesday, May 19, 1847
At Sea

I can't write down below. 'Tis too dark, and I can find no peace. At least on deck 'tis light.

There are times during the night when I awake with the shivers and can't breathe. There is no air, and it feels as if there is a heavy weight sitting on my chest. When that happens I can never go back to sleep.

Thursday, May 20, 1847
At Sea

Mr. O'Donnell is worse each day. God bless him, there is no doctor on board. No one to turn to for help.

Friday, May 21, 1847
At Sea

Each morning when I hear Molly and Sophie coming, I pretend I am still sleeping. They scream and jump in my berth to wake me.

They are the first twins I have ever known. Just because they look alike you think they would be alike, but they are not. Sophie is quiet and serious and doesn't like to be away from her ma. Molly is more playful than her sister. Being with them helps with the boredom of the voyage and brings me the deepest joy.

Monday, May 24, 1847
At Sea

I am tired.

I fear I might fall over my own shadow. I can barely walk without stopping to catch my breath.

When Molly and Sophie came to wake me this morning they brought the bouncing balls Sean had found for them. But I couldn't play. I was too weak to even tell them a story. Sadly I had to send them back to Mrs. Corcoran.

Sean came to see me but I sent him away, too.

Wednesday, May 26, 1847
At Sea

I am dizzy. 'Tis a trial to write. I thought 'twas because of the hunger. This morning the dizziness was so bad I couldn't walk. My body is on fire. My throat is sore, and my lips dry and cracked.

I fear I have gotten the ship fever. First Mr. O'Donnell, and now will it take me, too?

35

'Twas nothing anyone could do for him. None of the crew is any help. Sean is right, they care nothing for us.

Mrs. O'Donnell is overcome with grief. She is not feeling well herself at all. She asked me to go with Mr. O'Donnell when they put him out to sea. She did not want him to be alone. Mrs. Corcoran and the children are staying below.

I did as she asked, although if truth be told, I was weak as a kitten. I was afraid. Sean came with me. We stood by as the crewmen wrapped Mr. O'Donnell in an old canvas sailcloth. They placed a great stone at his feet and sewed up the sailcloth. The ship's bells were tolling as he was slipped overboard into the sea.

I said a prayer for him before returning to my berth.

At Sea

At times I don't know if 'tis day or night down here. I sleep so poorly. There is little light from the one swinging lantern. 'Tis nearly impossible to write.

At Sea

The awful creaking of the timbers. All night long.

By my faith, maybe I won't live to see America. Maybe Aunt Nora is wrong.

'Tis a long voyage, and I feel so far from home.

Monday, May 31, 1847
At Sea

I miss the children. Sean says they are asking why they can't see me. They want to know when I'll be all better.

Sean brought me some tea and a slice of bread with sugar on top.

'Tis a miracle because there is little food left and no tea. But a friend of Sean's uncle gave him some whiskey before he departed. To be sure, it has come in handy. Sean traded the whiskey for the tea and bread. Said the cook was most happy with the trade, thinking he had gotten the better of the deal. I laughed. I can't remember the last time I laughed.

Merciful Son of God, I have been spared.

My fever has passed.

Sean said he feared I would not recover. "The Holy Ghost looks after me," I told him.

We all went up on deck where Sean played his

fiddle. Sophie, Molly, and Brendan held hands and danced round and round while Mr. and Mrs. Corcoran clapped. Two of the sailors were tapping their feet as they mended the sails and tarred the ropes.

'Twas raining lightly, and Mr. Corcoran put his pipe upside down to keep it dry. Just like Da.

Monday, June 7, 1847
At Sea

The good Lord God took Mrs. O'Donnell today. 'Twas the ship fever. Once Mr. O'Donnell died she seemed to give up all hope.

I told Sean that somehow I had to find Alice O'Donnell when we arrived in Boston. The O'Donnells looked after me like I was their own. I must repay their kindness.

I can't bear the thought that the poor child will never see them again. She must know all they went through to be with her. 'Twas so sad it made me cry, something I never do.

I don't like to cry.

There is a man selling dolls. How I wished we were able to get one for Molly and Sophie. 'Twould so help make their time pass more pleasantly.

Sean came to see us this morning. He had something behind his back and a big grin on his face. The twins knew whatever he had was for them. They tried to see what it might be while Sean twisted this way and that. Molly and Sophie squealed with delight when Sean finally gave them the doll. I dare not ask where he got it.

Today Brendan said that Sean is going to teach him how to whistle.

The weather was fair today, and the captain allowed lines to be strung between the masts. I helped Mrs. Corcoran with the wash. We had to use sea water, which gives no suds. We did the best we could, beating the clothes against the decks. Mrs. Corcoran told me to be sure to shake them out once they were dry. This is to rid the salt from the sea water. She said they would burn our skin if we didn't.

Friday, June 11, 1847
At Sea

Mr. Corcoran was beaten by one of the crew two days ago. He lies in his berth all day and isn't speaking. No one knows what happened.

Sunday, June 13, 1847
At Sea

Sean heard one of the crew talking about Mr. Corcoran. He was found smoking his pipe below decks. Sean says the crewman talked about a fire aboard another ship earlier this year. The fire was put out and the ship returned to Cork. No one was hurt. 'Twas started by someone smoking in his berth. Just like Mr. Corcoran. There have been reports of fires on other ships bound for America. Ships that were lost at sea, with everyone perishing.

I am sorry for Mr. Corcoran, but not sorry his smoking below decks has stopped. Imagine the whole lot of us sinking because Mr. Corcoran was smoking his pipe.

Tuesday, June 15, 1847
At Sea

Sean put aside water so that we can wash before we reach Boston. We barely have enough to drink, down to a cup a day, we are, so it seems foolish to worry about washing. But Sean says his uncle warned him that your troubles are not over once you've reached harbor. If the authorities think you are ill, they will place you in quarantine or worse, send you back to Ireland.

The thought of being returned to Ireland after all this time and all I've been through is more than I can bear.

Thursday, June 17, 1847
At Sea

There is talk we are nearing land.

Many of the passengers are buying tickets for the lottery. They are trying to see who can guess when land will be sighted. A ticket is sold for each hour of the day. Those who have tickets for days past try to buy tickets for upcoming days. Tickets for daylight hours fetch the highest price. Especially the early-morning hours, when land is most likely to be spotted. Whoever has the winning ticket gets all the money.

Friday, June 18, 1847
At Sea

The ship is buzzing with excitement. Word is spreading like wildfire.

Mr. Corcoran has heard the rumors that we are nearing America. Now he stands on deck all day, one hand holding his ticket, the other the railing. He stares straight ahead, waiting. I don't know where he gets the strength.

Sunday, June 20, 1847
At Sea

Sean saw seaweed floating on the surface of the ocean.

We are indeed nearing land. Sweet Jesus, it's been so long, I dare not hope.

At long last, land.
Just saying the word. Land.
I feel like I've been on this ship for all eternity.

Lowell, Massachusetts

Glory be to God.

'Tis true.

America.

You could see it.

Everyone who could walk rushed up on deck, bringing their bundles and their cases with them. Many fell to their knees and gave thanks to the Lord in heaven. Others wept and embraced those around them as tears ran down their cheeks.

'Tis over, this horrible voyage is over.

My new life is about to begin. I give thanks to the Lord who mercifully granted me the good fortune to see this day.

Many were not so fortunate.

Wednesday, June 23, 1847
Boston

So much has happened. I must try to write.

When the medical officer and the other men

boarded the ship, the celebration ended. Everyone crowded together on deck, thinking the nearness would protect us.

The men stretched ropes across the ship so that there was only enough room for one person at a time to walk. They went to calling out names. Those whose names were called walked between the ropes to where the medical officer stood waiting. And quickly he worked. Those he judged healthy were allowed to leave. Those he thought ill or feverish were stopped and questioned.

One wee boy was found to be infected. His mother begged to remain with him. But her pleas were for naught. The boy was too sick to even cry out and was carried away. 'Twas his poor mother they held back. But little enough could they do to hold back her shrieks, which stabbed the air.

I tried not to watch but my eyes were fixed, like a moth to the flame.

Saddest of all were the Corcorans. First the medical officer examined the twins and Brendan. 'Tis a miracle the children have never had a day's sickness since the voyage began. Mrs. Corcoran looked drained but was not feverish. They were allowed to pass.

Then came Mr. Corcoran. He was having trouble standing. The medical officer was asking him questions but no answer was coming. He wasn't even looking at the officer. Looking right past him, he was, to America. He was still clutching his losing lottery ticket in his hand.

Suddenly he was pushed to the side and before anything could be done, he was led away. I began to move forward to help, but Sean was grabbing my arm. Mrs. Corcoran looked confused. Everything was happening so fast.

"Be on your way!" one of the men shouted. Mrs. Corcoran carried Sophie, while Brendan took Molly by the hand, and they made their way down to the wharf.

How will they find each other? I thought. What will happen to Mr. Corcoran? Where was he being taken?

"Mary Driscoll," the man called out.

"Go," Sean whispered. "Be brave."

Trembling, I was, while the doctor looked in my

eyes. He asked me to open my mouth and hold out my tongue. I prayed that I showed no signs of the fever. He was standing close and looking at me. His eyes were coal black and as hard as flint. Afraid to look at him, I was, but afraid not to. If I looked away he would think I did have something to hide.

Finally he looked down, wrote something on a piece of paper, put a blue tag on my shawl, and told me to move along.

Sean said to wait and not to let anyone help me no matter what. His uncle warned him that the runners will steal from you or try to take you to one of the boardinghouses. Then they will demand to be paid for their service. "America," he said, "is no place for a fool."

I waited for Sean while keeping a sharp eye out for Aunt Nora.

'Twas chaos all around me. Passengers streaming off the boat, people being greeted by their families and friends. 'Twas a scene of wildest excitement, I promise you that. Everyone running after one thing or the other. I didn't see how Aunt Nora would ever find me. But I stayed rooted to the spot just the same.

Suddenly a man appeared out of nowhere.

He snatched the bundle from my arms and told me he would be pleased to find me proper lodgings.

"We have no need of your services," someone behind me was saying. 'Twas Sean and with him, his uncle. Mr. Quinn was not as tall as Sean, but as thick as a stone wall, he was. His face wore a terrible look. He told the man we didn't need aid of any kind from the likes of him. Praise God, the man dropped the bundle, turned, and disappeared into the crowd.

I was still not seeing Aunt Nora. The docks had emptied. Only a few sailors and stragglers were still about. The sky was turning dark. "We must leave soon," Sean was saying. Where was it but to Aunt Nora's that I had to go? Why she was not there to meet me only God can say. What would I do? I didn't even know Kate's address.

I couldn't leave until Aunt Nora came. "Go on without me," I said. "I will be all right."

Sean said he would not be going without me. He would stay all night if waiting was my choice. "But," he said, "'tis a foolish thing to do."

Sean's uncle said 'twas not likely my aunt would be coming at this late hour. Missed connections are common now that so many Irish are coming to America. Sometimes a ship is late or a letter gets lost. He promised to place a notice in the Irish newspaper. "All will turn out well in the end, young lady," he assured me.

Mr. Quinn urged me to allow him to take me to his home for some food and a good night's rest. I was hungry and tired to the bone. I was sorely in need of shelter for the night. "'Tis a long road that has no turning," he said gently.

I accepted his kind offer.

The roads are not paved with gold as Aunt Nora said. I asked Sean's uncle if we would be coming upon them soon, and he laughed heartily.

There is so much to see and hear. The tall houses with their spires and chimney tops are piled one on top of the other. Everything is bigger than back in Skibbereen. The roads are filled with people rushing around, moving so fast — and all at the same time. Not one slowed to rest. Carts and carriages of every shape and size drive wildly, their warning bells ringing out. No one pays any mind.

They barely look before stepping into the road, the carriages flying past their noses.

Everywhere I looked there were Irish. 'Tis a wonder there are any of us left in Ireland. They seemed as worn and hungry as those I left behind in Skibbereen. Some were begging for food. Some were standing on the street corners. Still others simply stared out from doorways. Far from the kings and queens I expected to see dressed in their robes of red.

Friday, June 25, 1847
Boston

Sean's uncle was able to find out where Alice O'Donnell was living from a man he knows at his tavern. 'Tis a miracle if you ask me. We found the building, but there were so many rooms we didn't know where to begin.

Finally a man came out and told Mr. Quinn that Alice O'Donnell was in the cellar. She earned her keep doing the wash for a family with a flock of children that lives upstairs.

God help her, the poor child was curled up asleep on a mattress when we found her. 'Twas so damp, the mattress was soaked and her clothes were wet. Not a ray of light and precious little air to breathe down there.

When Mr. Quinn woke her, she opened her eyes wide. I could see the fear within. I reached for her, hoping she would take my hand. She made no move. 'Twasn't because of the fear. The poor child could not see.

Why Mrs. O'Donnell did not tell me her daughter was blind only the Lord can say. Her conditions, along with the state she was living in, grieved me terribly.

Mr. Quinn kept his wits about him. He told Alice O'Donnell we were her friends and we had come to help her. He asked if she could speak, but she said not a word. 'Twas plain for all to see she was horribly treated. Mr. Quinn and Sean left to find the family she worked for, while I tried to talk to her.

Alice O'Donnell remained crouched in the corner, her knees up to her chin, holding herself and rocking. I wanted dearly to find the right words to say. I wanted to tell her I knew her family and that she could trust me, but wasn't I afraid. How would I answer if she asked where they were? When they would be coming for her?

Gently I touched her hand, but she pulled back. I tried again, but still she withdrew. I didn't know if I were scaring her more than she already was. 'Twas then I decided to sing, hoping Ma's lullaby might soothe her:

> *On the wings of the wind*
> *Over the dark rolling deep*
> *Angels are coming*
> *To watch over thy sleep*
>
> *Angels are coming*
> *To watch over thee*
> *So list' to the wind*
> *Coming over the sea*
>
> *Hear the wind blow*
> *Hear the wind blow*
> *Lean your head over*
> *Hear the wind blow*

Still singing, I tried once more to touch her hands. I could see that some of the fear had fallen from her eyes. This time she let me stroke her fingers and press her hands in mine. She was listening carefully now to every sound. I could tell by the way she cocked her head. Slowly she reached out with her other hand and searched the air for my face. I leaned forward, and she found my chin. Then she felt for my mouth and my eyes. She stroked my hair, trying to see how long 'twas.

Then we both heard steps. 'Twas Sean and his uncle. Alice's hand remained in mine.

I don't know what Mr. Quinn said to the family, but when he returned he was pacing up and down like a caged animal. He said that Alice O'Donnell would be leaving with us. She would stay with him and his wife until it could be decided what was best for her. Then he looked at me. I wasn't sure what he wanted me to do.

I told Alice that we were her friends. That I had just come from Ireland. She felt my face again. I told her my name and promised that no harm would come to her.

She was tilting her head again. I wished she would talk to me. She moved her hand across my face, feeling the tears falling down my cheeks. "My name is Alice," she said in a whisper, and we stood up to leave.

Thursday, July 8, 1847
Lowell

Aunt Nora never received the letter telling her what ship I would be on. 'Twas only when she saw the notice in *The Pilot* — the one placed by Mr. Quinn — that she knew I was in America and sent Kate to get me.

As soon as Kate arrived at Mr. Quinn's, she made it plain that she was wanting to leave. So I hurried along as best I could.

Aunt Nora was unable to come herself. The journey would be too much for her bad leg. If only I had known 'twas Kate coming in her place, I would have found a way to get to Lowell on my own, to be sure.

" 'Tis glad I am to see my little sister after all

this time," Kate said. But she appeared to be no more glad about it than I.

The stagecoach ride to Lowell was a rocky one. The two men who journeyed with us seemed to welcome Kate's chatter. My sister still talks without end, choosing to use two words when one would do. Her favorite subject is still herself.

In that way Kate has changed little in the past two years. But she looks and sounds like a different girl. She fixes her hair in a braided crown now and dresses with great care. (She was wearing a fancy white dress.) She speaks with a wee singsong voice that sounds make-believe — like she were a fairy-tale princess. Everyone was always fooled by that round, milk-white, innocent-looking face, even Ma. But not me. My sister has two faces — one she wears on the outside, and one she wears when she thinks no one is looking. I can see she has taken easily to the ways of this new world. 'Tisn't surprising.

She went on and on about Mrs. Abbott. Mrs. Abbott and her children are visiting relatives in Philadelphia. Mr. Abbott is the agent for the Merrimack Mills. 'Tis thanks to him I will be working there. Kate said it was very kind of Mrs. Abbott to allow her to travel all the way to Boston to "fetch" me — like I were the hen for that night's supper. Proud, she is, that Mrs. Abbott favors her above the others. Mrs. Abbott considers Kate to be trustworthy. "Unlike other Irish," my sister said.

When she first went to work for Mrs. Abbott, she was cleaning and discovered a dollar under one of the beds. Kate had been warned that this was something Yankee women do. Mrs. Abbott had placed the dollar there on purpose — just to see if Kate would be tempted. That afternoon she gave her the dollar, telling Mrs. Abbott that someone must have accidentally dropped it under the bed and that she hoped Mrs. Abbott would be able to return it to its rightful owner.

"Aren't you an angel," Mrs. Abbott told Kate.

Kate lectured me about all the things Mrs. Abbott has taught her: how to set the table, where to place the wineglasses. She has learned how to polish fruit properly and arrange flowers. Kate says Mrs. Abbott likes everything just so. I would think she does.

There are times when Mrs. Abbott speaks to Kate like a friend. My sister is quite proud of this.

Mrs. Abbott also employs two cooks and a lady from England who looks after the Abbott children.

'Twas dark when we arrived in Lowell. We went in the back door and up the stairs — Mrs. Abbott does not allow the servants to use the front door — and down the hall to Kate's room.

Kate said that Aunt Nora picked a fine time to take to bed. 'Tis a great burden for her to take me to the mills in the morning, that much is plain. I don't know what to do. I would go myself, to be sure, but I don't know where they are or how to get there. We are going to see Mr. Fowler. He works for Mr. Abbott as the overseer.

I awoke at dawn. The early morning light was just beginning to come through the window. Not even a bird was awake. I was terribly confused. 'Twas like I was in a dream. I wanted to find a place to write because so much has happened.

Slowly I left the bed, being sure not to disturb Kate, who was still asleep in the bed beside me. I opened the door and went into the hall. I stopped and listened, but heard no sound other than my own breathing.

I found myself standing in front of the door that leads to Mrs. Abbott's bedchamber. Mrs. Abbott is away, I remembered Kate saying. No one would be in there. My curiosity was greater than my fear. I went in.

The room is big. A wide, white bed that has a white cloth stretched above it is in one corner. It looks like a heavenly carriage. Opposite the bed is a window framed by folds of blue shiny cloth. I parted the cloth and looked down on a beautiful garden enclosed by a white fence. This, I thought, must be what a garden in paradise looks like. *This* is what I pictured America to be.

The walls of the room are covered with paper. Different pleasant scenes are shown: animals in the forest, flowers in the field, and a picnic by the lake. Along one wall where the picnic is, I saw the most comfortable-looking ruby-red cushioned chair. I ran my hand over the cloth. 'Twas soft — like the fur of a baby animal. I sat down carefully and put my arms on the arms of the chair. I felt like a queen. I wondered what 'twould be like to live in this house.

Across the room is a tall chest of drawers with an oval mirror framed in swirling dark wood on top.

I went over to it. Lying on the top was a box made of different woods, some light, some dark. They were put together in a way that made a pattern. 'Twas an A for Abbott. The wood was smoother than any I have ever seen or touched. The box gleamed like still water reflecting the moonlight. What treasures, I wondered, would be kept in such a precious box? I hesitated, but I could not stop myself. I opened the box, not knowing what to expect.

Will you look at that, I thought. Jewelry. Lying on the rose-colored cloth within were shiny rings, golden bracelets, strings of pearls, and red and green necklaces. Even in the weak light of the coming dawn the contents of the glorious box shimmered, sparkly and golden. I gently pulled out a long, silver necklace with square green stones dangling along its length. I put it around my neck and looked in the mirror. I saw my face for the first time in a long while. My, how thin I look. I touched my cheeks. There is barely any skin on my bones.

What if these were my jewels and 'twas *I* who was preparing to dress for the evening?

Then I heard something.

The floorboards above were creaking. Someone was up and about. I closed the box and held my breath. I stood frozen, unable to move. What if someone heard me? Or saw me come into the room? What would they do to me? Why had I come in here? I should have known better.

Be still, a voice within me warned. I knew that if I were found out there would be the devil to pay. Perhaps 'twas just someone stirring in the night. Perhaps 'twas my imagination. I had heard nothing since. I was afraid to leave the room, but I knew the longer I stayed the worse 'twould be. The sky was growing lighter with every moment I delayed.

I turned the doorknob slowly and pulled the door toward me. Thank the Lord, it made no sound.

Being careful to close the door behind me I, tiptoed quietly and quickly down the hall and back to the room before anyone saw me. Kate, praise God, was still sleeping soundly. I crouched down by the window to get the light. I am writing quickly, not knowing how long 'twill be before my sister awakes.

Friday, July 9, 1847
Lowell

Mrs. Abbott's house is so near the mills we were able to walk there. On the way Kate reminded me to be polite and respectful.

I told her I hoped I would be acceptable, which caused her to laugh.

She said I should not concern myself with that. "The Yankee girls are leaving faster than they are coming," she said. "Mr. Abbott is eager to replace them with as many Irish girls as he can because the Irish won't complain about things the way the Yankee girls do."

What "things"? I wondered, but spoke not a word.

The bright redbrick building is so tall, it seems to reach the sky. I never dreamed earthly hands could make anything that big. It looked to me like all the people in Ireland could fit inside. 'Twas like a fortress. There were smokestacks blowing their blackness heavenward and darkening the sky.

I felt cold although the day was warm. A shudder rippled through my body. There is nothing to be afraid of, I told myself. What could be worse than what I had already seen back in Ireland?

I had to go through those gates.

The guard led us to see Mr. Fowler. He is the oddest-looking man. Bald as a crow, he is. The sunlight from the window above fell on his hairless head, causing it to glow.

Kate told him that I was Mary Driscoll, the girl Mr. Abbott mentioned. I think she was ashamed to say I was her sister. Mr. Fowler looked at me like that doctor did in Boston Harbor. I wonder, does everyone in America look at you this way?

Could I write my name? he asked. I told him I could. He handed me a paper and showed me where to sign, which I did without reading what it said. I was too afraid.

I start Monday in spinning room number three.

Kate left just as soon as she delivered me to Aunt Nora. "Only Irish live in the Acre," she said as we neared. 'Tis plain she doesn't like being in this part of Lowell. In such a rush, she was, that her heels nearly touched her head when she left.

The Acre is not far from the mills but it might as well be on the other side of the ocean. The roads are narrow, twisting, and muddy — not like the roads where Mrs. Abbott lives. The houses are crowded together, and goats, geese, chickens, and pigs roam everywhere. There are no houses such as Mrs. Abbott's in the Acre.

There must be two Lowells. One where Mrs. Abbott lives and one where Aunt Nora lives.

Perhaps there are two Americas.

'Twas sad to see that Aunt Nora uses a cane because of her bad leg. "Don't let it trouble you, child," she said when I asked her how she was feeling. "First come and give us a hug. Hasn't it been ever so long a time. I've missed you terrible. Why, bless us and save us, Quiet One, 'tis a pure joy to behold your angelic face. How lovely you've become. I've been as lonely as a church mouse these past six years. But now that you are here I'll be lonely no more."

Seeing Aunt Nora made me feel safe for the first time since I left home.

I am glad my coming to America is a help and not a burden.

I held back the tears from my eyes. Aunt Nora said that she knew it must be hard but that we would care for each other.

Just then the Delaneys came home. They are Aunt Nora's boarders.

Mrs. Delaney is old. Her face wears a thousand wrinkles, and her hair looks matted and dirty. Her son, John, looks like he wouldn't say boo to a goose.

"She's afflicted with the kind of complaint no one can understand," Aunt Nora said after they had gone into the other room.

Mrs. Delaney helps Aunt Nora care for the two pigs. Once in a while she gives a good sweeping to the kitchen. Mr. Delaney disappeared two years ago, and she and John have been staying with Aunt Nora ever since.

"Mr. Delaney was the laziest rogue that ever wore clothes and was fed," Aunt Nora said. She thinks Mrs. Delaney is better off without him. "Now he won't be pourin' the family's money down his throat all day. But she was left with a heavy handful."

It's her son, John, that Aunt Nora calls a heavy handful. "The boy's a little daft, though not totally useless. 'Twas him that whitewashed the cottage. And all by himself I might add. But he acts like something that fell of a tinker's cart and was never missed."

John seems harmless just the same. He has found work north of here. He leaves in the morning. My aunt can be a harsh judge when she has a mind to.

There are only two rooms. The Delaneys sleep on the floor in one and Aunt Nora and me in the bed in the kitchen. Beside the bed there are two benches, a table, and a rocking chair near the fireplace. Aunt Nora is proud of the large stone fireplace at the end of the room. She said 'tis a great comfort come winter. Winters can be fierce, she says. There is only one tiny window to let light in.

Aunt Nora urged me to go to bed. I told her I wanted to talk some more. I wanted to tell her about Alice O'Donnell. She said I could barely keep my head up, which was a fact, and that there would be plenty of time tomorrow.

Saturday, July 10, 1847
Lowell

'Twas the best night's sleep I've had in a long, long time.

I dreamed Molly and Sophie were safe at home. But not Brendan. I didn't know where he was and decided to look for him. 'Twas getting darker by the minute. I didn't want to leave the twins alone, but I had no choice. I had a serious talk with them. Got down on one knee, I did, so I could look both in the eyes. I told them I was going to look for Brendan. That he should have been home by now. They nodded like they understood but they can fool you, those little ones. I told them they had to promise not to leave and not to open the door for anyone, no matter what. I got up, put on my cloak, and wrapped it tight around me, for the night was cold. I turned to take one last look at their shiny faces. They smiled and said, "No matter what, Mary, no matter what," and then giggled. Then I awoke.

Aunt Nora was sitting in her rocking chair. It took me a while to remember where I was. Mrs. Delaney and her son were nowhere to be seen, praise God. I so wanted to talk to Aunt Nora about Alice O'Donnell.

I was only going to say a little. But once I began there was no stopping me. It just came spilling out. Aunt Nora, bless her heart, listened patiently while I told her the sad tale.

When I was done she asked if Mr. Quinn knew what had happened to cause the poor girl to find herself so all alone. I told her that he thought she must have come to America with someone. That her family must not have been able to care for her properly back in Ireland. They must have believed she would be better off in America. I remember Mrs. O'Donnell saying that. That 'twould be for the best. Mr. Quinn thinks whoever was with Alice O'Donnell did not survive the passage.

I told Aunt Nora that I could not bring myself to tell Alice about her ma and da. I pray that I made the right decision.

Sunday, July 11, 1847
Lowell

I don't have to go to church today. Aunt Nora said 'tis better I rest.

I am to be at the mills by five-thirty tomorrow morning. If I am late the main gates will be closed and I will have to enter through the counting house.

'Twould not be good to be late on my first day.

Monday, July 12, 1847
Lowell

Spinning room number three takes up the whole floor. There are long rows of machines lined up, one next to the other, as far as the eye can see. There are girls tending to them up and down the aisles. I cannot say how many machines there are, but there must be hundreds. Of that I am certain. Each was making the most awful hissing and whizzing sounds. This devilish noise came rushing down all around me like an endless waterfall. The sound was so great that the floor beneath my feet trembled. I could feel the thunderous sound come up my legs. I feared I would cry out and run from the room, just to be rid of it. God help me.

Mr. Fowler said that one of the girls would teach me my tasks. 'Twas nearly impossible to hear what he was saying. He had to holler right into my ear. He pulls on his red mustache and mops his damp brow with a handkerchief while he talks.

He warned me not to daydream. 'Tis important to pay strict attention at all times and not to hold up the girls.

I spied one of the Yankee girls watching me while Mr. Fowler yelled into my ear. She gave me quite a start. Seeing her was like looking into a mirror. She has the same green eyes and the same honey-red hair I do. Lucky girl, she does not have freckles. She looks older, maybe seventeen. Most of the girls look older than me.

The girl looked at me in a gentle way. (Many of the girls were not looking at me so gently.) My prayers were answered when Mr. Fowler called her over. She was waiting for his signal. Her name is Annie Clark. Mr. Fowler left us alone and returned to his desk at the far end of the room. He walks with his hands held behind his back, standing stiff and straight, like he must have swallowed a crowbar.

Annie Clark explained that I am to be a bobbin girl. She showed me the wooden crates on rollers where the empty bobbins are kept and how to doff the bobbins when they are filled with the spun yarn. Then I take them off the spinning frame and replace them quickly with empty ones. I must hurry so the spinning frames are not stopped long. While there are no bobbins to change, I can sit quietly and wait.

There are four or five other Irish girls who do the same thing. The others are Yankee girls.

A bell rang in the middle of the day, and Annie

said she would be going to dinner. She showed me where I could sit outside.

I watched her join the other Yankee girls who were streaming back into their boardinghouses while I ate the hard-boiled egg Aunt Nora had fixed. The girls are as fine as fine, one prettier than the next. And they wear the sweetest dresses. I wish I had something to wear besides these rags.

The boardinghouses are made of redbrick, just like the mills, but they are much smaller. There is row upon row of them, lined up neatly just across the canal. They are pretty, just like the girls who live there. I wonder what 'tis like inside.

Friday, July 16, 1847
Lowell

I have been too tired to write. Perhaps I will be able to on Sunday, my only day of rest.

Sunday, July 18, 1847
Lowell

Went to St. Patrick's for the first time with Aunt Nora. She sings in the choir, and 'tis a beautiful voice she has.

Tuesday, July 20, 1847
Lowell

A letter from Sean.

He and his uncle have found a convent in Arlington where Alice will be cared for. Mr. Quinn believes she is in the proper hands now, and he will keep watch over her.

Sean has had difficulty finding work. His first job was a long way from Boston. So many Irish were seeking work there that the promised wages were lowered to sixty-five cents a day. Sean said they had to take what was offered. There were plenty of men ready to take their places.

Sean found work in Somerville. The wages are

better, but the work is difficult due to the heat of the day and the swamp nearby.

He gives me no address. I do have Mr. Quinn's address in Boston so I can write him if necessary. I am glad that Alice O'Donnell is safe. By now she must know about her ma and da. Before I left Boston, Mr. Quinn asked me what I had decided, to tell Alice or not. Truth is I hadn't decided anything. I think Mr. Quinn could see that. "Leave it in my hands," he had said, and I was glad to do just that.

Saturday, July 24, 1847
Lowell

Kate visited today. She was having tea with Aunt Nora when I returned from the mills. Saturday work is only a half day.

As always Kate had much news about herself.

In three weeks she is going away with Mrs. Abbott to visit Mrs. Abbott's sister. She lives in Boston but spends her summers in Rhode Island. Mrs. Abbott has decided to join her because 'tis near the ocean and therefore much cooler.

Kate boasts about how much Mrs. Abbott needs her. Yankee ladies, she says, know that good help is precious. Kate thinks being a servant for a rich lady is better than being a mill girl. She thinks that if she works for Mrs. Abbott and lives in Mrs. Abbott's house she can act like Mrs. Abbott.

Aunt Nora says that Kate's head has swelled quite a bit since she came to America.

Mill work suits me just fine, 'twas all I said. I didn't want her to know that my bones ache, my ankles swell up, and my body throbs from head to toe at night. I didn't tell her that the spinning room is so noisy, I think it must be what hell itself sounds like.

Still, I prefer work in the mills. Once I am done, my time, such that 'tis, is my own.

Monday, July 26, 1847
Lowell

Aunt Nora's leg is on the mend.
Poor dear. It has never truly healed since she

tumbled on the rocks back home. But she is going around now without a cane.

Tuesday, July 27, 1847
Lowell

My heart is filled with joy. When I got home Aunt Nora was waiting with a letter from Skibbereen.

('Tis Father Mullaney who writes Ma's letters.)

She sends greetings from the Connellys. Maureen wishes she could be here with me. Not nearly as much as I do. Sadly Mr. and Mrs. Sweeney have fallen victim to the black fever. 'Twas to be expected. They were so very ill when I left.

Ma and Da have not been evicted from our cottage, thanks to the kindness of Mr. Hughes, the landlord.

I pray to the Heavenly Father each night that they will keep well even though they face great hardship. I pray I will be able to earn enough money to send for them before 'tis too late.

Friday, July 30, 1847
Lowell

Annie Clark spoke to me today. I have learned my tasks quickly and well. She said she is very proud of me, which made me blush, I'm sure. There is a need for another spinner, just like her, if I am interested. Spinning means I will be paid more money. So I said yes, I would like to be a spinner. Annie is going to speak to Mr. Fowler.

Monday, August 2, 1847
Lowell

Mrs. Delaney cries in the night because she has not heard from her son. I wish she wouldn't cry. It makes me think back to the nights I heard Ma crying.

'Tis raining again today. Rain all week.

Aunt Nora can put a fright into you if she has a mind to. She had a row with Mr. Byrnes, who is also a teacher at St. Patrick's.

She says Mr. Byrnes hit wee Liam O'Neil, one of the students. Mr. Byrnes got it into his head that Liam was making fun of him behind his back. Liam said he did not, but Mr. Byrnes hit him a number of times with a heavy strap.

Aunt Nora said he has no call to be carrying on like that, and she's going to make him scratch where he doesn't itch.

Friday, August 6, 1847
Lowell

Annie Clark has spoken to Mr. Fowler. He is
going to allow me to become a spinner. Annie has
been very patient with me. She showed me carefully how to tend the spinning frame. I am to
watch for breaks in the yarn. If there is a break, the
machine stops. I piece together the two ends of the
yarn with a small, special knot that Annie showed
me how to tie. Then I am to restart the spinning
frame.

Annie won't leave me on my own until I am
ready. God bless her.

Saturday, August 7, 1847
Lowell

I told Aunt Nora the good news. She is proud
of me, too.

After Mass I went for a walk in the woods near the canal. I came upon Annie Clark. I think we were both surprised. I would have liked to turn away, but the narrowness of the path did not allow for that.

"Good morning, Mary Driscoll," she said.

We discovered that this is our favorite path. In weeks past we must have missed each other only by a matter of minutes.

We fell to talking easily. Annie told me she thinks I am "catching on nicely." That's how she put it — "catching on nicely." She has such a fine way of talking. I told her that I was nervous at first, but that I am feeling more comfortable each day. She is going to leave me on my own soon.

She wanted to know if I missed Ireland, if 'twas hard coming to a new country, if I liked America. So many questions. Truth is I'm not certain, not yet, about America. And that's what I told her. She said I was a spunky one when I told her that.

Annie comes from the state of Maine. I asked her if *she* misses home. She doesn't. She likes being on her own.

'Twas late afternoon before I knew it. The air had turned cold and damp.

Annie has invited me to supper at her boardinghouse next Sunday. I said yes, but now I have only regrets. What will I say? What will I wear? Annie always dresses so prettily, as do the other girls, and my clothes are so ragged.

I told Aunt Nora about going to Annie Clark's boardinghouse. She says I should worry about tomorrow tomorrow. 'Tis good advice, but I'm not sure I'm up to it.

Friday, August 13, 1847
Lowell

Mr. Byrnes, the teacher who hit Liam O'Neill, was found dead yesterday morning. He fell from the roof of St. Patrick's. 'Tis a mystery what he was doing up there or how he fell.

Aunt Nora sang a tune all evening while I helped her cut and peel the potatoes.

All the boardinghouses on Dutton Street look the same. Annie's is the sixth one from the corner, so I counted and knocked. I hummed while I waited, and I prayed for the Blessed Virgin to help me.

The door was opened by Mrs. Jackson, the boardinghouse keeper.

She took me by the arm and pulled me into the hall, saying I could use some flesh on my bare bones.

The bonnets and shawls that all the Yankee girls wear hung neatly from the hooks on the hallway wall. Near them was a list of the rules the girls were to follow.

"My girls," Mrs. Jackson said, "are just now coming down." Indeed they were. Doors were slamming closed, and I could hear them on the stairs. All the girls seemed to be talking at once. Sounded like a flock of screaming seagulls, they did.

When I saw Annie, she squeezed my hand and whispered, "Just do as I do." I hurried along and sat down next to her at one of the two large tables the girls were crowding around. They began passing large platters of boiled beef, potatoes, and steaming bowls of cabbage and vegetables. Everyone helped themselves to bread and crackers and gobbled down their food faster than I thought possible.

American girls do everything quickly.

They were all dressed with care and fixed their hair so neatly. I don't know how they do it. Annie was wearing a plain blue dress and black slippers. Many of the girls were dressed fancier than Annie, but none shone as brightly. Like a fairy-tale princess, she is.

Annie introduced me to the other girls at the table. Ruth Shattuck, Eunice Currier, Laura Austin, and Clarissa Burroughs. I have seen Clarissa Burroughs before, with Annie.

'Twas that first day, I remember now, when Annie showed me where I could eat. Clarissa Burroughs was watching us. But she didn't see me seeing her.

Ruth, Eunice, and Laura are all kindly in manner. You could tell they were trying to make me feel at home.

Laura asked how I like mill work. 'Tis fine, I told her. She has a steady gaze, and her eyes can bore a hole through you. She wanted to know what is fine about it. Truth is I was hoping not to have to do much talking. Not with all those finely dressed Yankee girls listening. But Laura's voice was as calm and steady as her gaze. I knew she wouldn't be satisfied until I told her.

So I explained that the mills paid steady and good, and that I plan to earn enough money to send for Ma and Da.

That made Clarissa Burroughs laugh. I know the Yankee girls think I talk funny.

Laura Austin went on as if nothing had happened.

She said she can see why Annie likes me. 'Twas nice of her to say, especially in front of the other girls. I think Laura Austin was being nice because of Clarissa Burroughs.

Ruth asked if 'tis hard with all the new things I have to learn. I said that Annie is a good and patient teacher, which made Ruth laugh, though not the way Clarissa Burroughs did. Ruth was Annie's teacher when Annie first came to the mills.

Then Ruth got a faraway look in her eyes. Did I miss being home? she was asking. I don't think she heard me say there isn't much time left in the day for missing home.

Ruth has been working in the mills for five years. She misses her home and family. She has not been home for a visit all year. She said all this in a dreamy way.

Clarissa Burroughs wets her lips with the tip of her tongue and plays with her long, black hair while she talks. You can tell she thinks she's prettier than she is. Truth is she's harsh-looking. She watched me like a hawk the whole night, didn't take her eyes off me, not even while she was talking to Annie. She's a crooked one, that Clarissa Burroughs. If she swallowed a knitting needle 'twould come out a corkscrew.

Clarissa Burroughs and Annie Clark are as different as night and day. How they can be friends is a mystery to me.

I have never eaten so much food. My plate was bare, but then came dessert: coffee, tea, blueberry pie, and ice cream. To be sure, ice cream is so much better than potatoes. I wanted to take some home to Aunt Nora, 'twas that good.

After dinner the tables were cleared and placed against the walls. Mrs. Jackson brought out a pot of tea and then went into her room.

Ruth went upstairs to write some letters. I stayed and sat with Annie and the other girls.

Laura talked with two girls about a book they were reading while Clarissa boasted about a lecture she had been to. The other girls read or sewed or looked at magazines. 'Twas hard for me to understand what they were talking about. They all have that Lowell way of talking. So fast and so sure. I don't have enough learning to keep up.

Annie wanted to show me her room. Clarissa came with us. I think she just didn't want Annie and me to be alone.

Annie shares her room with Ruth, Laura, and Clarissa. 'Tis filled with beds, trunks, and band-boxes of all shapes and sizes. There is little room to spare. They use the trunks for seats and the band-boxes as writing tables.

The ceiling slopes down so much that we could only stand in the middle of the room.

Clarissa looked at the gold watch she wears and reminded Annie 'twas nearing ten o'clock. The doors have to be locked then because of the curfew. Clarissa said she was sure I didn't want to be stuck there all night.

Just as we reached the front hall, Ruth Shattuck came running down the stairs, calling that she hoped I would visit them again soon. 'Twas nice of her to say so. She reminds me of Maureen. Maureen's dreamy, too.

"Ruth has a pure heart," Annie said when we were outside. "Perhaps too pure."

I was about to be asking what she meant, but she told me to go, 'twas late enough.

The night was as black as can be. I could not see my hand in front of my face. As I came to the Acre I quickened my pace. Lately there has been much strife between neighboring clans. You would think they would have left these feuds back in Ireland. The Irish boys are forever throwing stones at each other over one slight or another. On my way home I spied one of the constables patroling the area. I was fortunate that I did not encounter any difficulty.

I slept little, thinking about my first American friend.

Monday, August 16, 1847
Lowell

Mr. Byrnes was buried today. Aunt Nora said you should never dig a grave on a Monday.

Wednesday, August 18, 1847
Lowell

Lord have mercy. I don't see how we all can fit into the Acre. There are already too many of us, and more Irish arrive every day.

Aunt Nora and I were seeing how our wee

neighbor Fiona Buckley is faring. She was walking home down Dublin Street last night and got caught in the middle of some Irish lads. They hit her in the head with one of their stones, and the poor girl bruised her knees when she ran and fell.

The Buckleys live at the end of a narrow lane, in a tar-paper shack, not a wood house like Aunt Nora's. They don't even have windows to let in the light. There was a piece of horseshoe nailed by the door. Aunt Nora says 'tis to keep bad spirits from entering the house.

Father Callahan was there when we arrived, seeing to the poor girl. She was sleeping soundly, and he said she was more frightened than anything else. I think he said that to quiet Mrs. Buckley. Who can blame her for weeping? Fiona is but a child.

So many people live with Fiona Buckley that there is barely room to stand. Fiona sleeps in a bed with her sister Kathleen and six others. The rest sleep on the floor.

We told Mrs. Buckley that we would be visiting again soon. Mr. Buckley just sat in the corner. He is as odd-looking as two left feet, that one. His black hair is plastered down so it looks like 'twould crack into a thousand pieces if you hit him with a hammer.

I told Aunt Nora that on the way home and we had a good laugh.

Thursday, August 19, 1847
Lowell

Aunt Nora claims to have knowledge of the future. She sees grave events looming on the horizon for me. Soon I will be faced with an important decision. "When the wheel has come full circle," she said.

'Tis putting a fright into me, this kind of talk. She was preparing to tell me more, and I put a stop to it. I have no need to see into the future — the present is quite enough, if you don't mind. I told her I wanted my life to unfold at its own pace.

She smiled and said, "So it will, dearest Mary, so it will."

Sometimes Aunt Nora gives me the chills.

I saw Eunice Currier today. She works in the dressing room, where the cloth is finished, and lucky, she is. The air is cleaner, and there is much less noise than in the spinning room. If I could work in the dressing room I would get more pay. But no Irish girls work there. Only Yankee girls.

Annie Clark invited me to visit the shops with her and Laura Austin tomorrow. I could barely stop from throwing my arms around her. Having Annie has made the world seem brighter.

She warned me that she and Laura usually don't buy anything. They just go to look. That suits me fine. Monday is my first payday. And I'm sure I have no money to spare, even if I should be paid at this very instant.

'Twas a fine day, the sun shining, the sky blue, and the trees trying to turn red and orange.

The streets of Lowell are clean and made of stone. How different from the Acre, where the streets are quick to turn to mud after a rain.

Merrimack Street is so wide and straight that horses, wagons, and shiny black carriages parade up and down. There are fancy ladies riding in the carriages. They wear wide-brimmed straw bonnets, and their cheeks are painted red.

I asked Laura and Annie why the fancy ladies paint their cheeks, and they both laughed. "To attract their prey," Laura said.

I must have looked puzzled.

"They are looking to snare a man," she said. Annie asked me if I thought they looked pretty. I wasn't sure of the right thing to say. I couldn't tell if they looked pretty or silly. I decided to be silent.

Annie and Laura showed me the library and a grand hotel called the Merrimack House. We went by the depot just in time. A long line of cars was only then pulling in. 'Twas like a giant iron serpent. How that one car pulls all the others is a mystery.

The shops all look new. Their windows show what can be found inside: dresses, shoes, boots, bonnets, combs, shawls, and jewelry. One store has jars of striped candy, chocolate, molasses, raisins, bread, crackers, and barrels of sugar, flour, and rice.

In America there is everything.

My favorite store had a wooden doll, sitting in the window, with bright red lips and yellow hair. For a sad moment I was thinking of the doll Sean got for Molly and Sophie. I wonder where they are. I hope they are safe, like in the dream. I hope Brendan and Sean are safe, too. 'Twould be nice to walk down Merrimack Street with Sean. I wonder if Laura and Annie would like him.

Annie wanted to stop in the bookstore. "Just for a look," she said. Laura tugged at my arm so we could lag behind. She whispered in my ear that Annie won't be able to resist buying a book. 'Tis a quick tongue Laura has and a ready smile to go with it.

'Twas like in a trance Annie was, once we were inside. She walked slowly by the books, as if they were colorful birds and she was choosing one for a pet. Pick one up, she would, read it a bit, and gently put it back down. I saw her draw one close and breathe deeply.

Glad, I was, that Laura Austin wanted to be leaving. I stood the whole time, watching the people passing by the storefront window. I find people so much more interesting than books.

Annie did buy a book. Laura was right.

Sunday, August 22, 1847
Lowell

Kate has come back. She was waiting when we returned from Mass.

On and on she went about Rhode Island. Mrs. Abbott's sister is even richer than Mrs. Abbott. Their house is grander, and they have more servants. Thanks to the beaches and the cool summer breezes they did not suffer because of the heat. Blessed Mother, how relieved I was to hear that.

Kate paints her cheeks now. Just like the ladies in the carriages.

Aunt Nora asked her if she would be staying for supper. I was stirring the stew pot hanging over the fire — there was plenty. But Kate said she wanted to be getting back before dark.

When she left, Aunt Nora said, "Those who travel seldom return holy."

Monday, August 23, 1847
Lowell

My first payday.

'Twas a long time to be waiting. Two weeks before I was put on the payroll. And then pay is once a month.

We lined up as soon as the closing bell rang. The line was so long, I feared they would run out of money by the time they came to me. When I reached the paymaster, he handed me my earnings. At last. How good it felt to hold it in my hands.

I have given the money to Aunt Nora for safekeeping. She put it with the money she is setting aside from her teacher's pay. We counted how much we have. 'Tisn't as much as I'd hoped. 'Twill be a long time before we can send for Ma and Da.

Tuesday, August 24, 1847
Lowell

One of the girls in the weaving room was hurt today. God help her, a shuttle flew off the loom and hit her above the eye. I did not see her, but Laura says she was hurt badly. Knowing how fast those shuttles fly, 'tisn't a surprise to me.

Laura works in the weaving room. She has been here three years. She says that the weaving room is even worse than the spinning room. 'Tis hotter and the noise is greater.

'Tis always hot in the mills. Today two girls fainted before the noon bell. Laura says the corporation doesn't want the thread to become brittle and break. I asked if they worried that we might become brittle and break.

Laura said the corporation won't allow water buckets in the rooms. They think we'll take too much time drinking water. Imagine. I am thirsty all the time now because my throat is so sore. 'Tis hard to breathe, and the lint flies everywhere. I stand on the staircase just to get some air.

My dress always soaks through. So do the other girls'. Some tuck handkerchiefs in their sleeves, but I don't. 'Tisn't a help. They just become soaked, too.

Thursday, August 26, 1847
Lowell

I went to work even though I feel poorly. If I don't work, I don't get paid.

Aunt Nora went to making raspberry leaves steeped in sugar-sweetened water. She gave it to me from her favorite tin cup. I am to gargle every evening for three days and take walks in the countryside after Mass on Sundays. Aunt Nora said she has seen too many girls get sick, working in the mills. Fresh air, "that's the ticket," she says.

Sunday 'tis walking with Annie, I am. I will get some air then.

Friday, August 27, 1847
Lowell

Aunt Nora made me an onion boiled in milk. 'Twas good, and I am feeling a wee bit better.

Saturday, August 28, 1847
Lowell

I am writing to Mr. Quinn. No letter from him in some time. I want to know how Alice O'Donnell is and how Sean is faring. I wish he were here. Lord knows there is work for him. The Irish lads are building all over Lowell. Working on the new canal, they are. Surely Sean could find work here.

If only Annie and Laura could meet him. They would like each other, now I am sure. They are all so true.

Aunt Nora is in great pain. She had to have a tooth out. The top of the tooth came off, wouldn't you know it, while the root remained. It took twenty-five pulls before 'twas over. So weak she was, she could not teach today. Aunt Nora doesn't like to miss school. The children mean the world to her. Her "little scholars," she calls them. Mrs. Buckley watched over her till I returned from the mills. (Mrs. Delaney was here all day, but 'tisn't saying much.) I was glad to hear Fiona is feeling much better, though she is still afraid to walk down Dublin Street alone. And who's to blame her?

My cough continues. I slept little and was tired in the morning.

Tuesday, August 31, 1847
Lowell

Aunt Nora is still in pain, with her cheeks all swollen. I begged her to stay home again today, but she was having none of it. Stubborn as a mule, she is.

Wednesday, September 1, 1847
Lowell

Mrs. Delaney is greatly relieved. A letter from her son came yesterday. She asked me to read it to her. John has found work digging holes in a cemetery. They work all day, and there is little time to rest, but he is thankful not to be working in a factory because one of his chums died from a boiler explosion. The poor boy was scalded so badly, they could not save him.

I didn't read that part to Mrs. Delaney. She'd just go to worrying. I read the rest as he wrote it.

The pay is good — eighty cents a day. He is

saving every penny and hopes to return home by Christmas.

"Sorry to be troubling you," she said. "You're a good lass." She gripped my arm tightly. It felt as if I were being held by the claws of an awful, big bird.

Thursday, September 2, 1847
Lowell

Mr. Fowler dismissed one of the girls. She has not been at work for the past two days. Laura says Mr. Fowler drives us so hard because of the premium the corporation pays him. The more work he gets out of us, the more money he makes.

My head aches terribly, but I am sure to come to the mills just the same. Lord knows I am used to hard work. But doing the same thing over and over is tiring.

Aunt Nora placed a cold cloth on my forehead, which stopped the throbbing, but only for a while.

Friday, September 3, 1847
Lowell

One of the girls was caught reading her Bible instead of tending her machine. Took the heavy end of the stick, she did. Mr. Fowler was so angry, I thought his eyes would pop right out of his head. He took her Bible and threw it into his desk.

Reading is not allowed in the spinning room. Some of the Yankee girls bring little clippings of poetry and favorite hymns. They paste them on the sides of the window, near the geraniums, and glance at them from time to time.

Mr. Fowler watched me all afternoon. No matter where he was in the room I could feel his eyes following my every move.

Sunday, September 5, 1847
Lowell

Talked about everything under the sun, Annie and me. Having to leave home. Working in the mills. The girls at the boardinghouse.

Annie says she doesn't mind mill work. It lets her lay aside enough money. She wants to work just one more year. Then she'll set off on her own.

She is lucky to be living at the boardinghouse. 'Tis so much nicer than the Acre. Annie said that it is. Mill work has helped her see that there is more to life than working on a farm. And for that she is grateful.

But she does not like having to go to church every Sunday, Mrs. Jackson keeping a sharp eye on their coming and going, and peddlers disturbing them at night, selling their ribbons, shoes, jewelry, and candy.

She can barely find the time to write her poetry. I told her about my diary. 'Twas the first time I ever told anyone. It just jumped out of my mouth. Annie said I never cease to surprise her.

What bothers her most is being with people all day, every day, even when she eats and sleeps.

I thought she liked Laura, Ruth, and Clarissa. I thought they were her friends. Annie said she does like Laura and Ruth. They are like sisters to her — and just as precious. Still, there are times when she wants to be alone.

Seemed to me all the Yankee girls were happy. They are always chirping away like little birds.

"Even the caged bird sings," Annie said, sounding just like Aunt Nora.

As for Clarissa, she said, nothing is worse than listening to her after she returns from one of her lectures. Annie says that Clarissa understands nothing but speaks at great length.

I wish I could be more like Annie. She is so sure of herself. She knows what she thinks and isn't afraid to say it. She says I am shy. I told her that I'm not shy, just quiet. At least I'm not as shy as I was, that's what Aunt Nora says. It seems I'm always talking about Aunt Nora, and now Annie wants to meet her.

I was thinking someone like Annie wouldn't want to come to the Acre. But she just stood there looking at me, so I invited her for a wee visit on Sunday. She said she would be "delighted."

Aunt Nora thinks 'tis a fine idea. "'Twill be nice to have a friend for your birthday," she said.

I had forgotten.
Next Sunday is my birthday.
I will be fifteen.

Monday, September 6, 1847
Lowell

One of the wee boys who cleans the machines got his finger caught today. It was snapped right off. Their hands are small enough to get into the hard-to-reach places, but they are in great danger because of this.

The lad was near me when it happened. As soon as I heard him cry out, I rushed over and picked him up in my arms. Mr. Fowler was there in a flash and grabbed the boy from me. He told me to return at once to my machine. I would have liked to stay with the boy, but Mr. Fowler looked at me with those dull gray eyes of his. He's all eyes and no sight, that one.

I said a prayer for the boy, but there is little I can do that will change anything.

Yesterday I heard Clarissa Burroughs talking about the Irish again. She didn't know I was near. She was talking so loud, 'twas hard not to hear.

She said that the mill agents like the Irish girls because we take all the lower-paying jobs and we have to take what we can get. "Just look where they live — in shantytowns like the Acre. That's where that Mary Driscoll lives." She started imitating how I speak. Everyone laughed. "The Irish should stay in Ireland, where they belong," Clarissa Burroughs said.

The hairs were standing along the back of my neck, and my cheeks were burning like red-hot coals. I went over to where she stood, tapped her on the shoulder, I did. When she turned around 'twas plain I was not who she was expecting to see.

I asked her if she would stay "where she belonged" if there was no food to eat and everyone around her was starving? If leaving was her only hope? "Would you stay, Clarissa?" I said.

She looked at me, her dark eyes blinking. 'Twas like she was trying to make me disappear. Her mouth stayed open, but no sound was I hearing. We were standing so close, I could smell her.

I was after raising my voice, and some of the Yankee girls had gathered around. They were staring and talking to one another and began moving aside to let someone through. 'Twas Annie. Before I knew it, she had joined us in the center of the ring I have never seen her look that way, like an animal sniffing the air, waiting to be sure before making a move.

She took my arm and pulled me away from Clarissa Burroughs. Then she stepped in between us. She was standing right in front of me, her back to Clarissa. "Pay her no mind," she whispered.

I wanted to tell Annie that I was sorry, but truly I wasn't. Annie didn't give me a chance. She left as suddenly as she had appeared. The other girls stepped aside, letting her pass through the same way she came.

I was once again facing Clarissa. She wasn't blinking anymore, but her mouth was still open.

She came to me, stopping just inches away. "I knew you were trouble the moment I saw you," she said. Her voice was shaking and so was she. "From the moment I saw you."

Then she turned quickly and walked away, making a swooshing sound with her skirt.

I told Aunt Nora everything. She looked sad. "If truth be told," she said, "Clarissa Burroughs is right. We Irish are not where we belong."

'Tis a sorrowful thought.

Wednesday, September 8, 1847
Lowell

I asked Annie why the Yankee girls don't like the Irish.

She said they blame us for what happened at the mills. They say that factory work was better before there were so many Irish. There was time to sit and rest. Now the corporation doesn't care about the girls the way they once did. There are enough Irish girls looking for work that they don't have to.

Why the Irish are to blame for all of this I wasn't understanding. Surely we aren't the reason the windows are nailed shut. Or why the rooms are always hot and so filled with dirt, you can hardly breathe. Is it our fault that the days are long? Wouldn't we prefer a ten-hour day, too?

But I was afraid to say any of that. The words were in my head clear enough, but I wasn't sure they would come out that way. I could feel my heart pounding in my chest.

Still, I decided to ask one question that would not wait.

"What about you? You talk to me, and I'm Irish."

"You're different," Annie said. "You're not like the rest."

Thursday, September 9, 1847
Lowell

Ruth Shattuck is ill with a fever. Annie says that she is delirious and sleeps fitfully. I went back with Annie to the boardinghouse during the noon meal. Ruth was sleeping, so we didn't disturb her. Annie is greatly troubled by her condition.

Friday, September 10, 1847
Lowell

The boy who got his finger snapped off was back in the mills today. When he saw me he came right over and said thank you, very politely. I asked him his name, and he said Sylvester Sawyer. Such a big name for such a wee boy.

Sunday, September 12, 1847
Lowell

At noon a knock was given at the door. We had just come home from Mass. 'Twas Annie, as planned. I was glad that she met with no difficulties.

Aunt Nora made a special birthday dinner. Corned beef, cabbage, and roast potatoes. There was more, too — a cake of fine wheaten bread mixed with honey.

Annie was surprised that I am only fifteen. She said I act older than my age. She said I should have told her 'twas my birthday. Now she wants to be thinking of a present for me. I told her there is no need, which is so.

Once Annie told Aunt Nora that she believes in ghosts there was no stopping them. They had a lively talk about what Annie calls "the spirit world." They agreed that ghosts are poor souls stuck between this life and the next.

The two of them are dear to me, but both live with their heads in the clouds.

After tea Annie asked if we would like to hear one of her poems. I'd never heard one before. She must have approved of Aunt Nora, else she wouldn't have offered, if you ask me.

She reached into her sack and took out her little poetry-writing book. Aunt Nora moved from the table to the rocking chair. Then she said there was nothing she liked more than to hear a fine piece of writing.

Annie read in her soft, soothing voice.

In the poem, a small girl gets lost in a thick forest. Trying to find her way back home, she comes upon a note tacked to a tree. The note invites her to climb to the top. Once there she will be able to see her future.

The tree is the oldest and tallest in the forest. But the branches are low and good for climbing. She climbs the tree to the very top, and when she gets there — just as the note promised — she sees all the days of her life laid out before her. "Like an endless sentence," is the way Annie says it.

Then, when she climbs down from the tree the note is gone. That's the end of the poem.

Annie asked if we liked it. Truth is I wanted to know what the girl saw and what happened to the note. If 'twasn't there when she came down, who took it then? But I held my tongue thinking these were silly questions.

Aunt Nora was wiping tears from her eyes. I didn't think the poem was sad. But I'm not one for poetry.

Annie asked Aunt Nora what she thought.

Aunt Nora said her niece was blessed to have found a friend such as she.

That's the only time I've ever seen Annie blush.

'Tis my first birthday without Ma and Da. We have not heard from them in some time.

Monday, September 13, 1847
Lowell

Everyone is talking about Clarissa Burroughs getting caught.

She was secretly meeting a boy in the mill yard when the night watchman came upon them. They were startled and ran from him. But when they tried to climb over the fence, Clarissa's dress got caught on one of the spikes. The watchman called for help. I understand it took quite a while to get her down.

Annie said Clarissa didn't utter a word to anyone last night and went to bed without eating. In the morning she remained in bed, saying she felt poorly. She is not in work today. Annie said Mrs. Jackson would surely have something to say about this. No one knows what has happened to the boy.

Wednesday, September 15, 1847
Lowell

Each day I am becoming better acquainted with my machines. That's what Annie says. I have nimble fingers and am doing better than she expected in such a short period of time.

Sometimes, however, I still fear I won't be able to do my tasks properly. Thank the Lord that this is only fleeting, and I tend to my machines without mishap.

Thursday, September 16, 1847
Lowell

Ruth is feeling better and is back at work. 'Twas so good to see her. I gave her a big hello, and she smiled.

Sunday, September 19, 1847
Lowell

Aunt Nora was eager to get to church this morning. St. Patrick's has a new organ now. Aunt Nora says the old one was too small.

Later I met Annie, and we talked away the afternoon.

I told her how much I miss Ma and Da. I have not said a word to anyone. Not even Aunt Nora.

Annie told me about her family. 'Tis a sad story.

Annie is the youngest and only girl. She has five brothers. Her mother used to hit her with a small branch she kept hidden in the kitchen. Annie couldn't understand why her mother hated her so.

Then one day she found out from Jed, her oldest brother, that she was not her real mother. Her real mother had died giving birth to her. At first Annie couldn't believe it. But the more she thought about it, the truer it became.

A week after she found out, she left to find work in Lowell. "Lowell was my salvation," she said.

She would like to write Jed but is afraid to let anyone know where she is.

Later, Annie gave me my present. 'Twas in a box all nicely tied up with violet ribbons. Inside was a delicate shawl wrapped around a book of poems. I threw the shawl over my shoulder, and Annie said not to forget about the book.

She is forever reading, and I know she thinks I should. Imagine spending money for a book. She said that 'tis every individual's responsibility to improve their minds. I have to bite my lip to keep from laughing when Annie talks like that. I told her I was more interested in improving my purse than my mind. She laughed and said, "I suppose you are, Mary Driscoll."

Then I hugged her by way of thanks.

Merciful Lord, a letter from Sean.

He is building a road. The bosses treat them like animals, and the people in town do not like them being around. They think there are already too many Irish. And they work cheap, and this makes it bad for everyone.

A boy from County Kerry was killed when a huge rock fell on him. 'Twas being lifted when the chain broke. Another boy was killed by a gunpowder blast. The blast sent rocks flying, and he was struck in the head while taking a drink of water. Bless us and save us, there are so many sad stories like these.

Sean says that Americans do not like the Irish. He's thinking now 'twas a mistake to come here. America is not the way he thought 'twould be. 'Tisn't the way I thought 'twould be, either, but better than back home. At least here there is food to eat and hope for tomorrow.

Sean has visited Alice O'Donnell. The convent is nearby, and he says she is being taken care of.

That puts my mind at ease. 'Twas good of Sean to go see her. He's a dear boy with a good heart. None better.

Mr. Fowler was eyeing me all morning. Buzzing around like a maddened fly, he was.

In the afternoon he crept up on me, silent as a mouse. I did not see him until he was right on me. I could feel his breath on my neck.

"Don't let your mind wander, Mary", he hissed into my ear. 'Twas a miracle I could hear him above the noise, but he was standing very, very close. I was as scared as a rabbit in its burrow.

Annie showed me the signal they use to warn each other that Mr. Fowler is coming. 'Tis making a circle with your arms over your head. I have always wondered why they do that. He won't catch me again.

Ruth Shattuck walked out today. Some of her bobbins began falling on the floor, making quite a clatter. She just stood there looking at them with that dreamy look in her eyes. Watched them fall like they weren't even hers. Then she ran out of the spinning room without an if-you-don't-mind to anyone.

I went back with Annie just as soon as the seven o'clock bell rang. Ruth was packing when we arrived.

Annie tried to convince her to stay, but she wasn't hearing any of it. Talking away, she was, while she packed. Annie and I sat on the bed and listened. 'Twas all we could do.

"I don't have eyes in the back of my head. I can't tend that many machines without going mad. I need fresh air. I am going home where there are no bells, bells, bells. Bells that tell you when you can open your eyes and when you can close them. When you can sleep and when you can eat.

I don't know if I'll ever get those bells out of my head."

Thanks be to the Lord, Annie was able to get her to wait till tomorrow. Then Annie will take her to the stagecoach.

I have never seen Annie this upset. Usually she runs as deep as the ocean.

Downstairs, as I was leaving, she said 'twas a shame, and Ruth is a fine girl. She is that.

On the way home, I thought about the look in Ruth's eyes. "I have been here too long," she said. I hope I'm not here too long.

Monday, September 27, 1847
Lowell

Another payday. Aunt Nora and I counted the money we have. Like a hive hoards honey, we lay away money for Ma and Da.

Clarissa Burrough's beautiful long, black hair was caught in her machine, and her scalp was pulled off. Glory of God, 'twas a frightful spectacle.

Her howls of pain were loud enough to be heard above the roar of the machines. It took forever to stop them. By the time Mr. Fowler cut off her hair and pulled her away, 'twas too late.

There was utter silence.

Mr. Fowler wasted no time. He was more concerned that the machines were down than the fate of the girl. As soon as her limp body was removed from the room, he pulled the cord and ordered everyone back to work.

Ruth had warned Clarissa not to wear her hair that way. She showed her how to fix it up so 'twouldn't get caught, because this has happened before. Ruth warned her how dangerous 'twas, but Clarissa would not listen. She insisted on leaving her hair loose because she was so proud of how long and shiny 'twas. But look where her pride has gotten her now.

I have not slept since this happened.

Kate came by for a chat.

Bless the day, she only stayed a wee minute. She was finding out if Aunt Nora knew any love potions. Wouldn't you know she did. Much good, Aunt Nora said, could come from sprinkling water that has washed a child's feet outside your door.

'Twas just what Kate was after. Having what she came for, she got up to leave. Aunt Nora asked her if she is planning to marry. Kate said she might be and left as suddenly as she came.

I told Annie about Kate and the love potions.

Annie asked if I wanted to marry. "I am too young," I told her.

"When you are old enough. Would you choose to then?"

"Marriage is fine if you're rich, like Mrs. Abbott. If you're not rich what do you have to look
forward to? Hoping your husband will provide?
'Tisn't enough for me," I told her.

Annie said 'twould be a shame if a pretty girl
like me never marries.

When I asked if Annie would marry, she said
she is a restless spirit.

She would like to be on her own for a while.
To live where she wants and go where she
pleases. She doesn't think you can do that if you're
married.

"But then," she said, "when I've had my fill, I'll
find my true love and live happily ever after." It
sounded like one of those books Annie gets from
the library.

"And what will your true love be like, dear
Annie?" I asked.

She grabbed my shoulders with both her hands
and said, "Why, just like Mr. Fowler, of course."

We went to laughing so hard that we fell down
on top of each other and rolled in the freshly
fallen snow.

Laura Austin fears her name is on the list because she was handing out a labor newspaper. There is a list of girls who the corporation thinks are troublemakers. If you are dismissed, they send the list to the other mills in the area. That way you can't find work and cause more trouble.

Laura was one of the girls in the turnout last year when they were striking for a ten-hour day. They got more time for their meals but 'twas all. Laura said they all signed the petition, but it came to nothing. "The corporation won," Laura said, "just like it always does."

When Laura first came to Lowell — six years ago — the girls stood by one another. Then, she said, no girl tended more than two looms. There was time to sit and rest. Now, she says, some girls tend four or five machines. The corporations speed up the machines and slow down the clocks so we work longer and get paid less.

'Twould be nice to work only ten hours. I can only imagine.

Still, if truth be told, I am glad not to have to sign anything. For myself, I would sign. I have nothing to fear. But I have Ma and Da to think about.

When I have enough money for their passage, when they are here beside me, then I can think of such things, but not now. That is not what I came to America for.

Friday, October 8, 1847
Lowell

Ma and Da will not be coming.

Something was terribly wrong, I just knew it. Aunt Nora is always so cheerful — humming a tune more likely than not. But she was sitting at the table, quiet, resting her head in one hand and holding a letter in the other. When she looked up, I could see that she had been crying. 'Twas like the light had left her eyes.

She didn't want me to read the letter. She said there was no need. 'Twas from Father Mullaney. He said little. Only what was needed. That they are gone.

I feel lost. I should never have left Ireland. Never.

Mrs. Buckley and Fiona visited. Later Annie came. 'Twas kind of her. She brought me chocolate and raisins. She worried when I wasn't in the mills. And then, last night, Aunt Nora went to Mrs. Jackson's to tell her. Dear Aunt Nora. Now she has gone to talk to Kate.

Annie and Laura came. They are so dear to take the time.

My cough has worsened, but 'tis best I return to work on Monday. There is nothing for me to do here. Staying in bed does no good. I think too much about Ma and Da.

Last night Aunt Nora held me and rocked me back and forth, singing Ma's lullaby:

> On the wings of the wind
> Over the dark rolling deep
> Angels are coming
> To watch over thy sleep
>
> Angels are coming
> To watch over thee
> So list' to the wind
> Coming over the sea

Writing down the words helps to calm me, for I can hear Ma's voice when I see the words on the page.

If only Ma could hold me one last time.

I cried so long and so hard that I cried myself to sleep.

Monday, October 11, 1847
Lowell

I do my work. It helps me pass the time. Knowing Annie is near also helps.

Thursday, October 14, 1847
Lowell

I look out the mill windows and wonder just how far Ireland is from where I am. It seems 'twas only yesterday Ma said I would be going to America. Now it feels like so very long ago, beyond my memory's reach. Like 'twasn't even me.

If Mrs. Delaney doesn't stop staring at me soon I'll go mad. John is returning next week.

Laura Austin said her name is on the list. One of the girls saw it. There is a check next to her name and then it says, "willful."

The oil lamps were lit this morning and again this evening so that we could work in the dark. Many of the girls complain. They don't like the foul smell, and they don't like being forced to work by lamplight.

I am worn. Standing all day has caused my feet to ache terribly. Nothing relieves the pain. Weariness has crept into my bones. My eyes feel as if they will burst from my head thanks to the endless noise. The lint flies everywhere. Breathing itself is a burden.

At night my chest heaves painfully. I wake as tired as when I lay down.

Thursday, October 28, 1847
Lowell

The trees are bare and covered with last night's snowfall. 'Tis windy and icy. I walk carefully so as not to fall.

Aunt Nora stuffed paper into the toes of my boots to help keep me warm. She reminded me to leave them in front of the fireplace when they are wet so they will be dry in the morning.

'Tis a chill I caught going from the hot spinning room into the cold night air. Aunt Nora rubbed my hands before we went to sleep. "God save the poor," she said when she was done.

'Tis dark in the morning when I leave and dark when I return. I hardly see the sun. It makes me gloomy.

I stirred the fire carefully before I slept. I was feeling poorly last night. My cough disturbs my sleep. When I awoke the fire had gone out. Aunt Nora had to send John Delaney to Mrs. Buckley's for some live coals.

I have read Mr. Quinn's letter over and over. I am pasting it here so I will never forget it.

Dear Mary Driscoll,

'Tis my unpleasant task to inform you of the sorrowful events that have recently taken place.

There has been much tension in the air. The Yankees seem to dislike we Irish more with each passing week.

On Monday past, a mob, angered by ru-

mors that Irish lads had treated an American flag rudely, formed in the streets of Arlington. Arlington, as you know, is the location of the convent to which Alice O'Donnell has been entrusted.

By nightfall the unruly mob was headed for the Irish district. They attacked homes and churches, destroying everything in their path. Many on both sides were bleeding and wounded. The melee continued for two days and two nights and grew more deadly with each passing hour. As darkness fell on the second night, the mob, having no regard for either man or God, made for the convent.

During the two days of rioting, word spread to nearby Somerville, where my nephew Sean was working. Fearing for Alice O'Donnell's safety, he made his way to Arlington. There he joined with others who were working to restore order. He helped evacuate the convent and saw to it that Alice was in safe hands.

He then returned to the convent. The mob

had set fire to the now-empty building, which was soon engulfed in flames.

Although, thank the Lord, none of the children were hurt, Sean and three other Irish lads have been charged as accessories to murder because two of the Yankees died from head wounds received during the rock-throwing riot.

Sean protested that he was not in Arlington at the time of the violence — he was still in Somerville — but his words fell on deaf ears as you might imagine.

I am presently occupied with trying to raise the bail money necessary to free Sean from his jail cell, where he awaits trial. The amount is quite steep, and although I am, of course, taking all necessary steps, I cannot say that I am hopeful. I am proceeding as quickly as possible for there is grave talk here that the boys will not be allowed to live long enough to stand trial.

Alice is with us now. She is sleeping near me as I write. She will, of course, remain here *as long as necessary, so have no fear in that regard.*

What the result of all this will be only heaven knows. The Lord will, I am certain, reward the good and condemn the evil to unceasing flames.

Respectfully,
Patrick Quinn

I ran all the way to Annie's. 'Twas cold and the snow was blowing in my face, making it hard to breathe. I hadn't given a moment's thought to what I would do if Annie wasn't there. Thankfully she was. Mrs. Jackson let me go right up.

Annie was writing in one of her books and Laura lay beside her, chatting away. I was glad, too, that Laura was there. They saw on my face that something was terribly wrong and Laura made room for me on the wee bed. I told them all that Mr. Quinn had written and my plan.

Laura said nothing, but Annie said right out she wouldn't let me go. I had to think of myself first, she said. Not Sean or Alice O'Donnell. She said she is sure Mr. Quinn will see to Alice's safety.

Maybe so. Maybe not.

And what of Sean? I asked her. What would I do, just let him sit in jail? Wait till Mr. Quinn writes me again, this time to tell me how the Yankees dragged him into the street and beat him to death just because he is Irish?

I cannot see with anyone's eyes but my own. I must go to Boston. I must take the money I put aside for Ma and Da and bring it to Sean.

Suddenly Laura broke her silence. "I'll go with you," she said. I could hardly believe my ears. "'Tis just a matter of time before I am dismissed, and I have always wanted to see Boston. And now," she said, "I will."

Annie looked shaken by this turn. She asked me if I had told Aunt Nora. I think she hoped Aunt Nora would be able to stop me. I haven't told her because truth be told, I am afraid she will not approve. But I am going whether she approves or not.

I told Aunt Nora I would only take my pay, but she said to take it all. With the Delaneys' board and her own wages, she will have enough.

She hugged me, and then Annie and Laura started to cry. 'Twas a sight. Annie said we'd best be leaving for the depot.

They waited outside while I said one more good-bye to Aunt Nora.

"Quiet One," she said. "Always remember one thing. The Lord would never close one gate without opening another."

The same as Ma said when I left home to come to America. 'Tis true, I hope.

Epilogue

Nora Kinsella, Mary's aunt, continued to teach school in Lowell for thirty-two more years.

Kate Driscoll worked for Mrs. Abbott until 1851 when she met and married Dennis Kelly. They had two children.

Sean Riordan fled Boston as soon as Mary provided the necessary bail money. His whereabouts after 1847 are unknown.

Annie Clark left the mills in 1848, as planned. She traveled west, stopping in Racine, Wisconsin. There she married Silas Marks, one of the town's leading lawyers. She and her husband had no children.

Patrick Quinn's tavern grew in size, doubling as a grocery store by day. He became a wealthy man of property. Although he never ran for elective office, he was so influential in Boston politics that it was said, "You can't win without Quinn." He was loved and respected throughout the Boston Irish community.

Laura Austin and Mary Driscoll, with Quinn's help, placed Alice O'Donnell in the capable hands of the Perkins Institute for the Blind. There Alice learned the manual alphabet and other ways of improving her communication with the outside world. She was well cared for.

Mary Driscoll died in the cholera epidemic of 1849.

She was seventeen.

Life in America
in 1847

Historical Note

Beginning in 1845, Ireland experienced an extended crop failure that became known as the Great Famine. Over the next five years, one million of Ireland's nine million citizens died, and almost two million emigrated to other countries.

The Great Famine was the result of two terrible forces. First, potatoes, the basic crop of Irish tenant farmers, were attacked by a "blight" or fungus. Because the Irish farmers were unable to plant new healthy potato crops, their primary diet, there was widespread starvation. Second, Ireland, subject to British rule since the beginning of the nineteenth century, consisted of large estates owned and managed by English landlords. These estates were divided into small farms, rented at high rates to poor Irish farmers. When half the oat crop failed, farmers were unable to pay their rents, and many landlords evicted them.

Initially, there was little help from the British government. Their "laissez-faire," or "hands-off" approach allowed the large land owners to run their own affairs. As starvation and evictions worsened, the British prime minister, Sir Robert Peel, set up public works programs. Irish men were hired as laborers on make-work construction projects such as "famine roads," which were created more to keep the men busy than to build functioning roads. The wages were very low, not nearly enough to prevent starvation or evictions. What Ireland needed was food and a new farming system.

By 1847, conditions in Ireland had reached catastrophic levels. Many people were reduced to eating seaweed and cabbage leaves, even grass and tree bark. Women with children often left their husbands to move into poorhouses or workhouses for the homeless. Diseases such as typhus, relapsing fever, and dropsy were rampant, bringing death. Public works programs were stopped, and soup kitchens were set up to feed the starving. Each person was allowed to receive two meals of free soup a week. Help came from churches and governments around the world, and the United States Congress authorized millions of dollars for famine relief. These efforts eventually ended the Great Famine, but for many it was too little too late.

The town of Skibbereen in County Cork was the hardest hit in all of Ireland, and the area was known as "the fatal district." So many people died that there weren't enough coffins in which to bury the dead. For the people of Skibbereen and many other parts of Ireland, the only choice was to leave their country. By the early 1850s, approximately one quarter of Ireland's population had left.

The British government encouraged emigration of the Irish to other countries as the solution to their "troublesome problem." Ticket prices for ship passage were kept low. In some cases, English landlords purchased tickets for their tenant farmers, grateful to get rid of them. For most immigrants, however, tickets were bought with money raised by selling their few remaining belongings or with money sent to them by relatives in other countries. A popular saying was, "The only place in Ireland a man can make his fortune is in America."

The voyage to America took at least six weeks, and sometimes more than three months. The cheapest passage was in old wooden slave ships, called "coffin ships," or in steerage on sailing sloops. Passengers were crowded into tiny closed living quarters with little ventilation. Food and water on these ships were scarce. Water was stored in barrels that had formerly carried products like vinegar and turpentine, making it unfit for drinking. On long voyages, meat became tainted, and bread and flour crawled with insects and vermin. Cattle and pigs were treated better than the passengers. Fire was a constant danger, and cooking and smoking were extremely risky. There were few facilities for washing, and because the steerage was so filthy, diseases spread rapidly. In 1847, the worst year of the Great Famine, 7,000 immigrants perished aboard ships, and another 10,000 died after landing in America.

Upon arriving in the United States, immigrants underwent a medical examination. Those who were sick and did not pass the examination were either placed in quarantine until they were well or turned away. Those turned away frequently sailed on to Canada.

In the large port cities of Philadelphia, New York, and Boston, the new immigrants, with high hopes, little money, and few skills, were easily victimized. Their Catholic religion was feared and often scorned, and they faced harsh discrimination and prejudice. When seeking work, they were often rejected by "NINA" signs, which meant "No Irish Need Apply."

In the 1820s, the Industrial Revolution began in Lowell, Massachusetts at the Pawtucket Falls on the Merrimack River. It was a factory in the wilderness, started by young adventuresome investors from well-to-do Boston families. They brought together a new system of textile manufacturing using power looms, a primarily female workforce, and venture capital in order to make money. They were extraordinarily successful.

By 1847, Lowell, a city of 30,000 people, was the center for textile manufacturing in the United States. The Lowell textile mills employed 15,000 workers, two-thirds of whom were young women, between the ages of fifteen and thirty, from New England. Work in the mills was hard, but provided young women with one of the few chances to earn cash wages. To recruit young women to work in the textile mills, the corporations built large, well-run, brick boardinghouses. They encouraged the establishment of churches, and sponsored schools, libraries, hospitals, health clinics, charitable organizations, reading rooms, and lectures. The lectures included popular writers, educators, and activists such as Ralph Waldo Emerson. In the evenings and on weekends, "improvement circles" were held in churches and reading rooms, and young women were encouraged to write poetry and short stories.

These young female workers had a strong sense of independence. They fought for better working conditions, a ten-hour workday, and higher wages. Although not always successful, they used petitions, legislative hearings, walkouts, newspaper editorials, and journal articles to fight for their rights. They published a prolabor newspaper, the *Voice of Industry*, and a literary magazine, *The Lowell Offering*.

When the textile corporations entered upon a major expansion program, they needed additional workers to meet their ambitious plans. The enormous numbers of unskilled famine Irish immigrants who were pouring into America, desperate for jobs, became that new source.

The Lowell factory system began to change in the 1850s. New advanced technology enabled less skilled workers to produce more cloth at lower wages. The directors of the corporations were more interested in profit than in the workers' welfare. Life in the mills became less desirable for the Yankee girls, and mill management shifted recruiting efforts toward immigrants. The poor, uneducated, and unskilled famine Irish had little choice but to endure these hardships in order to survive in their new homeland.

From the founding of Lowell, small numbers of Irish immigrants had come to help construct the power canals and brick mills and boardinghouses. They had established two Catholic churches, opened shops and businesses, and attended city Irish schools taught by Irish women and men. In some ways, these early Irish immigrants paved the way for the famine Irish who followed.

Thousands of Irish immigrants flowed into the United States, surviving and overcoming terrible conditions. Unskilled jobs with low wages required entire families — mothers, fathers, and older children — to work in order to earn a living wage. Discrimination forced families to live in deplorable housing in overcrowded neighborhoods. Religious prejudice and language (many Irish immigrants spoke the Irish language) often isolated and segregated the Irish community. But ultimately, with citizenship and the vote, the Irish gained the opportunity to participate as equals in the American system. Still, even 150 years later, it would be hard to find people of Irish extraction who don't remember the famine and the many hardships their ancestors endured on the way to becoming full-fledged American citizens.

The potato, a cheap but nutritious food, was the principal diet of the poor in Ireland until 1845, when a fungus destroyed most of the crop. The failure of the potato crop was the cause of the Great Famine, in which almost a million Irish people starved to death.

Desperate for basic survival, nearly two million Irish fled their homeland, and half of them came to America. Passage cost little, but the wooden ships were terribly uncomfortable, grossly unsanitary, and easily caught fire. Tens of thousands died at sea.

Lowell, Massachusetts, was the center of textile manufacturing in the 1840s. As workers in the mill, young single women were taught skills of the trade, as well as reading and writing.

One of the most important inventions of the Industrial Revolution was the power loom, which enabled one person to supervise several mechanized looms at once. With fewer workers, textile mills were able to churn out bolts of fabric more quickly. This had an obvious result: profit.

Mill owners, motivated by profit and greed, showed little concern for their workers' welfare. Labor newspapers, such as the Voice of Industry, *provided workers with a forum for speaking out against inhumane working conditions.*

The "mill girls" wore simple dresses. They kept their long hair pinned up, in order to avoid the dangerous possiblity of getting it caught in the machines.

There was a hierarchy of workers in the mill, according to their skills—
from the lowest bobbin girl, who replaced the empty spools, to the weavers,
whose skill and practiced eye created the patterns of fabrics. In between,
there were spinners, who spun yarn, and drawing-in girls, who threaded
yarn for the weavers.

Merrimack was one of the many internationally-known manufacturers
of textiles in Lowell, Massachusetts, during this period of time. Cloth
fabrics from Lowell were sold and shipped to all parts of the world from
nearby ports.

TIME TABLE OF THE LOWELL MILLS,

To take effect on and after Oct. 21st, 1851.

The Standard time being that of the meridian of Lowell, as shown by the regulator clock of JOSEPH RAYNES, 43 Central Street.

	From 1st to 10th inclusive.				From 11th to 20th inclusive.				From 21st to last day of month.			
	1st Bell	2d Bell	3d Bell	Eve. Bell	1st Bell	2d Bell	3d Bell	Eve. Bell	1st Bell	2d Bell	3d Bell	Eve. Bell
January,	5.00	6.00	6.50	*7.30	5.00	6 00	6.50	*7.30	5.00	6.00	6.50	*7.30
February,	4.30	5.30	6.40	*7.30	4.30	5.30	6.25	*7.30	4.30	5.30	6.15	*7.30
March,	5.40	6.00		*7.30	5.20	5.40		*7.30	5.05	5.25		6.35
April,	4.45	5.05		6.45	4.30	4.50		6.55	4.30	4.50		7.00
May,	4 30	4.50		7·00	4.30	4.50		7.00	4.30	4.50		7 00
June,	"	"		"	"	"		"	"	"		"
July,	"	"		"	"	"		"	"	"		"
August,	"	"		"	"	"		"	"	"		"
September,	4.40	5.00		6.45	4.50	5.10		6.30	5.00	5.20		*7.30
October,	5.10	5.30		*7.30	5.20	5.40		*7.30	5.35	5.55		*7.30
November,	4.30	5,30	6.10	*7.30	4.30	5.30	6.20	*7.30	5.00	6.00	6.35	*7.30
December,	5.00	6.00	6.45	*7.30	5.00	6.00	6.50	*7.30	5.00	6·00	6.50	*7.30

* Excepting on Saturdays from Sept. 21st to March 20th inclusive, when it is rung at 20 minutes after sunset.

YARD GATES,

Will be opened at ringing of last morning bell, of meal bells, and of evening bells; and kept open Ten minutes.

MILL GATES.

Commence hoisting Mill Gates, Two minutes before commencing work.

WORK COMMENCES,

At Ten minutes after last morning bell, and at Ten minutes after bell which "rings in" from Meals.

BREAKFAST BELLS.

During March "Ring out"........at....7.30 a. m......... "Ring in" at 8.05 a. m.
April 1st to Sept. 20th inclusive.....at....7 00 " " .... " " at 7.35 " "
Sept. 21st to Oct. 31st inclusive.....at....7.30 " " .... " " at 8.05 " "
Remainder of year work commences after Breakfast.

DINNER BELLS.

"Ring out" ....12.30 p. m......... "Ring in".... 1.05 p. m.

In all cases, the *first* stroke of the bell is considered as marking the time.

A worker's life was strictly regulated by the clock. Bells were rung to designate each change of activity and workers were fined for lateness.

LOWELL OFFERING

December, 1845.

"Is Saul also among the prophets!"

A REPOSITORY
OF ORIGINAL ARTICLES, WRITTEN BY
"FACTORY GIRLS."

LOWELL: MISSES CURTIS & FARLEY.
BOSTON: JORDAN & WILEY, 121
Washington street.
1845.

*This popular magazine was written by and for female mill workers.
It became an outlet for creative expression, and featured poetry, short
stories, essays, announcements of cultural activities, and advertisements.*

The town of Lowell was the hub of social activity and a cultural center.
The "mill girls" enjoyed a certain independence and could use their wages
as they pleased. They went downtown to buy clothes and books; to attend
theater, concerts, and poetry readings; and to have tea after church.

St. Patrick's Church became
the center of the Irish immi-
grant social world as well as
their religious sanctuary.

Mill agents provided clean, supervised, pleasant boarding houses where the "mill girls" ate together, shared rooms, and had curfews, almost as if they were living in college sororities.

The famine Irish lived mainly in impoverished neighborhoods like the Acre, shown here. Though the photos on this page were not taken until the 1930s, the buildings remain much the same as they were in 1847.

HEAR THE WIND BLOW

Music has always been an important part of Irish culture, and many popular American folk songs have their roots in Ireland. This is one of many songs the Irish brought to the United States, and it was sung wherever they settled from Massachusetts to California.

1. On the wings of the wind
   Over the dark rolling deep
   Angels are coming
   To watch over thy sleep

   Angels are coming
   To watch over thee
   So list' to the wind
   Coming over the sea

   Hear the wind blow
   Hear the wind blow
   Lean your head over
   Hear the wind blow

2. On wings of the night
   May your fury be crossed
   May no one that's dear
   To our island be lost

   Blow the winds gently
   Calm be the foam
   Shine the light brightly
   To guide them back home

3. The curraghs are sailing
   Way out in the blue
   Laden with herring
   Of silvery hue

   Silver the herring
   Silver the sea
   Soon there'll be silver
   For baby and me

   Hear the wind blow
   Hear the wind blow
   Lean your head over
   Hear the wind blow

4. The curraghs tomorrow
   Will stand on the shore
   And he'll go sailing
   And sailing no more

   The nets will be drying
   Nets haven't passed
   Contented he'll rest
   Safe in my arms

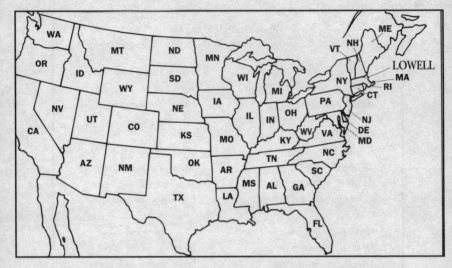

Modern map of the continental United States, showing the approximate location of Lowell, Massachusetts.

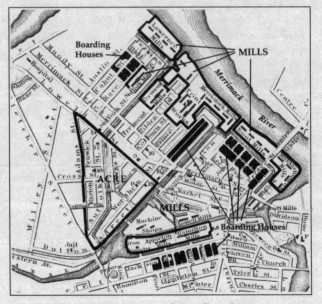

This map shows the main streets of Lowell as they were in 1847.

About the Author

Barry Denenberg is the author of several critically acclaimed books for middle-grade and young-adult readers, including one other book in the Dear America series, *When Will This Cruel War Be Over?: The Civil War Diary of Emma Simpson*, which was named an NCSS Notable Children's Trade Book in the Field of Social Studies. Widely praised for his rigorous research, he has written about many important areas of American history, from the Civil War to Vietnam.

"*So Far from Home* illuminates three critical and fascinating aspects of American history," he says. "First, the Lowell mills marked the beginning of the Industrial Revolution in America. Second, the girls who came to work in those mills earned and saved their own money and went on to help shape American society. Lastly, Mary Driscoll can tell us what it was like to be forced to leave the country of your birth and come to the United States with no money, little or no knowledge of the language, few friends, and fewer prospects for earning a living.

"For four hundred years, America has been the land of hope for an incredibly diverse group of immigrants. It is, I think, what makes us unique."

Denenberg's works of nonfiction include, *An American Hero: The True Story of Charles A. Lindbergh*, an ALA Best Book for Young Adults and a New York Public Library Book for the Teenage; and *Voices from Vietnam*, an ALA Best Book for Young Adults, a *Booklist* Editor's Choice Book, and a New York Public Library Book for the Teenage. He lives with his wife and their daughter, Emma, in Westchester County, New York.

To the memory of
my grandfather, Louis Denenberg

Acknowledgments

The author would like to thank Martha Mayo at the Center for Lowell History for graciously sharing her intelligence and time.

Grateful acknowledgment is made for permission to reprint the following.

Cover portrait: *Gulnihal* by Frederic Lord Leighton. Exhibited 1886. Oil on canvas. Collection of Andrew Lloyd Webber, Switzerland, by courtesy of Julian Hartnoll.
Cover background: *The Dinner Hour, Wigan* by Eyre Crow. Manchester Museum of Art. Used by permission of Bridgeman/Art Resource, New York.

Page 153: Famine drawing, Library of Congress
Page 154: Passenger ship en route to America, *Harpers Weekly*
Page 155 (top): Merrimack Mills and boarding house, American Textile Museum, Lowell, Massachusetts
Page 155 (bottom): Power loom, ibid.
Page 156 (top): *Voice of Industry*, Lowell Historical Society, Lowell, Massachusetts
Page 156 (bottom): Mill girls at loom, American Textile Museum, Lowell, Massachusetts

Page 157 (top): Factory worker daguerreotype, ibid.

Page 157 (bottom): Merrimack label, ibid.

Page 158: Time table of Lowell Mills, ibid.

Page 159: *Lowell Offering*, ibid.

Page 160 (top): Town of Lowell with shops, Lowell Historical Society, Lowell, Massachusetts

Page 160 (bottom): Saint Patrick's Church, ibid.

Page 161 (top): Lowell boarding house, ibid.

Page 161 (bottom): Famine Irish neighborhood, the Acre, ibid.

Page 162: Music to "Hear the Wind Blow," from The *American Song Treasury* by Theodore Raph, Dover Publications, Inc., New York, New York

Page 164 (top): Map by Heather Saunders

Page 164 (bottom): Map of Lowell, 1845, Lowell Historical Society, Lowell, Massachusetts

ISBN 0-439-34192-2

Copyright © 1997 by Barry Denenberg.
All rights reserved.
Published by Scholastic Inc. SCHOLASTIC, DEAR AMERICA,
the DEAR AMERICA logo, and associated logos are trademarks
and/or registered trademarks of Scholastic Inc.

12 11 10 9 8 7 6 5 4 3 2 1   1 2 3 4 5 6/0

Printed in the U.S.A.   40

First Scholastic paperback printing, October 2001

The display type was set in Tiranti Solid.
The text type was set in Berling.
Book design by Elizabeth B. Parisi